2006–2007 Annual Supplement to

THE PIANO BOOK

BUYING & OWNING A NEW OR USED PIANO

LARRY FINE

BROOKSIDE PRESS • BOSTON, MASSACHUSETTS

Brookside Press
P.O. Box 178, Jamaica Plain, Massachusetts 02130
(617) 522-7182
(800) 888-4741 (orders: Independent Publishers Group)

info@pianobook.com
www.pianobook.com

Printed in the United States of America

Distributed to the book trade by Independent Publishers Group,
814 North Franklin St., Chicago, IL 60610
(800) 888-4741 or (312) 337-0747

ISBN 1-929145-19-5 (print edition)
ISBN 1-929145-20-9 (electronic edition)

NOTICE

Reasonable efforts have been made to secure accurate information for this publication. Due in part to the fact that manufacturers and distributors will not always willingly make this information available, however, some indirect sources have been relied upon.

Neither the author nor publisher make any guarantees with respect to the accuracy of the information contained herein and will not be liable for damages—incidental, consequential, or otherwise—resulting from the use of the information.

INTRODUCTION

Given the long time span between new editions of *The Piano Book,* it's impractical to provide in the book itself the detailed model and price data that piano shoppers increasingly seek. Similarly, updated information about manufacturers and products is needed in a timely manner. This *Annual Supplement to The Piano Book,* published each summer, is designed to fill that information gap. I hope this modest companion volume will effectively extend the "shelf life" of *The Piano Book* as a valuable reference work, and serve as an additional information resource for piano buyers and piano lovers.

Larry Fine

June 2006

CONTENTS

MANUFACTURER and PRODUCT UPDATE

This section describes changes to companies, products, and brand names since the fourth edition of *The Piano Book* went to press in the Fall of 2000. This section is cumulative; that is, information contained in last year's *Supplement*, to the extent it is still accurate, is repeated here and changes that have occurred during the past year have been added. If a company or brand name is not listed here, it means that there is nothing new of substance to report. "New Listing" means that a listing is entirely new since publication of the fourth edition of *The Piano Book*.

It is not intended, of course, that the information in this update section take the place of the reviews in *The Piano Book*. With some exceptions, the update is limited to changes of a factual nature only, whereas the main book contains, in addition, critical reviews, ratings, and recommendations. Readers should understand that, in most cases, changes in the quality of any particular brand of piano occur very slowly, over a period of many years, if at all. Only where there has been an abrupt change in company ownership, or a period of rapid technological or economic change in the country of origin, is there likely to be a change in quality worth worrying about. For that reason, the reviews in *The Piano Book* can still be considered reliable unless otherwise noted here.

Trends

Pianos made in China continue to improve and make inroads into the North American market. By some estimates, more than a third of all new pianos sold in the U.S. in 2005 were made in China. As recently as 2001, most pianos from China, though technically acceptable, were not musically desirable. Over the past few years, however, the musical qualities have taken a big leap forward. Though nearly all makes have improved, and most are acceptable, the best vertical pianos from China are probably the Perzina and Palatino brands. The best grands are from the Dongbei factory, sold under the names Nordiska, Everett, Hallet & Davis, Hardman & Peck, and Story & Clark, among others. Pearl River and Ritmüller (by Pearl River) are also among the better ones. The jury is still out as to whether these pianos will hold up over the long term and in demanding climates and situations. Anecdotal reports suggest less consistency than with pianos from other countries, and the need for thorough pre-sale preparation by the dealer (and sometimes the dealer needs to weed out the bad ones and return them to the factory), but otherwise few major problems. Prices are so low, however, that for many entry-level buyers these pianos are an excellent value despite some uncertainty about their longevity. At least as short-term investments, and in milder climates and less demanding situations, they are probably fine.

(*The Piano Book* contains brand ratings organized by "group," each group representing a level of quality. At the time of publication, I placed most Chinese pianos in Group 5, the lowest level. At the present time, I would probably place most in Group 4, "Medium quality consumer-grade pianos." Although some actually exhibit the performance characteristics of higher grade instruments, due to their short track record caution would dictate describing them as Group 4 instruments for the time being. See *The Piano Book* for details.)

Chinese piano manufacturers have been quite aggressive at acquiring piano-making knowledge, and are happy to use their alliances with U.S. distributors to that end. However, the distributors frequently complain that agreements as to technical specifications, quality, and exclusivity of relationship are routinely disregarded by their Chinese business partners. Once the Western inspectors leave the factory, the Chinese managers do whatever they feel is in their own best interest, which often amounts to maximizing production at the expense of quality. The distributors have gradually discovered that the only way to overcome this problem is to own the factory themselves, to maintain a constant presence at the factory, or to constitute such a large percentage of the Chinese company's business that they (the Westerners) can control production. Alternatively, a U.S. company can examine all the pianos in the U.S. before sending them on to dealers, but this is less satisfactory than stopping problems at the source. Western distributors of Korean pianos used to complain of a similar problem with Korean piano-factory managers during the height of that country's piano industry in the 1980s and '90s.

For the consumer, there are two lessons to take from this. First, although the average quality is quite reasonable, depending on how well the distributor handles the quality-control issue, and how well the dealer examines and prepares the pianos, you may find a fair amount of variation among Chinese-made pianos as you shop (this is in addition to whatever variation naturally exists between brands). Therefore, it may be in your best interest to hire a piano technician to examine one of these pianos before purchase. Second, statements by salespeople as to particular specifications or exclusivity of relationship ("Of all the brands that ZYX Piano Co. makes, this is the only one with a cantilevered bridge") should not be relied upon as true in every case, even though such statements may be made in good faith. Buy what you can see with your eyes and hear with your ears.

There has been an explosion of different brand names under which Chinese-made pianos are being marketed, there now being about a dozen Chinese manufacturers making pianos for export to the U.S. Piano shoppers should keep in mind, however, that cosmetics aside, if two brands of piano originate in the same factory, they are probably very similar, perhaps identical.

On the other end of the price spectrum, European piano makers seem to be in a race to redesign their pianos for better sound projection and sustain, à la Steinway. While the European piano market is languishing, the U.S. market for high-end pianos, relatively speaking, is thriving, and for a number of companies, Steinway is the principal competitor. Considering how tradition-bound these companies are, this degree of activity is unusual. Some of the redesigns—new models from Seiler and Schimmel come to mind—have been terrific musical successes. My only worry is that the palette of available piano tonal qualities is becoming smaller and more homogeneous as the old-world sounds pass away.

Changes in China and in Europe, and their far-reaching consequences, are causing a paradigm shift in the piano industry that is making it more difficult to give advice to piano shoppers. (A paradigm is a theoretical framework from which generalizations are formulated.) For many years, the paradigm for piano quality has been an international pecking order with pianos from Russia and China (and, more recently, Indonesia) at the bottom, followed by Korea, Japan, Eastern Europe, and finally Western Europe (mostly Germany) at the top, with pianos from the United States scattered here and there depending on the brand. While this pecking order has never been foolproof, it has served its purpose as a generalization well enough for use by a generation of piano buyers.

Now these distinctions are being blurred by globalization. Unable to escape the high cost of doing business at home, some Western European manufacturers are developing satellite operations and more affordable second product lines in Eastern Europe and third product lines in China. Some makers of high-end instruments are also quietly beginning to source parts and subassemblies from Asia and elsewhere. To the extent they can afford it, they are also investing in high-tech equipment to reduce the expense and inconsistency of hand labor, even while continuing to tout their status as makers of "hand-made" instruments. Some Korean and Chinese manufacturers, on the other hand, are importing parts and technology from Germany and Japan, producing instruments that when well prepared by the dealer rival the performance qualities of far more expensive pianos from Japan and, occasionally, Europe. The most we can say is that their longevity is unknown, an argument that, while true, becomes weaker with each passing year. In addition, global alliances such as that between Samick and Bechstein (described elsewhere in this *Supplement*) are sure to bring new products to the market that are more hybridized than anything we've seen before. Although the old paradigm still has validity, the number of nonconforming situations is increasing, all of which will cause temporary confusion in the marketplace until such time as a new paradigm emerges.

At the same time that quality differences between low-end and high-end instruments are becoming narrower, price differences are greater than they've ever been, bringing issues of "value" into greater prominence. Eastern European quality in some cases now closely approaches that of Western Europe, but at a price comparable to that of Japan. Some of the better pianos from China, Korea, and Indonesia have specifications equal to almost anything from Japan, and workmanship nearly as good, at a fraction of the price. Caught in the middle, the Japanese are gradually being squeezed out of the piano market despite their perennially good quality.

Another consequence of globalization has been the diminishing number of independent suppliers of parts and materials (actions, hammers, pinblocks, soundboards, keys, plates, etc.) to the piano industry. (Actually, the enormous Chinese piano industry has numerous parts suppliers, but most of these supply parts only for pianos sold in the domestic Chinese market, not internationally.) At one time there were large differences in quality between suppliers, but globalization has reduced and sometimes eliminated those differences. For example, as recently as a few years ago, Detoa (Czech) actions were markedly inferior to Renner (German) actions, and Chinese-made actions were terrible. Now there is at most only a small difference in quality between Detoa and Renner, virtually all Chinese actions are acceptable, and at least one Chinese supplier is said to be producing perfect-looking knockoffs of Renner actions.

At the same time, many manufacturers continue to use a "recipe" approach to differentiating differently-priced piano lines: Choose an action (Renner, Detoa, Chinese), combine it with a hammer (Renner, Abel, Tokiwa), add a pinblock (Delignit, Dehonit, Bolduc), and so forth, to produce a piano at a particular price. But with fewer suppliers to choose from, and less difference between them, the implied difference in quality at different price points is threatening to become more a matter of image than actuality. Image has always been important in differentiating one piano brand from another, in part because even real differences can be subtle or highly technical and not obvious, especially to those who don't play the instrument well. But with even real differences evaporating, image-spinning is reaching new heights.

The above notwithstanding, differences still do exist. The most important is that between consumer-grade pianos on the one hand (Groups 3, 4, and 5) and performance-grade pianos on the other (Groups 1 and 2). There have been some fairly successful attempts by makers to bridge this gap (i.e. Knabe by Samick and Kawai's Shigeru Kawai), but for the most part, the two different types of manufacturers still live in two different worlds. The difference between the two worlds is less than it used to be, but still exists in the form of selection, drying, and use of wood; final regulation and voicing; and attention to technical and cosmetic detail; in other words, the difference is more than just the "recipe." Theoretically, it would be possible for, say, a Chinese company to duplicate the finest pianos. But the market for these instruments is small, and some have unique and idiosyncratic designs that are not amenable to mass production. Therefore, it is always likely to be more of a niche market entered into by those whose profit-seeking is mixed with a love for the instrument and perhaps a desire to carry on a family business. At this point in time, such businesses are more likely to be Western than Asian, but who knows . . . that may one day change.

As I mentioned, globalization means more than just Chinese pianos, and in general it should not be feared. A German company making pianos or parts in a Czech or Polish factory it owns or controls is not much different from an Ohio company sourcing parts from a factory over the border in Kentucky. These days, among the countries of Europe, there is enough of a commonality of business practices, laws, culture, and attitudes toward quality that geographic differences carry little meaning, except as to labor costs, where the savings may be great. (In fact, it's not unusual for an Eastern European piano manufacturer to make parts for its Western European competitors.) When a Japanese or Korean piano maker sets up shop in China or Indonesia, it tends to transplant the entire culture of its home factory to the new one, including machinery, managers, and quality standards. After a short period of start-up problems, the quality will usually be comparable to what is produced at home.

The phenomenon of Western makers of high-end pianos sourcing parts in China may be inevitable, but it does trouble me a little more than the other manifestations of globalization. For one thing, most of the Western companies are small and their orders are not likely to constitute more than a tiny fraction of the output of their Chinese suppliers, providing them little leverage with which to control the quality of the goods they receive. I don't want to be alarmist about this because I know that the Western makers are intelligent and don't want to sully their reputation for short-term gain. I'm sure they carefully examine and test each and every item they purchase from a new supplier. But there's no test like the test of time, and when one is investing tens of thousands of dollars on a luxury item, one has a right to expect the manufacturer to use only the most time-tested methods and suppliers, regardless of cost. I have no doubt that parts from these new suppliers will work fine in the short and medium term. But we know from past experience that good piano parts can, under the right conditions, last fifty or even a hundred years. How confident are these manufacturers that the new parts will last that long?

For another thing, luxury goods are sold in large part on image. They have to be because the difference in quality between the luxury goods and the next less expensive alternative is usually not great enough to justify to the consumer the steep difference in price unless supplemented by appeals to vanity, security, prestige, and so forth. In the world of luxury pianos, this appeal is generally phrased in terms of "tradition," "hand-made," and "old-world European (or American) craftsmanship," to name a few buzzwords. Dealers often make a point of promoting these pianos as an all-European or all-American alternative to a mass-produced, Asian piano. Now, no one is so naïve as to believe that every screw in these pianos is made locally or by hand. But when a large percentage of critical parts is imported from Asia without disclosure and assembled in the West, at what point does the image-making begin to border on misrepresentation – even if the product quality is good and no laws have been broken?

This is by no means a complete discussion of the issue. For example, parts vary in how critical they are to the piano and in how sensitive they are to issues of quality. If a pinblock or plate fails, the piano must be rebuilt or junked. If a minor piece of hardware fails, on the other hand, it can easily be replaced and little harm will have been done. I'm particularly concerned about action parts, which are especially sensitive to the issue of selection and drying of wood, must be machined and adjusted to extremely tight tolerances, and are constantly subjected to use and abuse. It's not unusual for well-made wooden action parts and their cloth action centers to still be in good shape after a half-century or more of use. Will action parts from new suppliers not accustomed to Western standards of quality last that long? In the interest of fairness toward the manufacturers, the following topics should also be discussed: Are Western sources of supply disappearing or deteriorating, forcing manufacturers to look to the East? Are some Chinese industries actually more advanced than their Western counterparts? Are some "traditional" Western suppliers themselves secretly buying their parts from China?

Some of you reading this may consider the above concerns about quality and image to be old-fashioned and romantic, and would prefer to just trust the manufacturers and be spared the details. After all, if the piano works well, who cares where the parts come from? My point in this article is not to bash manufacturers who source parts from China, but rather to promote greater transparency on the issue and to foster dialogue on both the manufacturing and retail levels about the pros and cons of this phenomenon. Ultimately, this issue will be resolved in the marketplace, but only if consumers are informed about it. To that end, I asked most of the makers of higher-end (Group 1 and Group 2) pianos to tell me if they procured parts for their pianos from China and, if so, which ones.

Boy, this was a pot that did not want to be stirred! Although most makers told me (usually honestly, I believe) that they do not use Chinese-made components, several would not answer my question, answered vaguely, or (it would appear) lied. None answered in the affirmative. More than one manufacturer has intentionally left its distributor and dealers completely in the dark on this issue so as not to have its secret revealed inadvertently. Usually I learned much more from a company's competitors, suppliers, former suppliers, and other industry insiders than from the company itself. In a few cases, I've noted the response of the manufacturer (or lack of it) in the brief product updates that follow this section. Because I don't know how important this issue is to consumers, however, rather than ruffle feathers unnecessarily, I have decided to recommend the following market-oriented approach:

If the issue of Chinese parts in higher-end pianos is important to you (and only if it is), then before agreeing to purchase a European or higher-end American piano, you should ask the dealer to supply a written statement from the manufacturer detailing the country of origin of the piano's major components, and perhaps reasons for sourcing them from non-traditional or Chinese suppliers where applicable. If this statement is satisfactory to you and inspires confidence, then buy the piano. If not, or if no statement is forthcoming, then move on to another brand. Forward-looking manufacturers may wish to proactively supply their dealers with such a statement.

ALTENBURG

Distributed by:

Wyman Piano Company
P.O. Box 218802
Nashville, Tennessee 37221

941-661-0200
george.benson@wymanpiano.com
Correction to web site address: www.altenburgpiano.com

Altenburg pianos are now being distributed nationwide, not only through the company's retail stores in New Jersey.

The F.E. Altenburg line of pianos made by Niendorf has been discontinued.

The Beijing Hsinghai Piano Group is making a new line of Altenburg pianos, some of which are special designs for Altenburg, with individually-hitched strings. Grand models up to 5' 3" use a laminated soundboard, larger models use solid spruce.

ASTIN-WEIGHT

Due to storm damage to the factory, Astin-Weight is currently engaged in limited production from several temporary locations. Current contact information is:

Astin-Weight Piano Makers
P.O. Box 65281
Salt Lake City, Utah 84165

801-487-0641
New e-mail address: gr8pianos@networld.com
Change to web site address: www.astin-weight.com

Production of the 41" console has been discontinued.

BALDWIN

including D.H. Baldwin, Hamilton, Howard, Chickering, Wurlitzer, ConcertMaster

New address, phone, and ownership:

Baldwin Piano Company
309 Plus Park Blvd.
Nashville, Tennessee 37217

615-871-4500
800-876-2976

800-444-2766 (24/7 consumer hotline)

Owned by: Baldwin Piano, Inc., a wholly owned subsidiary of Gibson Musical Instruments, Inc.

Shortly after the fourth edition of *The Piano Book* was published in early 2001, the Baldwin board of directors hired a new management team to try to stave off impending bankruptcy caused by a series of costly mistakes and prior poor management. Avoiding bankruptcy turned out not to be possible, and the company filed for protection under Chapter 11 of the U.S. bankruptcy laws in May of 2001. On October 16, 2001, Baldwin's major creditor, General Electric Capital, purchased the company's assets at a court-ordered liquidation sale and then sold them to the Gibson Guitar Corporation on November 9, 2001.

Gibson owners Henry Juszkiewicz and Dave Berryman purchased Gibson in 1986 when it was in complete disarray and turned it into an extremely profitable and well-respected company. They feel that there are many parallels between Gibson's situation at that time and Baldwin's present situation, and expect to be able to turn Baldwin around as well.

Baldwin's new owners say they have made large capital investments to improve product quality. In order to make production more efficient, grand production has been moved from Conway, Arkansas and consolidated with vertical production in the company's Trumann, Arkansas facility. A woodworking plant in Greenwood, Mississippi closed in mid-2000 has had its functions transferred to a new woodworking plant in Trumann. The Juarez, Mexico action-making facility has been closed and its equipment divided between Baldwin plants in the U.S. and China. Additional cost savings have been realized by the transfer of all Baldwin sales, marketing, and administrative functions to Gibson headquarters in Nashville.

In 2004, Baldwin formed a joint venture with a piano manufacturer in Zhongshan, China, to be called Baldwin Zhongshan China, to produce pianos for the Chinese domestic market. In time, this factory is also expected to produce pianos and parts for Wurlitzer and other Baldwin-owned piano brands sold in the United States.

Prior to the management reorganization and subsequent bankruptcy, Baldwin had announced a number of changes to its product line, some of which were reported in *The Piano Book*. These changes were never fully realized due to the bankruptcy. The new owners plan to complete implementation of some of these changes (see comments below), and other changes are to be expected as Baldwin's reorganization evolves.

Baldwin's line of digital pianos has been discontinued.

The Eurostyle consoles and studios (E100, E101, E102, E250, E260) have been discontinued.

In the grands, the new model 225E is the model M (5' 2") in French Provincial styling. Model 226E is the model R (5' 8") in French Provincial styling. Model 227E is the model R with round, fluted, tapered legs. The 7' model SF-10 has been renamed SF-10E in honor of its adoption of the enhanced features of the upgraded Artist series grands (see *The Piano Book* for details).

The Chickering grands reported on in *The Piano Book* have been withdrawn. They were to be replaced by three new models—5' 4", 5' 9", and 6' 2"—made by Samick in Korea, with some cosmetic features taken from old Chickering designs. Due to Baldwin's bankruptcy, however, Baldwin never took possession of these pianos, so they were sold and warranted by Samick under license from Baldwin while supplies lasted. Baldwin still retains ownership of the Chickering trademark and may use it again in the future.

Also in the grand department, Baldwin has introduced a Custom Grand Finishes program, allowing customers to design their own grand piano. Four levels of customization are available: 1) wood-finish accents on regular grands; 2) colors (Jubilee Red, Golden Honey, Evergreen, Beale Street Blue, Madeira); 3) exotic wood veneers; and 4) anything you want. Some of the Custom Grand Finishes are also available in regular inventory. A Custom Vertical program includes the limited edition Gibson studio, each one signed by guitarist Les Paul; the Elvis Presley Signature model, authorized by the Presley estate; and a new B.B. King model (also available as a grand).

Baldwin has developed a new "Stealth"™ action, now used in all Baldwin vertical pianos. The "Full Blow" action, in use since 1939, has been updated with a Schwander-style hammer-butt return spring and other changes for improved quietness, responsiveness, durability, and ease of servicing. You can recognize the Stealth™ action by its visually striking black and deep blue colors. In addition, vertical pianos with the new action have model numbers ending in "E."

Baldwin has introduced several new lower-cost lines of piano. The first of these is the "Hamilton." Not to be confused with the famous Hamilton model studio piano Baldwin has made for decades with "Baldwin" on the fallboard, these new Hamiltons say "Hamilton" on the fallboard. Currently they are made in China by Sejung to Baldwin's specifications. The verticals are available in both continental and American furniture styles, have a solid spruce soundboard, and come with a ten-year parts and labor warranty. A 73-note spinet is part of this line. The company says that except for the number of notes, this short-keyboard instrument is a true acoustic piano with all the features of a full-size piano. This year a 47" studio was added to the line. The grands feature solid spruce soundboards and a ten-year parts and labor warranty.

As for Baldwin's Wurlitzer line of pianos, they are no longer made by Samick in Korea. Like the Hamiltons, Wurlitzer pianos are made in China by Sejung. However, whereas the Hamilton pianos are made with Sejung-designed scales and plates, the Wurlitzer pianos are made with Baldwin-designed sand-cast plates based on old Chickering scale designs. The pianos, all grands, come in six sizes, from 4' 7" to a 9' 1" concert grand.

Another new line is the "D.H. Baldwin." Those in the piano trade may recall this as a name Baldwin used on a line of pianos made in Korea. The new D.H. Baldwin line, however, is made in Arkansas and is based on the Baldwin Acrosonic vertical piano scale. The company says these new models are essentially like their higher-priced cousins musically, but with scaled-down cabinetry. Also made in Arkansas are pianos with a variety of minor brand names Baldwin owns and uses at dealer request, such as Ivers & Pond, Cable, J & C Fischer, and others. These are essentially the same as the D.H. Baldwin pianos.

Lastly, a new "Howard" line is made in Arkansas, complementing the D.H. Baldwin verticals with a U.S.-made line of grands. Currently the Howard line consists of two models, 5' 2" and 5' 8".

The ConcertMaster electronic player piano system has a new optional feature available that provides piano accompaniment to a number of popular music CDs available on the general market. When a customer plays one of the CDs, ConcertMaster links the accompaniment, located on the system's hard drive, to the CD and plays them together.

When Gibson acquired Baldwin, it acquired only its assets, not its liabilities. Therefore, the company is not required to honor warranty claims for pianos purchased prior to the acquisition date. Pianos purchased by the consumer from an authorized dealer on or after November 9, 2001 are eligible for warranty coverage, even if the dealer purchased the piano before that date. Warranty coverage for pianos purchased by the consumer before November 9, 2001 will only be considered on a case-by-case basis.

In mid-April 2002, Baldwin cancelled agreements with most of its dealers, retaining only the most active ones. Since then the company has been steadily rebuilding its dealer network, inviting new dealers to demonstrate their commitment, in part by making large purchases from the company. Baldwin says, however, that it *will* honor the warranty on pianos purchased from "cancelled" dealers, even though, technically, they are no longer "authorized" dealers.

BECHSTEIN, C.

New North American distributor:

SMC (formerly Samick Music Corp.)
575 Airport Road
Gallatin, Tennessee 37066

615-206-0077
800-592-9393
www.bechstein-usa.com
www.bechstein.de

In 2002, Korean piano maker Samick purchased a majority interest in C. Bechstein by acquiring shares held by Karl Schulze, Bechstein's largest shareholder and CEO. Schulze also purchased an interest in Samick. Since then, Schulze has repurchased some of the Bechstein stock such that each party now holds about a fifteen percent interest in the other. Samick is helping Bechstein increase production, diversify its product line, and sell in North America, and Bechstein is providing Samick with technical assistance and helping it market its pianos in Europe. Bechstein remains a separately-managed German corporation. SMC, Samick's North American distribution arm, markets and distributes Bechstein pianos in the U.S. and Canada.

Like other European manufacturers, Bechstein has expanded in recent years to produce pianos for other markets in other parts of the world. It shares a plant in China with Samick to produce inexpensive pianos for the Chinese domestic market, makes the less-expensive Euterpe brand in Indonesia, manufactures the medium-quality W. Hoffmann line in the Czech Republic (this line was once distributed in the U.S. and Canada but has been discontinued), and makes the Zimmermann brand in Germany. In 2006, the company purchased a 49 percent share of the Bohemia Piano Company in the Czech Republic.

Over the past few years, all Bechstein grands have been redesigned with a capo bar (eliminating the agraffes in the treble), higher tension scale, and duplex scale for better tonal projection and tonal color. Also, unlike older Bechsteins, which had an open pinblock design, in the redesigned grands the plate covers the pinblock area. This year the 7' 7" model C-232 was redesigned in this manner and reissued as 7' 8" model C-234.

Bechstein has introduced a series of very beautiful designer verticals called "ProBechstein" in 45½", 46½", and 49" sizes. In the Pricing Guide section, they are the models called "Balance," "Avance," and "Ars Nova." "Elegance" is a more traditional version of the 49" model.

The verticals mentioned above, plus the 51½" Concert 8 vertical, and the fully-redesigned grands, are called the "Concert Series" and say "C. Bechstein" on the fallboard. The regular verticals and partially redesigned versions of the old grand models are known as the "Academy Series" and say only "Bechstein" on the fallboard.

There has been some confusion, as evidenced by internet messages and customer feedback, about the difference between the C. Bechstein and Academy series models. The company's original plan, reported in last year's *Supplement*, was to reduce cost by sourcing some parts and subassemblies for the Academy series in other parts of the world, and to put all the best components in the C. Bechstein models. This plan was altered somewhat before production began in earnest. The older versions of the grands were partially redesigned and updated for the Academy series and many of the same components are installed in both piano lines. The company says that both lines are made in their entirety at the Bechstein factory in Seifhennersdorf, Germany. (I question the truth of that statement because I know the company has cabinet parts and rims for many of its less-expensive pianos made in the Czech Republic, but I don't regard that discrepancy as being significant.)

Looking at the specifications for the two lines, the difference in musical quality appears to be smaller than anticipated, with most of the difference belonging instead to the realms of tonal philosophy and cabinetry. According to the company, the C. Bechstein line was designed with a higher tension scale for better projection and with various components that would result in the greatest usable palette of tonal color. To that end, the soundboard in the C. Bechstein line is tapered, whereas that in the Academy series is not, though both lines use the same quality soundboard wood. The C. Bechstein bridges are of vertically laminated beech with a hornbeam cap, whereas the Academy series bridges are of solid beech with a beech cap. Hammer shanks in the C. Bechstein are mostly of the stiffer hornbeam, as opposed to the maple shanks in the Academy series (the stiffness of the shanks affects the tone). Both lines use the same quality Renner-made hammers, though the C. Bechstein may need more voicing due to the scale design, and both lines have beech rims, though the rims in the C. Bechstein line are beefier to accommodate the higher-tension scale. (Interestingly, the larger C. Bechstein models also have two laminations of mahogany sandwiched in with the beech to produce some desired tonal effect, I'm not sure what.) Contrary to what one might expect, the Academy series uses a Steinway-like expansion-type keybed, whereas the C. Bechstein series uses a more expensive, veneered, solid keybed. Bechstein thinks the solid kind transmits sound better throughout the structure and is more stable. The same quality pinblock and strings are used in both lines.

As for the actions, Bechstein says only that the actions in both pianos are "Bechstein" actions, but won't say where the parts come from. The C. Bechstein actions say "Gold Line" and the Academy series actions say "Silver Line." It is known that at least some of the parts are made by Renner, probably for some of the C. Bechstein pianos. It is widely speculated that most of the parts are made in China, probably for the Academy series pianos and perhaps for some of the C. Bechsteins. Although experts can often tell them apart, it's next to impossible for the average person, either looking at them or playing them, to tell which actions are Renner and which are not. Both appear to be well made, and both are of the Renner design and so have the smooth, responsive touch characteristic of that design. Of course, I would have more confidence in the long-term reliability of Renner action parts than those of unknown origin. (See the "Trends" section, pages 5–12, for commentary on this subject.) As mentioned above, for tonal reasons there is a difference in the wood used in the two actions. Both have the same quality spruce keys, although the C. Bechstein keys still use leather key bushings, whereas the Academy series keys use the more conventional cloth bushings. Bone keytops are an option on the C. Bechstein pianos only.

The C. Bechstein cabinetry is much sleeker and more sophisticated than the plain Academy series, though both cabinets are finished to the same standards. The C. Bechstein plates receive the royal hand-rubbed finish; the Academy series plates are just spray finished in the conventional manner.

The Academy series pianos cost 40 to 45 percent less than the C. Bechsteins of similar size.

A 7' 6" model 228 will be added to the Academy line in Fall 2006.

BECKER, J.

Distribution of these pianos in the U.S. has been discontinued.

BEHNING

Distribution discontinued. See "Weber"

BEIJING HSINGHAI (new listing)

Beijing Hsinghai Piano Group, Ltd., part of the Beijing Hsinghai Musical Instruments Co., has been producing pianos since 1949 and manufactures more than fifty thousand vertical and grand pianos annually. They are available throughout the world under the Otto Meister and Hsinghai (sometimes spelled "Xinghai") labels, as well as under various other labels as joint ventures with other manufacturers and distributors, including Heintzman (in Canada), Story & Clark, Steigerman, and Wyman. Kawai also has a joint venture with Beijing, though the pianos are distributed only in Canada and Europe, not the U.S. (at one time they bore the name "Linden").

The assets of Canadian piano manufacturer Heintzman were purchased by a Chinese company and moved from Canada to Beijing, where pianos are now produced under the Heintzman name in joint venture with the Beijing Hsinghai Piano Group by a firm known as Beijing Heintzman.

BERGMANN

See "Young Chang"

BLONDEL, G.

Distribution of Blondel pianos in the U.S. has been discontinued.

BLÜTHNER

The name of the U.S. distributor has been changed to Blüthner USA LLC, but the contact information otherwise remains the same.

In Canada, contact Blüthner Agency, Canada at 416-236-8870; web site www.bluethner.ca.

In honor of the company's 150th anniversary, Blüthner has introduced a Jubilee model with a commemorative cast-iron plate in the style of the special-edition pianos of a century ago. Available only in model 6 (6' 3"), it can be ordered in any style and finish.

In what is perhaps a world's "first," Blüthner has designed and built a piano for left-handed pianists. This is a completely "backwards" piano, with the treble keys, hammers, and strings on the left and the bass on the right. When it was introduced, a pianist gave a concert on it after only a couple of hours of practice! It is currently available in the 6' 10" and 9' 2" sizes by special order (price not available).

BOHEMIA (new listing)

German American Trading, Inc.
P.O. Box 17789
Tampa, Florida 33682

813-961-8405
germanamer@msn.com

Pianos made by: Bohemia Piano Co., Hradec Kralove, Czech Republic

The factory that makes Bohemia pianos began production in 1871, after World War II becoming part of the Czech state-owned enterprise that included the better-known Petrof. Privatized in 1993, Bohemia now makes 2,500 verticals and 500 grands per year. Originally it exported to the U.S. under the name Rieger-Kloss, a name now used only in other markets. The name Bohemia is derived from the original term used by the ancient Romans for the part of Europe that is now the Czech Republic.

Specifications for the instruments include Czech solid spruce soundboards, Czech-made sand-cast plates, either Czech actions on Bohemia action frames or Renner parts on Bohemia action frames (the latter denoted by "BR" in model numbers), and either Renner or Abel hammers. All pianos come with a leather upholstered adjustable artist bench, and the grands all have slow-close fallboards.

The Bohemia grands I played at a trade show a few years ago sounded and felt very good, with a nice, bright, singing treble tone.

Warranty: Ten years, parts and labor.

[Note: I spoke with a Bohemia company official and with other Czech piano-manufacturing executives about changes to the Bohemia piano. Unfortunately, the information from Bohemia just doesn't add up, leaving me to wonder where the various piano parts are made. Bohemia says that its Czech actions are no longer being made by Detoa (Detoa confirms this), but instead are coming from another Czech supplier. However, no one else I spoke with knows of another Czech manufacturer of action parts, especially one that could supply parts on the scale Bohemia would require. There is only a small supplier of repair parts for technicians, whose parts, I'm told, are imported from China. (Bohemia says that the parts for the models advertised as having Bohemia/Renner actions continue to come from Renner.)

There are other parts for which there appear to be discrepancies, particularly grand piano rims, but that requires an explanation too lengthy to publish here. Suffice it to say that all the other manufacturing executives I spoke with speculated that Bohemia must be getting its actions and most of its rims from China or elsewhere in Asia, but the Bohemia executive flatly denies this and insists that everything comes from Europe. (See the "Trends" section, pages 5–12, for commentary on this subject.)]

BÖSENDORFER

New U.S. distributor contact information:

Bösendorfer USA
1771 Post Road East
Suite 239
Westport, Connecticut 06880

203-520-1801
usinfo@bosendorfer.com
www.bosendorfer.com

In January 2002, Bösendorfer was purchased from Kimball International by the BAWAG - P.S.K. Group, Austria's third largest banking group. Bösendorfer has a special place in Austrian history and culture, and although the company had thrived under Kimball's ownership, for some time there had been a desire on all sides to return Bösendorfer to Austrian hands. The new owner says it intends to maintain the same high standards of material and workmanship for which the company is renowned. It will also continue the new marketing course of the last few years, including the redesign of existing models, a new "Artisan" series of art case pianos, and the Conservatory series of cosmetically reduced, less expensive versions of some of its models. [In early 2006, the new owner announced that Bösendorfer is up for sale once again.]

In 2001, Bösendorfer introduced a new 9' 2" model 280 concert grand, and in 2002, a 6' 1" model 185 grand. These and other new and redesigned models share a new design philosophy in which the treble soundboard area is increased for better tonal projection by reducing excess cabinet distance between player and strings, and the bass soundboard area is increased for better bass response by joining the wide tail to the spine at a sharper corner. Action geometry has been improved, the company says, on all models. In 2005, a maple cap was added to the inside top edge of the bent side and tail of the model 280 rim. The company says the added rigidity and mass should increase the concert grand's tonal projection and sustain.

The new model 280 concert grand replaces the 9' model 275. Unlike the 275, however, which had 92 keys, this new model has only 88 keys. Its scale design also features a front duplex. The company says the new model is intended for concert pianists who would otherwise be distracted or intimidated by the presence of additional keys in the bass. To my ears, the new piano has better sustain in the treble than I usually find in Bösendorfer pianos, but otherwise has a characteristic Bösendorfer sound and feel.

During the past few years, Bösendorfer has introduced a number of interesting instruments in new cabinet styles. These include a Porsche-designed modern piano in aluminum and polished ebony (or special-ordered in any standard automobile finish color); a Victorian-styled piano called "Vienna;" a "Liszt" model that is similar to "Vienna" but less elaborate (available standard in model 185 and as a special order in other sizes); and a model called "Yacht" (available in models 170 and 200) in wood finish with brass inlay that can be ordered without casters to be bolted to the deck of a ship! The Conservatory series models described in *The Piano Book* are now limited to models 200 and 214.

There have also been a number of special, limited-edition models, including two 175th anniversary models, now retired, limited to a production run of 175 instruments each, and the first of a projected series of art-case "Artisan" pianos with elaborate marquetry. A "Mozart" edition, introduced in 2006, commemorates the 250th anniversary of the birth of Mozart and is limited to twenty-seven individually numbered instruments, one for each Mozart Piano Concerto. They are ordered by Concerto number, which is individually inscribed on the cheek block of the piano. Available only in the model 214 size (7'), the case has subtle modifications, including gold leaf trim, round legs and lyre posts, and a carved music desk.

The SE Reproducer system, out of production for a number of years, has been replaced by an all-new design called "CEUS (Create Emotions with Unique Sound)" with updated electronics and solenoids. The visual display is discreetly located on the fallboard and is wireless, so the fallboard can be removed for servicing the piano without the need to disconnect wires. Player controls for recording, playback, and data transfer are by means of a combination of keystrokes on the sharp keys, pedal movements, and fallboard touch sensors. Optical sensors measure key position and movement (both down and return), hammer velocity, and pedal movement at an extremely high sampling rate for maximum accuracy and sensitivity to musical nuance. A number of different interfaces and mediums are offered for data transfer and storage. Bösendorfer says it intends to build a library of recordings for CEUS, and that the system will also play standard MIDI piano files. CEUS is available in every grand model Bösendorfer makes and adds about $60,000 (list) to the price of the piano. At some point, it may also become available as a retrofit into existing Bösendorfers.

BOSTON

The 49" vertical model UP-125 has been replaced with a completely redesigned 50" model UP-126. In the redesign, the wooden back has been made much heftier and the plate much more rigid to better resist torsional and bending stresses. Similar changes have also been made to the 52" model UP-132E, and the 46" model UP-118E. In the two larger models, the bass scale has been reworked with reduced string tension for smoother bass tone, and the soundboard taper and rib placement have been refined for better treble tone. Lastly, the music desk for the European-style case design has been improved so that it holds music more securely. Boston says it has plans to redesign the grands over time using the same structural analysis software employed in the design of its Essex line of pianos.

In 2005, Boston replaced its 7' 2" model GP-218 with a newly redesigned 7' 1" model GP-215 grand. The company says that a modified rim shape and bracing, increased string length in the mid-treble, overall increased string tension, and other technical changes have resulted in a piano with better mid-range and treble sustain and more "bite" to the bass.

BREITMANN (new listing)

Blüthner USA LLC
5660 W. Grand River Ave.
Lansing, Michigan 48906

517-886-6000
800-954-3200
info@bluthnerpiano.com
www.bluthnerpiano.com

Pianos made by: Yohahy Piano Factory in Guangdon Province near Guangzhou

Breitmann is a brand associated with Blüthner and made in China. Features include Delignit pinblocks, laminated spruce soundboards, German strings, Abel hammers, and Renner parts in the grands.

THE BRITISH PIANO MANUFACTURING COMPANY LTD. (new listing)

This was, for a time, the new name for the company formerly known as Whelpdale, Maxwell & Codd. This company produced Welmar, Knight, Broadwood, Bentley, and Woodchester pianos. It purchased Woodchester in 2001 and moved the manufacturing facilities for all its brands to the Woodchester factory, formerly the Bentley factory (see *The Piano Book* for history).

In April, 2003, this company ceased operations. Its assets were purchased by a piano distributor in the United Kingdom, who said he has no immediate plans to reissue the brand names.

Clarification: In *The Piano Book* entry for Whelpdale Maxwell & Codd, I wrote that John Broadwood & Sons was established in 1728. It has been brought to my attention that this is not possible because Broadwood was not born until 1732. The 1728 (or 1729) date is widely used, however, and it probably represents the date of establishment of the shop of Burkat Shudi, with whom Broadwood apprenticed (1761), and of whose business

Broadwood later became partner (1770) and, eventually, sole proprietor (1782).

BRODMANN (new listing)

Piano Marketing Group, LLC
752 E. 21st Street
Ferdinand, Indiana 47532

812-630-0978
gtrafton@pianomarketinggroup.com
www.brodmann-pianos.com

World Headquarters: Joseph Brodmann Piano Group, Victorgasse 14, 1040 Vienna, Austria. Phone: +43-1-890-3203.
christian-hoeferl@brodmann-pianos.com

Joseph Brodmann was a well-known piano maker in Vienna in the late eighteenth and early nineteenth centuries. Ignatz Bösendorfer apprenticed in Brodmann's workshop and eventually took it over, producing the first Bösendorfer pianos there. Today's Brodmann is a new company, headquartered in Vienna, started by two former Bösendorfer executives, pursuing a direction they say was planned as a possible second line for Bösendorfer a number of years ago, but never acted upon.

There are three lines of Brodmann pianos. One is made in Hubei Province, China by a manufacturer not affiliated with other brands distributed in the West. The pianos are designed in Europe and use European components in critical areas, such as Strunz soundboards, Abel hammers, Röslau strings, and Langer-designed actions (Renner in the 7' 6" grand, a Chinese action in the verticals). Brodmann has its own employees in the factory for quality control purposes.

The other two lines, all verticals, are known as "European Premium Pianos." One is made in a small factory in Vienna and specializes in making pianos with stunning wood veneers, such as Bubinga, Pyramid Mahogany, Pommele, and Brazilian Rosewood. All the pianos have a traditional Viennese curved leg. The other line, made in Germany, features vertical pianos with a straight-leg design in Ebony, Mahogany, and Walnut. Both European lines have the same high-quality components as those listed above, but with a Renner action.

Warranty: Ten years, parts and labor.

CABLE, HOBART M.

See "Sejung"

CABLE-NELSON

See "Yamaha"

CHASE, A. B. (new listing)

Musical Properties, Inc.
949 French Drive
Mundelein, Illinois 60060

773-342-4212

Pianos made by: Dongbei Piano Co., Dongbei, China

A. B. Chase is an old American piano name, formerly owned by Aeolian Pianos but to the best of my knowledge not used since that company's bankruptcy in 1985. Since 2001, the brand has been used by Musical Properties, Inc. on pianos from the Dongbei piano factory in China.

CHICKERING

See "Baldwin" and "Samick"

CONN

Distribution discontinued

CRISTOFORI (new listing)

Jordan Kitt's Music
9520 Baltimore Avenue
College Park, Maryland 20740

800-466-9510 x1267
(Chris Syllaba)

Schmitt Music
Butler's Square, Suite 850B
100 North 6th Street
Minneapolis, Minnesota 55403

800-920-9540 x2372
(Wayne Reinhardt)

info@cristoforipianos.com
www.cristoforipianos.com

Pianos made by: Sejung Corporation, Qingdao, China

Names used: Cristofori, Vivace, Opus II (name discontinued)

Originally issued under the name "Opus II," the Cristofori piano is a joint venture between Jordan Kitt's Music and Schmitt Music, which own and operate a combined twenty-five piano dealerships throughout the country. At present, Cristofori pianos are sold only in their stores. (Cristofori was, of course, the inventor of the piano.)

Cristofori pianos are made by Sejung in China (see "Sejung"). They are differentiated from Sejung's regular pianos by upgraded feature specifications such as: the use of Mapes' highest-quality strings; action parts made from German hornbeam instead of maple; reinforced, T-fastened, double-felted hammers from Japanese felt; and premium solid Siberian spruce soundboards for the grands and taller verticals (veneered spruce soundboard for the smaller verticals). Some vertical models have cabinets that are custom-designed for Cristofori. Grands are pre-marked for more accurate PianoDisc installation should it be desired later by the customer or dealer. Each piano is individually inspected in the Sejung factory by an American piano technician before being boxed and shipped.

"Vivace" is a lower-cost 4' 8" grand similar to Sejung's Hobart M. Cable brand, except with a veneered spruce soundboard. The piano says "Vivace" at Jordan Kitt's stores and "Cristofori" at Schmitt Music stores.

Warranty from Jordan Kitt's Music: Twelve-year full (transferable) warranty on parts and labor.

Warranty from Schmitt Music: Ten-year limited (non-transferable) warranty on parts and labor.

DISKLAVIER

See "Yamaha"

DONGBEI (new listing)

The Dongbei Piano Co. in Dongbei, China makes pianos that are sold in North America under a variety of names, including Nordiska, Everett, Story & Clark, Hallet & Davis, and Hardman & Peck, among others (see listing under each name).

Dongbei recently changed its grand piano designs to utilize a focused beam structure that concentrates the piano's structural support toward the nose flange of the plate, a design used by Steinway and others that is thought to increase the tonal projection of the instrument by making the frame more rigid. This design was first brought out under the Nordiska brand name (see

"Nordiska"), but may be available to other Dongbei-made brands. You can tell if the Dongbei-made piano you are looking at uses this improved system by looking up at the beam structure of the piano from underneath. If all the beams are more or less parallel to each other, the piano is of the old design. If several of the beams converge toward the front of the instrument, the piano is of the new design.

EBEL, CARL

See "Perzina, Gebr."

ESSEX

Steinway, through its Boston Piano Company subsidiary, introduced several "Essex" models in early 2001 and 2002. These are manufactured by Young Chang to Steinway's specifications. They include 5' 3" and 6' grands and 42" and 44" verticals. The vertical models are of identical scale design, but the smaller one is in a continental-style cabinet. Some of the vertical cabinets look backward to styles of past decades of the twentieth century. At present, the verticals are manufactured in Young Chang's factory in China.

The grands are available in both traditional and Art Deco styles, the difference being in the styling of the music desk. They are made by Young Chang in Korea. Like Boston pianos, the Essex line was designed with a lower tension duplex scale and a larger, tapered solid spruce soundboard, for potentially better sustain. The grands utilize rosette-shaped flanges for better action stability. Steinway says it designed these pianos using state-of-the-art structural analysis software.

In mid-2006, Steinway will begin selling Essex pianos made in China by Pearl River, designed by Steinway. Steinway will also continue its collaboration with Young Chang. Both companies will make Essex verticals in China. Essex grands will be made by Young Chang in Korea and by Pearl River in China. Although plans and prices were not firm at press time, the company says it will be adding a model 116 (45½") and 123 (48½") to the current vertical-piano offering, plus various new furniture styles, such as French Formal, French Country, English Country, and Contemporary. The grand line will receive two new models, 155 (5' 1") and 173 (5' 8") in French Provincial and English Regency, in addition to the current Neoclassic style.

ESTONIA, LAUL

In 2001, having purchased the remaining shares in the company from the company employees, the former majority owner became the sole owner of the company. The name of the company has been changed to reflect his ownership.

New U.S. distributor contact information:

Laul Estonia Piano Factory
7 Fillmore Drive
Stony Point, New York 10980

845-947-7763
laulestoniapiano@aol.com
www.laulestoniapiano.com

The company reports that it has made a large number of changes and improvements during the past four years, among which are: rescaling the bass and upgrading bass string making machinery; improving the method of drilling pinblocks; stronger plates and improved plate finishes; thicker inner rims on the 5' 6" grands; improved fitting of soundboard to rim; concert-grand-quality soundboard spruce on all models; quarter-sawn maple bridge caps; an adjustable duplex scale; wood for legs and keyslips treated to better resist moisture; Renner Blue hammers on all models; better quality metal hardware that resists oxidation; suede-covered music desk tray; improved satin finishes; establishing a quality control department headed by the elder Mr. Laul (both he and his wife are professional musicians); higher-grade and better-prepared veneers; and establishing a U.S. service center for warranty repairs. All pianos are now accompanied by a quality control certificate signed by a member of the Laul family. The name on the piano has been changed to "Laul Estonia."

Concerning the criticisms in *The Piano Book*, technicians report that Estonia pianos are now arriving at the dealer well-prepared, and seem not to have problems anymore with uneven tuning pin tightness. Based on technical improvements the company has made and new information from technicians, I would raise both the "Confidence" and "Quality Control" ratings of Estonia pianos to four and a half stars (see *The Piano Book* for details about the rating system).

ETERNA

Distribution discontinued. See also under "Yamaha."

EVERETT

New distributor phone number: 800-445-0695

Most Everett models are made by the Dongbei Piano Co. in Dongbei, China.

FALCONE

See "Sejung"

FAZIOLI

Fazioli pianos are now being distributed directly from the factory:

Fazioli Pianoforti srl
Via Ronche 47
33077 Sacile (Pn), Italy

+39-0434-72026
info@fazioli.com
www.fazioli.com

Corrections to review: Three lids are optional on the 10' 2" grand. The 5' 2", 6', and 6' 11" models utilize a Delignit pinblock as mentioned, but the larger models have Bolduc (Canadian) pinblocks. The Fazioli warranty has been increased to ten years.

Additional web site address: www.fazioli.com

FEURICH

New U.S. representative:

Unique Pianos, Inc.
159 Parkhill Blvd.
Melbourne, Florida 32904

888-725-6633
321-725-5690
www.feurich.com

Pianos made by: Feurich Klavier-u.Flügelfabrikation GmbH, Gunzenhausen, Germany

This venerable German manufacturer is once again making pianos in its own factory. The models being offered at this time are 5' 8" (F172) and 7' 5" (F227) grands and a 49" (F123) vertical.

FÖRSTER, AUGUST

New distributor email address: germanamer@msn.com
New web site address: www.august-foerster.de

GROTRIAN

Grotrian now distributes directly from the factory:

Grotrian Piano Company
P.O. Box 5833
D-38049 Braunschweig, Germany

+49-531-210100
+49-531-2101040 (fax)
contact@grotrian.de
www.grotrian.de

The "Friedrich Grotrian" is a new 43½" vertical with a beech back frame but no back posts, and a simpler cabinet, at a lower price than regular Grotrian pianos.

Grotrian has introduced the Duo Grand Piano, two grand pianos placed side by side with keyboards at opposite ends, as in a duo piano concert, with removable rim parts, connected soundboards, and a common lid (price not available).

A 6' 10" grand model called "Charis" will be available in Fall 2006.

GULBRANSEN (new listing)

QRS Music Technologies, Inc.
2011 Seward Avenue
Naples, Florida 34109

800-247-6557
www.gulbransen.com

Pianos made by: Sejung Corp., Qingdao, China

Founded in 1904, Gulbransen was a well-regarded piano and organ manufacturer of the early twentieth century, and at one time was the world's largest maker of player pianos. In more modern times, the company was known for its electronic organs and MIDI products. In 2004, QRS Music Technologies, maker of the Pianomation player piano systems and distributor of Story & Clark pianos, purchased Gulbransen's MIDI products and company name.

QRS is using an innovative distribution strategy to market Gulbransen pianos. QRS sells the pianos online through Amazon.com at a fixed, non-negotiable price and, working with area piano dealers, through special events at Sam's Clubs. When sold through Amazon.com, a QRS dealer in the customer's area will provide delivery and after-sale support. If there is no dealer in the area, QRS will provide delivery and support directly from its national headquarters.

Currently the Gulbransen line consists of two sizes of grand, both with and without player systems, and two sizes of vertical, made by Sejung. The pianos are tuned, inspected, and adjusted at the Story & Clark facility in Pennsylvania prior to being shipped to the dealer or customer.

HAILUN (new listing)

Hailun Distribution, LLC
4002 Highway 78
Suite 530
Snellville, Georgia 30039

770-484-8104
atlnet@mindspring.com
www.hailunusa.com

Pianos made by: Ningbo Hailun Musical Instrument Co., Ningbo, China

Ningbo Hailun began making piano parts in 1986 under the Ningbo Piano Parts Factory name. Ningbo is a city near Shanghai which, the company says, is the birthplace of the maker of the first pianos built in China. In the mid-1990s, the company began assembling entire pianos. Most of its production is for export to Asia and Europe. This is its first foray into the U.S. market.

The Ningbo Hailun factory has over 400,000 square feet of production capacity and 800 employees. Since 2001, the company has invested heavily in digital equipment and has hired a trio of experts from Japan, Austria, and the United States to help it reach the highest quality standards.

At present, the company offers three sizes of vertical pianos and three sizes of grands to U.S. customers. The distributor says the models offered in the U.S. are aimed at the mid-level market.

HALLET, DAVIS & CO.

New contact information for distributor:

North American Music Inc.
11 Kay Fries Drive
Stony Point, New York 10980

800-782-2694

The Dongbei Piano Co. in China is now making the Hallet & Davis pianos. Most of the pianos are similar to those built by Dongbei under other names for several other distributors.

HARDMAN, PECK & CO. (new listing)

Hardman Pianos
11 Kay Fries Drive
Stony Point, New York 10980

800-782-2694
www.hardmanpiano.com

Hardman, Peck & Co. was an old American piano company whose roots go back to 1842. In the early twentieth century it was absorbed into the Aeolian Corporation, which went out of business in 1985. Current Hardman, Peck pianos are made for the distributor by the Dongbei Piano Co. in China. Most of the pianos are similar to those built by Dongbei under other names for several other distributors.

HAZELTON BROS.

Discontinued. See "Samick"

HEINTZMAN

See "Beijing Hsinghai"

HOFFMANN, W.

See "Bechstein, C."

HSINGHAI

See "Beijing Hsinghai"

HYUNDAI

Distribution discontinued.

IBACH

New U.S. distributor information:

Resource West, Inc.
2295 E. Sahara Avenue
Las Vegas, Nevada 89104

702-457-7919
800-777-6874
info@ibachpiano.com
www.ibachpiano.com

The real German Ibach pianos are once again being distributed in the United States. Resource West says it will be distributing these fine pianos through interior design professionals and some smaller piano dealers. No investment is needed by the dealer. In lieu of stocking the pianos and receiving a regular retail markup, the dealer instead refers interested customers to the Resource West/Ibach showroom in Las Vegas and receives a substantial commission when a sale is made. Resource West prepares the pianos and delivers them to the customers. The price list in this *Supplement* is the suggested retail price at the Las Vegas showroom.

The Ibach-Daewoo joint venture mentioned in *The Piano Book* was discontinued and the Korean manufacturing operation was sold by Daewoo to an investment group that continued to manufacture pianos in Korea on a limited basis. These pianos were distributed for a time in the U.S. under the name Bachendorff (an arrangement now discontinued) and in Canada under the name Royale. A distributor operating under the name Persis International, Inc. says it will be having this Korean company make pianos under the Sohmer name (see "Sohmer").

IRMLER

The name of the U.S. distributor has been changed to Blüthner USA LLC. The contact information otherwise remains the same.

The Chinese-made Irmlers have been discontinued. The European Irmlers are made in Poland with the technological assistance of Blüthner. Final action assembly and regulation are performed in the Blüthner factory in Germany.

KAWAI
including Shigeru Kawai

Additional web site address: www.shigerukawai.com

Kawai has opened a factory in Indonesia, where it is making many of the piano models sold in the U.S. The company has closed its North Carolina plant and has moved all its U.S. manufacturing and much of its Japanese vertical piano manufacturing to Indonesia. Kawai says the Indonesian factory is a "transplant" of the Japanese factory. Kawai also produces several vertical models in joint venture with the Beijing Hsinghai Piano Co. in China. These pianos are known as the KX models, and are sold in Canada and Europe, but not in the U.S. At one time these pianos bore the name "Linden," but use of that name has been discontinued. (The country of origin is shown on a label on the back of every Kawai vertical piano.)

True to its reputation, Kawai continues to make changes to its product line. Currently, model 506N is a 44½" vertical in a simple, studio-style cabinet. Although called a "studio" because of the cabinet style, it has a compressed action characteristic of a console. Model 508 is the same as the 506N, except with a slightly fancier cabinet. Model 607 is also the same design internally with a furniture-style cabinet. Model K-15 (44") is the 506N in a continental style (no legs). All are made in Kawai's Indonesian factory. Previously-listed console/studio models 505, 605, 606, and 608 have been discontinued.

Popular school studio models UST-7 and UST-8, formerly made in the U.S., are now being made in Indonesia. The 46½" furniture-style studio model 902, changed a few years ago to model 906 with a stiffer back structure, all ABS action parts, and new cabinetry, will be reissued as Indonesia-made model 907 in Fall 2006. Upright models UST-10 and UST-12 have been discontinued.

Among the Japanese-made models, model K-18 is the 506N in a Japanese-style, polyester-finished cabinet. It replaces the recent CX-10 and its predecessor, the popular model CX-5H, as Kawai's low-priced "studio." Model K-25 is like the 48" model K-30 (discontinued), except in a simpler cabinet. Beginning in Summer 2006, Kawai will replace K series models K-25 and larger with a new series (K-3, K-5, K-6, and K-8) with new cabinets and a new carbon-fiber action. The prices on these new models were not available at press time, but are expected to be slightly higher than the models they replace.

Kawai has invented a variable-touch action for vertical pianos in which the player can vary the touchweight by sliding a lever. The lever operates a set of sliding weights behind the fallboard. The touchweight varies depending on the point at which the keys contact the sliding weights. The touchweight can be adjusted from 48 to 70 grams (normal for Kawai is 56 grams). The "Vari-Touch" feature is currently available only on the 46" UST-8 upright (model VT-118).

In the grands, the 5' model GM-2A has become model GM-10. The original model GM-10C had a non-movable music desk (a nuisance) and a plain cabinet. This model was later upgraded to the GM-10LE with a movable music desk and a nicer cabinet. The current version (same features) is the GM-10K, made in Indonesia. The GM-12 is the same basic piano, but made in Japan with Kawai's new action (see next paragraph) and NEOTEX keytops. The 5' 1" model GE-1A has been replaced by the GE-20, which has the features of the former GE-1AS model mentioned in *The Piano Book*. A new 5' 5" model GE-30 has been introduced. It has the same scale as the model RX-1, but is like the other GE models structurally and in terms of its features (see *The Piano Book* for details on the differences between the RX, GE, and GM models).

As explained in *The Piano Book*, Kawai uses ABS Styran plastic as the material for many of its action parts. In 2004, the company introduced a new generation of these parts, which it calls the "Millennium III" action, made of ABS Styran mixed with carbon fibers. The carbon fibers allow the parts to be more rigid with less weight and to be more finely engineered for shape and texture, resulting in a faster, lighter action and more consistent touch. I played two pianos of identical model, one with the older parts and one with the new, and could sense a substantial difference. At present, the new parts are found in all Kawai grands made in Japan.

From time to time, Kawai makes available several of its grand and upright models in limited quantity as "Conservatory" and "Promotional" versions. The Conservatory model uprights have a wider music rack than the regular models, usually larger or double casters and a lock, and sometimes cabinetry or aesthetics that are slightly simplified. Promotional models have a regular (not soft-fall) fallboard and some other simplified features. Prices were not available at press time, but are expected to be about the same or slightly less than regular models.

Kawai's high-end Shigeru Kawai line of pianos is now available in six different models from 5' 10" to 9' 1". New for 2005 were two special finishes in the Shigeru VII (7' 6") – Pyramid Mahogany and Classic Noblesse (with inlaid walnut burl).

KEMBLE

Kemble is now acting as its own distributor for the U.S. The factory contact information is:

Kemble & Company Ltd.
Mount Avenue
Bletchley, Milton Keynes MK1 1JE
United Kingdom

+44-1908-371771
+44-1908-270448 (fax)
brian.kemble@gmx.yamaha.com
www.kemble-pianos.co.uk

The 43" "Oxford" is now available with a beautiful marquetry inlay. The "Traditional" model has been discontinued. The 52" model K131 vertical, formerly available only as a limited-edition designer model, is now available as a regular model. There is also a new 48" Shaker-styled designer upright called "Vermont" designed by the famous British designers Conran and Partners, a 45" black polyester and chrome model called "Classic-T," and a 49" model called "Quantum II" with a sound-escape mechanism. In 2006, the company introduced a 49" "Conservatoire" model with "softline" design (rounded edges and profile), brass inlay, and upgraded hammers.

Kemble has introduced its first grand piano, a 5' 8" model KC173, in cooperation with Yamaha, which owns a majority interest in Kemble. The grand is like the Yamaha model C2, with design differences such as plate color and music desk shape. It is also voiced to Kemble's specs, sounding to me more "European," i.e. a mellower bass.

KIMBALL

Brighton Music, Inc.
823 S. Sixth Street
Suite 100
Las Vegas, Nevada 89101

773-342-4212

As described in *The Piano Book*, Kimball International ceased making pianos in 1996 and has stated that it has no plans to reintroduce Kimball brand pianos. The trademarked name has been registered by a different distributor and is being used once again on pianos. The distributor says it has entered into a joint venture partnership in China and is producing its own American-designed pianos. Some American materials, including the strings and soundboard, are being used in their construction. The first two models are the 4' 10" model K1 grand and a series of 44" model K44 American furniture-style consoles.

KINGSBURG

This brand is no longer being distributed in the U.S.

KLIMA (new listing)

Klima was a small Czech piano manufacturer established in 1991 when the state-run piano manufacturing apparatus was sold off to several private firms, including Petrof. Several generations of the Klima family had been Petrof employees. Klima pianos were distributed in the United States for a brief period of time before the company discontinued production in 2004.

While they last, Klima vertical pianos are also available under the Fandrich & Sons label with a Fandrich vertical action installed. See *The Piano Book* for details and contact information.

KNABE, WM.

Contact information for new U.S. distributor:

SMC (formerly Samick Music Corp.)
575 Airport Road
Gallatin, Tennessee 37066

615-206-0077
800-592-9393
New web site address: www.smcmusic.com

The Wm. Knabe piano line made by Young Chang for PianoDisc has been discontinued, and Samick has acquired the Wm. Knabe name from PianoDisc. Samick is now using this name on the pianos formerly sold as the "World Piano" premium line of Samick pianos (see *The Piano Book* for details). Several of the grands have been redesigned, the new models based on the original nineteenth and early twentieth century Knabe scale designs and cabinet styles in use when the company was based in Baltimore, with sand-cast plates, lacquer finishes, Renner actions and hammers, maple and oak rim, and other high quality features. At present, this redesign has resulted in the 5' 8" (WKG-58) and 6' 4" (WKG-64) models, with the other grand models in the Knabe series not resembling old Knabes, but instead designed by Samick. The pianos are serviced in Samick's U.S. facility before being shipped to dealers. Samick expects to begin moving production of the Wm. Knabe line from Korea to its new manufacturing facility in Tennessee in 2007, though some parts and subassemblies may continue to be made elsewhere.

I have watched the Knabe line develop over the last couple of years and have noted many improvements. Some of these improvements are the result of collaboration with Bechstein engineers in the Samick factory. The instruments I have played have been impressive, especially for a Korean-made piano. I also made inquiry among my sources around the country. The pianos arrive in very good condition cosmetically. Most are also well-prepared technically, though not always. In a few cases, technicians found it necessary to completely re-weight the keyboard after correctly regulating the action. A few pianos in bone-dry regions have experienced structural and mechanical problems in the winter, including cracked soundboards. The dealers diligently repaired or replaced the affected pianos, and Samick responded by switching soundboard suppliers to avoid further problems. Other parts of the country did not report problems. When well prepared, most observers thought the pianos to be very musical, well designed, and a good value. For the time being, I would recommend paying special attention to humidity control in dry climates.

KRAKAUER

Distribution discontinued.

MASON & HAMLIN

In 2004, Mason & Hamlin reintroduced its 6' 4" model AA grand piano, a model the company manufactured during the first half of the twentieth century. The current version is modified somewhat from the old, but does have features typical of the company's other models, such as a wide tail, a full-perimeter plate, and the patented "tension resonator" crown retention system. In the process of developing the model, the company says, it standardized certain features, refined manufacturing processes, and modernized jigs and machinery, improvements that will now be applied to the other models the company makes. Other technical refinements to the grands include reducing mass in the action and tapering the soundboard. I played a prototype of the AA at a trade show and think it has the potential for becoming the company's most popular model.

In January 2005, the company reintroduced the 9' 4" model CC Concert Grand, not produced since 1984. It has the same features typical of the company's other models. However, its length requires the use of a double tension resonator.

The model 50 vertical piano has been redesigned, with longer keys for a more grand-like touch, and improved pedal leverage. Satin ebony and satin mahogany finishes have been added.

In the early part of the twentieth century, Wessell, Nickel & Gross was a major supplier of actions to American piano manufacturers, including Mason & Hamlin. Over the years, the name fell into disuse. In 2004, Mason & Hamlin revived the name by registering the trademark, which now refers to the design and specifications of Mason & Hamlin actions.

Concerning the "China question" discussed in the "Trends" section (pages 5–12), Mason & Hamlin says it has a policy of not disclosing where it sources its materials and components. However, a company statement reads, in part,

> "… we are pleased to say that we source our materials, brass, iron, steel, hard wood, felt, leather etc. and components from the four corners of the earth in an effort to maintain steady production and to control quality and price levels. Likewise as the artisans who built Mason & Hamlin pianos in the early Boston days, immigrants and direct descendents of immigrants, we are proud to report that the artisans who build our instruments today continue to represent a diverse mix of cultures and races from many parts of the world."

My understanding is that the owners of Mason & Hamlin have a strong connection with China and over the past few years have actively sought out piano components from that country, including but not limited to cast-iron plates, action parts, and metal hardware. As the company probably maintains multiple sources of supply for major components, it may also obtain some of these parts from Western suppliers.

MEISTER, OTTO (new listing)

The Piano Group, Inc.
P.O. Box 14128
Bradenton, Florida 34280

941-794-5157
thepianogroup@yahoo.com
www.ottomeisterpianos.com

Otto Meister pianos are made by the Beijing Hsinghai Piano Group, Ltd. in Beijing, China. See "Beijing Hsinghai."

MILLER, HENRY F. (new listing)

Henry F. Miller
236 West Portal Ave. #568
San Francisco, California 94127

800-511-0083
info@henryfmiller.com

Henry F. Miller is the name of an old American piano maker dating back to 1863. The name eventually became owned by Aeolian Pianos, which went out of business in 1985. The name is now owned by the Sherman Clay chain of piano stores and used on a mid-priced line of pianos carried by these and other major piano retailers around the country. Current Henry F. Miller pianos are made by Pearl River in China. Some models are similar to pianos sold under the Pearl River name. The 4' 10" and 5' 3" grands feature solid spruce soundboards.

NIENDORF

No longer in production

NORDISKA

New email address: pianos@geneva-intl.com

Web site: www.geneva-intl.com

Nordiska has introduced several new grand and vertical models including, in 2006, a 4' 8" grand and a 52" vertical. All models have Abel hammers except the 43" model 109 console.

Nordiska grands now utilize a focused beam structure that concentrates the piano's structural support toward the nose flange of the plate, a design used by Steinway and others that is thought to increase the tonal projection of the instrument by making the frame more rigid; and a maple rim, heavier plate, and better plate cosmetics. They also now feature the same leg plates used on Petrof pianos. The 7' and 9' models also feature Renner actions assembled by Renner, Kluge keys and key frame, and a Bolduc (Canadian) white spruce soundboard. The company says that imported American veneers are being used on all grands. The 7' grand has an especially good sound and touch, the best yet on a Chinese-made piano.

For some time I have been telling people that Nordiska grands are identical to all the other-named Dongbei grands except for Nordiska's use of Abel hammers. The importer has politely informed me that this is not accurate. According to the company, Nordiska grands use a higher grade of felt, cloth, and buckskin throughout the action, keys, and key frame, resulting in an action that is quieter and more durable than that of its competitors. The Nordiska division gets to use the best-quality soundboard wood and the most experienced technicians. Finally, only the Nordiska pianos utilize the Petrof leg attachment system. Other exclusive upgrades are planned for the future.

OPUS II

See "Cristofori"

PALATINO (new listing)

The Music Link
P.O. Box 162
Brisbane, California 94005

888-552-5465
piano@palatinousa.com
www.palatinousa.com

Pianos made by: AXL Musical Instruments Co., Ltd. Corp., Shanghai, China

Although this company is new to the piano world, it is not new to music. For some time, AXL has been manufacturing a full range of musical instruments under its own name and under OEM agreements with other companies. The company says that its factory is very automated, employing CNC routers from Japan and Germany, and that it sources materials for the pianos from around the world.

At present the company makes three sizes of vertical piano and three sizes of grand. Specifications include solid spruce soundboard in both verticals and grands, hard rock maple pinblock and bridges, adjustable artist bench with all models, and a ten-year transferable warranty. A slow-close fallboard is standard on all models.

Several verticals I inspected at a trade show were definitely better than the average piano from China and had apparently arrived in excellent condition, needing hardly any preparation. It seems this was not an isolated case, as other people are starting to report similar observations. This is a brand to watch.

PEARL RIVER
including Ritmüller

New contact information for U.S. distributor:

Pearl River Piano Group America, Ltd.
2260 S. Haven Avenue, Suite F
Ontario, California 91761

909-673-9155
800-435-5086
sales@pearlriverusa.com
www.pearlriverpiano.com

Pearl River has added 5' 7" and 6' 4" grands to its line. The company says these models are scaled to sound like Japanese or American pianos, whereas the other models are more European sounding. The 7' and 9' Pearl River grands now come with Renner actions. The company is in the process of changing the specifications of the 7' and 9' Pearl River and Ritmüller grands to include solid spruce soundboards; all other Ritmüller grands will follow in 2006. Pearl River no longer uses Czech-made Detoa actions. Most models come with a Pearl River action, with Renner action available as an option in some models.

A 49" vertical model 126R has been added to the Ritmüller line. The vertical is based on the model 125M1 joint venture piano (with Yamaha), but with agraffes throughout the scale. Renner action is standard on the 7' Ritmüller grand, and available at additional cost on the smaller models.

PERZINA, GEBR. (new listing)

Piano Empire, Inc.
13370 E. Firestone Blvd., Ste. A
Santa Fe Springs, California 90670

800-576-3463
562-926-1906
info@perzinapianos.com

Pianos made by: Yantai-Perzina Piano Manufacturing Co., Ltd., Yantai, China. Some names formerly made by Yantai Longfeng Piano Co.

Names used: Gebr. Perzina, Carl Ebel, Gerh. Steinberg.

The Gebr. Perzina (Brothers Perzina) piano company was established in the German town of Schwerin in 1871, and was a prominent piano maker until World War I, after which its fortunes declined. In more recent times, the factory was moved to the nearby city of Lenzen and the company is now known as Pianofabrik Lenzen GmbH. In the early 1990s, the company was purchased by Music Brokers International B.V. in The Netherlands. Eventually it was decided that making pianos in Germany was not economically viable, so manufacturing was moved to Yantai, China, where a range of verticals and grands were made for a number of years by the Yantai Longfeng Piano Co. under the Perzina name. In 2003, Music Brokers International established its own factory in Yantai, called Yantai-Perzina Piano Manufacturing Co. Ltd., where it now builds the Perzina, Carl Ebel, and Gerh. Steinberg pianos. (Note: Do not confuse Gerh. Steinberg with Wilh. Steinberg, a German piano brand.)

The Carl Ebel and Gerh. Steinberg pianos are based on the same scale design, but the Perzina scale design is different. Further technical differences revolve primarily around the choice of action, hammers, and soundboard design, among other things. In particular, the Perzina brand is distinguished by use of a solid, tapered, Austrian white spruce soundboard in both verticals and grands, whereas the Carl Ebel and Gerh. Steinberg soundboards are of veneered laminated Austrian white spruce. In addition, the Perzina verticals have several interesting features rarely found in other pianos, including a "floating" soundboard that is unattached to the back at certain points for freer vibration, and a reverse, or concave, soundboard crown. (There may be something to this, as the Perzina verticals are the best sounding verticals from China, the bass being particularly notable.) The Perzina grands are available with either Detoa ("G" models) or Renner ("E" models) action. The company says that the Perzina pianos also receive a higher level of attention to detail at the end of the manufacturing process than do the other two brands.

The company's European headquarters says it ships many European materials to Yantai, including Roslau strings, Delignit pinblocks, Abel hammers, English felts, European veneers, and Austrian white spruce soundboards. New machinery is from Germany, Japan and Italy. According to the company, all the piano designs are the original German scales. The Renner actions used in some of the Perzina grands are ordered complete from Germany, not assembled from parts.

PETROF
See also "Weinbach"

New email address: pianos@geneva-intl.com
Web site address: www.geneva-intl.com
Also of interest: www.petrof.com

Petrof has designed new grand and vertical actions, which it calls "Petrof Original." The geometry in the action for the smaller vertical has been re-designed to function more like the larger verticals, i.e. a full-sized jack and longer hammer shank. Several of the parts, both grand and vertical, have been re-designed to achieve greater rigidity and less weight. The actions are being manufactured in a separate section of the Detoa factory under the supervision of Petrof engineers. They can be identified by a "Petrof Original" label on the action. All Petrof pianos use the new action design.

Petrof has also invented and patented a version of its new grand action, the "Sterling Original" (formerly called "Magnetic Accelerated Action"), that uses tiny opposing magnets on the wippens and wippen rail. These magnets allow for the removal of the usual lead counterweights in the keys and, according to the company, significantly alters the dynamic properties of the action. "The hammer receives an inertial boost from the magnets as the key begins to move from the rest position. When the key is fully depressed, the effect of the magnets is minimal, allowing gravity to work in giving the hammer another inertial boost on the way down. The effect is faster repetition, less fatigue, and less physical work needed to reach higher dynamic levels." The new action also furthers the European Union's stated environmental goal of phasing out the use of lead in pianos. The action is adjusted in the factory for a standard touchweight. If necessary, it can be adjusted up or down five grams by a technician (not the customer) in an hour or so. Otherwise, the action can (and should) be serviced in exactly the same way as a standard action. The Sterling Original action is an option on Petrof grands in the 5' 3", 5' 8", and 6' 4" sizes.

Petrof has introduced a concert grand called the "P1 Mistral." The company says the instrument utilizes a more rigid brace and frame and front and rear duplex scales, among other features. Also relatively new is a 53" vertical model P135. It has a full sostenuto, a soft-close fallboard, and a newly-designed adjustable music desk, among other features. Several of the vertical models are now available with designer panels with inlays. A 4' 8" grand model VI was introduced in 2006.

All Petrof grands are now being shipped with Abel hammers. They should be easier to voice than the harder hammers previously used. Consequently, piano shoppers are now more likely to find individual Petrof grands with a mellower tone.

Also introduced in 2006 is the 6' 10½" "Pasat B" grand. This piano is the result of years of research and testing by the Petrof research and development department, one of the largest such departments in the piano industry. The piano contains a myriad of novel and interesting technical features, more than can be described here. For starters, the inner rim is built up by hand of alternating layers of solid pieces of red beech and spruce instead of consisting of laminations bent around a mold. The company says this is the way several piano makers formed their grand rims in the nineteenth century before modern technology made the bent-lamination rim possible, and that this method results in a more stable, stress-free rim. The bridges are of solid maple, but the treble bridge is capped with solid ebony wood to increase sound projection of the higher frequencies. The piano is single-strung with front and rear tuned duplexes (duplex scale) throughout the treble. The solid spruce soundboard is asymmetrically crowned, and each soundboard is custom-tapered based on tests of its vibrating characteristics. The cut-off bar that separates the live and dead portions of the soundboard is contoured to more accurately perform its function. The piano utilizes a focused beam structure that concentrates the piano's structural support toward the nose flange of the plate, a design used by Steinway and others that is thought to increase the tonal projection of the instrument by making the frame more rigid. However, in the Pasat B, the tension is spread over a greater area of the belly rail via a large steel plate for increased rigidity. A densified beam of red beech further stiffens the treble area to enhance projection of the treble tone. Like the other Petrof grands, the Pasat B comes with a Petrof Original action and Abel hammers. For cosmetics, the inner rim is lined with macassar ebony veneer. A representative I sent to a trade show where the piano was introduced was very impressed with the piano's sound.

Note that the Weinbach piano is no longer identical to the Petrof. See its separate listing under "Weinbach."

PIANODISC

PianoDisc offers several different systems for installation on new or existing pianos. The flagship is the Opus7 system, which was released in 2004. In addition to the PianoDisc playback system and SymphonyPro sound module, Opus7 features a wireless, internet-ready, Web Tablet with touchscreen and full color, high resolution graphics as the system's "Conductor." It has the ability to download music and system upgrades directly from PianoDisc's website, and surf the web and receive email (broadband users only), among other features. The Opus7 system is invisible — mounted completely out of sight under the piano — but with an access panel that allows the user to connect the included floppy and CD drives for copying music to the system's "MX3" music storage hard drive. The MX3 hard drive comes with forty hours of pre-loaded music. Its MX3 media format will accept Standard MIDI files type 0 and 1 available from a wide variety of Standard MIDI file publishers, PianoDisc CDs, and standard audio CDs. (The company says while playback of non-PianoDisc media is supported, it is not guaranteed.) Music saved to the MX3 hard drive from diverse sources can be organized into separate "libraries" and played back from a single source for convenience. The MX3 format provides many hours of true digital stereo sound with piano accompaniment without having to change CDs. Music can also be purchased online from PianoDisc's new "eMusic" store and downloaded directly to the Opus7 and stored on the MX3 hard drive. Opus 7 has a "Schedule" feature that allows one to program a start time and end time for selected music to play.

In 2005, PianoDisc introduced "PianoSync" software for the Opus 7. PianoSync is a MIDI-controlled piano performance that synchronizes with a commercially-available audio CD of a major recording artist. When you purchase a PianoSync performance from PianoDisc's growing collection, Opus 7 will recognize the matching audio CD and accompany the original recording on your piano whenever the CD is played. Both can be copied to MX3 for more convenient playback.

Using "PianoCast" and broadband internet, Opus7 can connect to PianoDisc's internet radio station. The station will feature special events, interviews, and performances, combining a traditional audio broadcast with a piano performance that will play the Opus7.

A "Performance Package" option includes the TFT MIDI record strip, mute rail, and headphones for recording one's own playing or for use as a QuietTime system or MIDI controller.

Opus7 comes in two versions, "Opulence" and "Luxury." Opulence is the full system. Luxury is designed to integrate with home automation systems, and so does not come with the web tablet, router, or floppy and CD drives, as it is assumed that the home automation system will already include these or similar interfaces. Owners of 228CFX or PDS128 PianoDisc systems can upgrade to Opus7 at a modest discount to the full system price. Note, however, that PianoDisc will continue to produce and sell the (current) 228CFX and PianoCD systems. Opus7 is distributed through an exclusive network of authorized dealers.

PianoDisc has replaced the PDS128 Plus system with the 228CFX. The main difference between the two is that the 228CFX has both a floppy drive and a CD drive as standard equipment, so it is unnecessary to plug in your own CD player (although you can do so if you have a multi-disc CD changer you want to use). The company says that the control box is the smallest such box with both floppy and CD drives on the market. It can be mounted on the piano or can be located up to 100 feet away and operated with the included infrared wireless remote control.

The 228CFX has several options available that allow you to customize the system to your needs. The MX Platinum option utilizes 64 MB of flash memory to store hours of music and play it back without ever having to change a disk. MX Platinum comes with 35 hours of pre-selected music (589 songs), to which one can add music from floppy disks, TFT MIDI Record, and standard MIDI files (but not PianoDisc CDs). PianoDisc's regular MX feature with 32 MB of flash memory and 25 hours of music still remains available as an option. The SymphonyPro option is a GM sound module and provides orchestrated accompaniment. The TFT MIDI Record option allows you to record your performance or use your keyboard as a MIDI controller.

PianoDisc's entry-level player system is PianoCD. PianoCD is an easy to use system for those who wish to have a player system but don't want or need the advanced features of PianoDisc's other systems.

For a limited time, PianoDisc is offering one thousand dollars in free music software with each PianoDisc system purchased. See your dealer for details.

Note Release Control (NRC) has been developed by PianoDisc to reduce noise made by the keys when they are released. This is achieved by pulsing the solenoid during key release to slow the key down. This new feature is compatible with all PDS128+ and 228CFX Silent Drive systems, and is added by using the Flash Memory feature that allows for convenient software upgrades. To add NRC at no charge, get the PianoDisc Update 4.2 and Silent Drive CPU Update F from the PianoDisc web site or from an authorized PianoDisc installer.

In 2006, PianoDisc introduced a new QuietTime system called the "GT-2." The GT360 and GT90 systems have been discontinued. GT-2 is a silent system for pianos and can be installed in virtually any new or used piano. Once installed, you can mute your acoustic piano and listen to your performance through headphones. The GT-2 has a control unit with two sounds, a piano sound and a church organ sound. It also includes a metronome with adjustable beat, rhythm, and volume. A key sensor system is installed under the keys, and a padded mute rail prevents the hammers from hitting the strings while still allowing the motion and feel of the piano action. The rail is activated by moving a small lever under the keyboard. The GT-2 comes with a control unit, power supply, MIDI cable, a MIDI strip, pedal switches, headphones, and a mute rail.

A question often arises concerning the relationship of the PianoDisc system components to the QuietTime system. The answer is that if you purchase the PianoDisc playback system with the SymphonyPro Sound Module, the TFT MIDI Record system, and the PianoMute Rail, you have purchased virtually all the components of the QuietTime system and have therefore acquired the QuietTime system virtually "free." The separate listing for QuietTime in the price list is for those who wish to purchase it without the PianoDisc playback.

Also recently introduced is the AudioForte speaker system, originally developed by Schimmel and described in an earlier edition of *The Piano Book*. AudioForte is a system of specialized speaker drivers mounted under the piano that turn a piano soundboard into spectacular stereo speakers.

PLEYEL

The company is currently distributing to dealers directly from the factory. See the Pleyel web site (www.pleyel.fr) for a list of U.S. dealers, who can be contacted for further information.

The Pleyel factory currently employs about 85 workers, who build about 1,300 vertical pianos and 50 grands a year using a blend of high-tech machinery and hand craftsmanship. Some interesting new art case models include a 47" vertical model P118 in luxury leather and a 6' 3" model P190 grand in bird's-eye poplar. Other new models include a new line of contemporary verticals, a 5' 8" model P170 grand, and a 9' 2" model 280 concert grand. The concert grand has white keytops made of mammoth bones, comparable in feel to ivory. The larger uprights are particularly nice-sounding instruments.

PRAMBERGER

See "Young Chang" and "Samick"

QRS / PIANOMATION

New phone number: 800-247-6557

QRS has made changes to its line of Pianomation® player piano systems since publication of the Fourth Edition of *The Piano Book*. As mentioned in the book, Pianomation consists of a basic MIDI-compatible playback engine common to all its systems plus a choice of several different front-end controllers that determine the input to the system.

The simplest and least expensive controller is the model 2000C. The control box is hidden under the piano. It has no built-in disk drives, but instead uses your own off-the-shelf stereo components to play QRS CDs and DVDs. The background music comes from your own stereo system, while a wireless transmitter sends the piano data to the Pianomation system, even through walls.

The model 2000CD+ is like the 2000C, above, but has a controller box with a slim profile of just two inches and includes its own CD drive for playing audio CDs. It is most often installed with an optional speaker. Its "plug and play" simplicity has made it a popular entry-level system.

The Petine, introduced in 2005, is just over one and a half inches tall, and includes both a DVD ROM drive and a compact flash reader. The drive will play both audio CDs and data CDs (CD ROMs), the latter potentially containing thousands of MIDI files on a single CD. This controller will also play Standard MIDI files type 1 and 0. Control is by means of a data wheel and a three-digit LED display. The Petine has a headphone output, microphone input for karaoke, and a 1.44 megabyte internal memory storage capacity. The operating system is flash upgradeable.

The Ancho controller has all the functionality of the Petine, but with the more user-friendly, 20-character alpha-numeric display plus dedicated transport controls, unique among Pianomation controllers. It comes standard with a sound card (optional on the Petine).

Both systems are most often installed with an optional speaker. Both the Ancho and Petine have mixed and unmixed audio outputs so that the background music track and the piano track can be mixed for piping around the house, but the piano track can be omitted from the speakers located in the room containing the piano. Individual sources of audio sound can be finely adjusted so they will sound properly balanced at any volume level. On board but not yet implemented on both controllers are dual USB ports and an S-video output.

Sync-Along CDs play on the Ancho and Petine as well as the discontinued Chili and Serenade Pro controllers. QRS has prepared a piano track in MIDI format, stored on a CompactFlash card, to go along with each of a number of popular audio CDs available on the general market. When the owner plays the CD, Sync-Along links it with the stored piano track, enabling Pianomation to accurately play along with the CD. A Transcription series, similar to Sync-Along but without the background music, is also available. A solo performance audio CD is transcribed and offered as a Pianomation CD so the customer can hear the performance on his or her own piano.

Qsync™, expected to be available in stores by mid-year, is a DVD interface designed to implement QRS' patent-pending DVD SyncAlong technology. With the addition of Qsync, a Pianomation player piano will play along with any of a number of popular concert DVDs available to the general market. The owner plays the DVD on their own DVD player, which is hooked up to the Pianomation system. Qsync links it with the stored piano track, enabling Pianomation to accurately play along with the DVD.

The QRS record option used to be offered in both "LiteSwitch" and "OptiScan" versions. These have been discontinued and replaced with QRS' own optical recording strip called PNOscan™.

Pianomation systems and controllers, excluding the Ancho, can be ordered or installed through any dealer doing business with QRS. The Ancho can be purchased through Story & Clark dealers only.

QRS has introduced its "NetPiano™" service through which customers can download any of the thousands of songs from the QRS library to their Pianomation-equipped piano through their personal computer. A wireless transmitter plugged into the computer's audio jack transmits the music to the piano. The service is subscription based, and allows the customer to have access to songs anytime, day or night, without having to build their own CD library. Subscriptions are available only through QRS dealers or through the QRS web site.

QRS also has available the Qtouch Tablet™, an optional tablet remote control with a Media Player plug-in, from which the user can control Pianomation, access NetPiano, or surf the web via the user's computer from anywhere in the home.

Apart from its player piano systems, QRS is constantly inventing new gadgets and gizmos for pianos that can be installed independently of Pianomation. Recent inventions include a Grand Mute Rail for quieting the sound of a grand piano (these have existed for verticals before, but not for grands); a Grand Fallboard Closer that allows a grand fallboard to close gently and avoid hurting the player's fingers (available on many new pianos for some time, but not previously as an add-on accessory); the PNObar™, a bar attachment designed to fit any Story & Clark grand piano, creating a natural setting for socializing (it comes with four bar stools); and GloKeys™, a customized keyboard option where the black keys have been replaced by clear keys that are illuminated using state-of-the-art Superflux RGB LED (red, green, blue light emitting diode) technology to produce a wide array of dazzling colors and effects.

REMINGTON

See "Samick"

RIDGEWOOD

Weber Piano Co., distributor of Ridgewood pianos, has gone out of business, and with it has gone the Ridgewood name. See "Weber."

RIEGER-KLOSS

The Rieger-Kloss name is no longer being used on pianos sold in the U.S. The Bohemia Piano Co. is now making and distributing pianos under its own name. See under "Bohemia" in this section for more information.

RITMŰLLER

See under "Pearl River"

SAGENHAFT

Weber Piano Co., distributor of Sagenhaft pianos, has gone out of business, and with it has gone the Sagenhaft name. See "Weber."

SAMICK

including Kohler & Campbell, Conover Cable, Remington, Pramberger, and others. See also "Knabe, Wm." and "Sohmer".

New contact information for U.S. distributor:

SMC (formerly Samick Music Corp.)
575 Airport Road
Gallatin, Tennessee 37066

615-206-0077
800-592-9393
New web site address: www.smcmusic.com

Samick Music Corporation, the North American marketing arm of the Korean company, is now known as SMC, and distributes Samick, Kohler & Campbell, Conover Cable, Pramberger, Remington, Wm. Knabe (see "Knabe, Wm."), and Sohmer & Co. (see "Sohmer") pianos in North America. Under an arrangement with Baldwin, SMC temporarily distributed Chickering pianos left over from a production run never claimed and paid for by Baldwin after its bankruptcy (see "Baldwin"). Samick has also recently acquired an interest in the C. Bechstein company, a major German manufacturer. See under "Bechstein, C." Samick is no longer making pianos under the Bernhard Steiner name. The Hazelton Bros. name is no longer being used.

SMC is in the process of building a new manufacturing, warehousing, and office facility in Tennessee. It says it intends to begin making the Wm. Knabe, J.P. Pramberger, Sohmer & Co., and some Kohler & Campbell Millennium series pianos there in 2007. These pianos are currently made in Korea, shipped to the U.S., and inspected before going to dealers. With the cost of labor in Korea approaching that in the U.S., and the added cost of duty and freight to import the pianos from Korea, SMC determined that it would be more cost-effective to manufacture the pianos in this country. State and local government in Tennessee provided incentives to make the move more attractive. SMC will be using modern CNC technology it developed in cooperation with Bechstein. Some parts and subassemblies will continue to be made in other parts of the world, especially Indonesia, and Samick will continue to make pianos in Korea for the Korean domestic market.

In March 2004, Samick acquired a controlling interest in its competitor Young Chang, and SMC briefly took over distribution of Young Chang and Bergmann pianos in the United States. However, court rulings in Korea and the United States temporarily ended this arrangement in March 2005, and an arbitration panel ruling in April 2006 permanently ended it. Young Chang and Bergmann pianos are once again being distributed by Young Chang's U.S. distributor, AND Music Corporation (see "Young Chang" for details).

Samick has acquired the rights to the Pramberger name. Pramberger was a name used by Young Chang under license from piano engineer Joseph Pramberger. When Mr. Pramberger died in 2003, his estate had the opportunity to terminate its relationship with Young Chang and did so. Samick quickly licensed the rights to the Pramberger name. However, Young Chang still holds the rights to the original designs, so Samick has designed new pianos to go with the name. The resulting "J.P. Pramberger" piano is a higher-end instrument made in Korea; production will be moved to Samick's new Tennessee facility beginning in 2007. Several American technicians who had known and worked with Joe Pramberger went to Korea at Samick's request to design this piano. The technicians benefited from work previously done by Bechstein engineers in the Samick factory. They began with a modified Bechstein scale, then added several features found on current or older Steinways, such as an all-maple rim, a tapered white spruce soundboard, vertically laminated maple and mahogany bridges with maple cap, and duplex scaling. Renner action and Renner hammers rounded out the list of features. One of the technicians told me the group feels that its design is an advancement of Mr. Pramberger's work that he would have approved of. The "J. Pramberger" is a more modestly-priced instrument from Indonesia. Its design is based on the former Young Chang version of the Pramberger piano.

SMC has created a new Pramberger division within its company for distribution of Pramberger, Sohmer & Co., and Remington pianos. Remington is a new line of low-cost pianos made in Indonesia.

Samick has discontinued a number of models in its Samick, Kohler & Campbell, and Conover Cable lines and has come out with some new ones as well, both Korean and Indonesian. In general, it is continuing its trend of moving most of its production to Indonesia, while concentrating its Korean production on higher-end models. At the present time, all Samick and Conover Cable brand pianos are made in Indonesia. Regular Kohler & Campbell verticals (KC models) and grands (KCG models) are made in Indonesia. Kohler & Campbell Millenium series verticals are made in Korea (KMV) or Indonesia (KM); grands are made in Korea (KFM) or Indonesia (KCM).

For its higher-end pianos, Samick is now using what it calls a "Pratt Reed Premium Action." This is not to be confused with the Pratt-*Read* action used in many American-made pianos in the mid to late twentieth century and eventually acquired by Baldwin. Samick says its Pratt Reed action is made in Korea and designed after the German Renner action.

SAUTER

New U.S. representative:

Sauter USA
P.O. Box 1130
Richland, Washington 99354

509-946-8078
csauter1819@aol.com
www.sauter-pianos.de

Several special models are to be released in 2006. "Amadeus" is a special edition in celebration of the 250th anniversary of Mozart's birth. Although the piano is musically identical to the 6' 1" model 185, the styling is reminiscent of that in Mozart's time. The natural keytops are of polished bone, the sharps of rosewood with ebony caps. Only thirty-six are to be made – one for each year of Mozart's life.

Two more Peter Maly-designed instruments are now available. The 48" model 122 vertical, known as "Vitrea" after the Latin word for "glass," has a veneer of greenish glass covering the front of the cabinet. The 7' 6" "Ambiente" grand is curved on both the bass and treble sides – but not symmetrically – and has other unusual but elegant ornamentation. Musically it is the same as the 7' 3" model 220. In the recent past, Sauter has won several prestigious design awards for its Peter Maly-designed pianos.

In *The Piano Book*, Sauter was listed in Group 2 (High-performance pianos), but some familiar with the European piano scene would place it closer to Group 1 (Highest quality performance pianos).

SCHIMMEL
including Vogel

New address for U.S. distributor:

Schimmel Piano Corporation
577B Hackman Road
Lititz, Pennsylvania 17543

Schimmel has developed several new upright models based on a more traditional philosphy of construction. These are the models K122 (48"), K125 (49"), and K132 (52"). Older models in the same or similar sizes continue to be produced, however. In the older models, the plate is the main structural support and contains a pocket for the pinblock. In the new models, traditional back posts assume a greater role for support, and the pinblock and soundboard are attached to the posts. The company says that the joining of wooden structural and acoustical parts enhances the tone. The new models also incorporate duplex scaling.

Schimmel has created a "trilogy" of redesigned grands by marrying the front end of its 7' grand to two new grand models: a 5' 7" model 169 and a 6' 3" model 189. The company says the new models have the same treble scale and action as its 7' grand, and so have a similar sound and touch. To obtain a larger soundboard, the case sides are angled slightly, a technique now applied to all the grand models. The soundboard and ribs were also modified for tonal improvement. The 6' model 182 has been discontinued. An example of the new 5' 7" grand I played was typically bright, but had very good sustain and the feel of a larger piano. In 2006, a new model 280 9' 2" concert grand was introduced. The piano features a tunable front duplex scale, stronger keys, and bone keytops, among other features.

In 2002, Schimmel acquired the PianoEurope factory in Kalisz, Poland, a piano restoration facility and manufacturer of the Meyer piano brand, one not generally found in the U.S. Schimmel is using this factory to launch its "Vogel" brand, a less expensive line named after the company's co-president. Schimmel says that although the skill level of the employees is high, lower wages and other lower costs results in a piano approximately thirty percent less costly than the Schimmel. Vogel pianos feature Renner actions and other parts from Schimmel or local Polish suppliers. Schimmel may gradually introduce older Schimmel scales into the Vogel pianos, which have received praise from many quarters.

SCHUBERT

U.S. distribution of Schubert pianos from Belarus has been discontinued. For several years, Schubert pianos were made by the Beijing Hsinghai Piano Group in Beijing, China, but these, too, have been discontinued.

SCHULZE POLLMANN

New contact information for U.S. distributor:

North American Music Inc.
11 Kay Fries Drive
Stony Point, New York 10980

800-782-2694
www.schulzepollmann.com
www.namusic.com

Schulze Pollmann has introduced a 5' 3" model 160 grand. As of June 2006, all grands will come with a Renner action; models with the Detoa action are being discontinued. The 46" model 117 and the 50" model 126E verticals have been redesigned. They have new scale designs with agraffes and one-piece solid lock (laminated) backs, and have been redesignated as models 118/P8 and 126/P6, respectively. A new entry-level 45" model 114/P4 has a traditional back, Renner hammers but not a Renner action, and a lesser-quality solid spruce soundboard, among other differences.

Italian auto manufacturer Ferrari Motor Car has selected Schulze Pollmann as a partner in the launch of its new Ferrari 612 Scaglietti series of automobiles. For the occasion, Schulze Pollmann has crafted a limited edition grand piano whose case sports the Ferrari racing red while the cast-iron plate is in the Ferrari gray carbon, the same as the engine of the Scaglietti. The car and the piano are being exhibited together in cities around the world.

SEIDL & SOHNE

New email address for distributor: germanamer@msn.com

SEILER

New U.S. representative:

Piano Marketing Group, LLC
752 E. 21st Street
Ferdinand, Indiana 47532

888-621-1137
america@seiler-pianos.com
www.seiler-pianos.com
www.seilerdirect.com

All Seiler grand models have been redesigned with a duplex scale, longer strings, larger soundboard area, longer keys, and a lighter touch. 5' 11" model 180 has become 6' 1" model 186; 6' 9" model 206 has become 6' 10" model 208; and 8' model 240 has become 8' model 242. There is a new 9' 1" concert grand model 278, and in 2006, a new 5' 6" model 168 grand. I have had an opportunity to play models 208 and 242. Musically, both of these redesigned models are very successful. They retain the typical Seiler clarity, but with longer sustain and a marvelously even-feeling touch — a real pleasure to play.

Seiler has introduced its "Value Added Warranty." The warranty states that at the end of ten years from the date of purchase, a purchaser who has maintained his or her Seiler piano as required under the terms of the warranty may trade it in toward a new Seiler and receive a credit of the full original purchase price paid.

Seiler has established a selection center in Scottsdale, Arizona to enable prospective purchasers without a local Seiler dealer the opportunity to view a large selection of Seiler pianos, and to purchase a piano at a sharply discounted price through its Seiler Direct program. Those with a local dealer but desiring to see a larger selection than available locally may also utilize the selection center by making arrangements through their dealer. For details, see the Seiler Direct web site (above).

Correction: Seiler makes approximately 2,000 pianos a year.

SEJUNG (new listing)

America Sejung Corporation
295 Brea Canyon Road
Walnut, California 91789

909-839-0757
866-473-5864
sales@ASCpianos.com
www.ASCpianos.com

Pianos made by: Sejung Corp., Qingdao, China

Names used: Falcone, Hobart M. Cable, Geo. Steck, Sejung (discontinued), Vivace (discontinued)

Sejung is a Korean-based textile, construction, and information technology business that was established in 1974, but the musical instrument portion of the business began only in 2001. In that year, the company's chairman received a proposal from an old friend with extensive experience in piano and guitar manufacturing to enter those businesses in a big way by manufacturing in China. Within a year, the company had partnered with a Chinese manufacturer (necessary for doing business in China); built a 700,000 square foot factory in Qingdao, a port city on the Eastern coast with a temperate climate; hired dozens of manufacturing managers who had once worked for Young Chang and Samick, and staffed the factory with some 2,000 workers, whom the company also feeds and houses in dormitories (necessary to attract good labor and reduce turnover). Although wages are incredibly low in China (less than one dollar per hour), the company says it has invested millions in automated production equipment in areas where precision counts, rather than just relying on cheap labor. The company produces just about every piano component in its own factories, and has a goal of producing 1,000 grand pianos and 2,000 verticals per month.

The first pianos from Sejung were shown in the U.S. in early 2003, less than one year after production began. I and other technicians examined a number of instruments at a trade show. Although still a little rough, they were definitely competent, and remarkably good for having been only an idea in someone's head less than two years earlier! Since that time, the quality has further improved. The general consensus seems to be that Sejung is destined to be a major force in the world piano market.

For marketing the pianos in the U.S., Sejung has licensed the Falcone and Geo. Steck names from PianoDisc/Mason & Hamlin and the Hobart M. Cable name from Story & Clark (see "Mason & Hamlin" and "Story & Clark" in *The Piano Book*). The names Vivace and Sejung were used briefly but have been discontinued (the Vivace name is now used as part of the Cristofori line of pianos – see "Cristofori"). Initially, the pianos were sold primarily under the Falcone and Hobart M. Cable names, and the two lines were very similar. When use of the Geo. Steck name began in early 2004, the Geo. Steck and Hobart M. Cable pianos became similar (with some style differences), and the Falcone line was upgraded slightly. Specifically, most of the Falcone models have a slow-close fallboard, cast pedals and maple trapwork on the verticals, and slightly nicer cabinets. In addition, a new Falcone Georgian (FG) series includes such features as Abel hammers on grands 5' 4" and larger, upgraded soundboard material, bubinga veneer on the inside of the grand rim, real ebony sharps, and gold-colored hardware.

For model and price information, see under "Falcone," "Cable, Hobart M.," and "Steck, Geo." in the Model and Pricing Guide section of this *Supplement*.

Warranty: Twelve years on parts and ten years on labor. The warranty is not transferable.

SHERMAN CLAY

Correction: I have been told that for much of the 1970s and 1980s, pianos sold under the Sherman Clay label were made by Kimball or Aeolian. In the mid to late 1980s, some Sherman Clay pianos were made by Daewoo (Sojin).

SOHMER (& CO.)

Pianos are again being made under this venerable name, once considered among the finest of American-built instruments. However, there appears to be a dispute over the ownership of the Sohmer trademark, with pianos bearing this name being manufactured and distributed by two different companies.

SMC, distributor of Samick pianos, says it holds a license from the Burgett brothers, owners of PianoDisc, to use the Sohmer name. The Burgetts acquired the Sohmer trademark registrations when they purchased the assets of Mason & Hamlin out of bankruptcy in 1996. A distributor doing business under the name Persis International, Inc., who applied for the Sohmer trademark in 2001, claims that the registrations acquired by the Burgetts are expired and have been legally abandoned, not having been used since the 1994 closing of the Sohmer factory in Pennsylvania. The U.S. Patent and Trademark Office confirms that the government considers all past registrations of the Sohmer trademark to be expired or canceled and that the Burgetts' new application was refused. Further action on Persis' application has been temporarily suspended pending the Burgetts' appeal. At press time, the application process was still ongoing and it may be some time before the issue is settled for good. In the meantime, piano shoppers may find two "Sohmer" pianos in the marketplace. (Note: Persis' pianos are labeled "Sohmer" and SMC's are labeled "Sohmer & Co.") Both companies submitted product information, including model and price data, for this *Supplement*.

Persis International, Inc.
3540 N. Southport #116
Chicago, Illinois 60657

800-445-0695

Sohmer pianos from this distributor are manufactured by Royale, a Korean firm that is descended from the now-defunct joint venture between Ibach and Daewoo (see "Ibach"). Models include a 50" vertical and 5' 3", 5' 10", and 7' 2" grands. The pianos have high quality components, such as Renner actions, Abel hammers, Delignit pinblocks, and Ciresa soundboards.

SMC
575 Airport Road
Gallatin, Tennessee 37066

615-206-0077
800-592-9393
www.smcmusic.com

The Sohmer & Co. model 34, a 42" vertical, features full-length backposts, a sand-cast plate, exposed 16-ply pinblock, and a slow-close fallboard— virtually identical (except for the slow-close fallboard) to the original, highly regarded Sohmer & Co. console. A new Sohmer & Co. studio piano has a design based on the Bechstein 116 centimeter scale. At present, the consoles are made in Indonesia, the studio pianos in Korea. Sohmer & Co. grands are similar to the pianos Samick made for Baldwin under the Chickering label. They have maple outer rims, sand-cast plates, spruce beams, solid brass hardware, agraffes, lacquer finishes, and other higher quality features, and are available in a variety of furniture styles. Sohmer & Co. grands are made in Korea. Production of all Sohmer & Co. pianos will be moved to SMC's new facility in Tennessee beginning in 2007.

STECK, GEO.

PianoDisc has discontinued its Geo. Steck line of PianoDisc-equipped, Chinese-made pianos. The name has been licensed to new Chinese manufacturer Sejung. See "Sejung."

STEIGERMAN

New distributor contact information:

Steigerman Music Corporation
4902 – 217B Street
Langley, British Columbia
Canada V3A 9K1

888-651-8119

pianos@steigerman.com
www.steigerman.com

Steigerman pianos are currently made by the Beijing Hsinghai Piano Group in Beijing, China. The company says it has two full-time inspectors at the factory. See "Beijing Hsinghai."

STEINBERG, GERH.

See "Perzina, Gebr."

STEINBERG, WILH.

New North American representative:

Piano Marketing Group, LLC
752 E. 21st Street
Ferdinand, Indiana 47532

812-630-0978
gtrafton@pianomarketinggroup.com
www.Wilh-Steinberg.com

The name of the manufacturer has changed from Wilhelm Steinberg Pianofortefabrik Gmbh to Thüringer Pianoforte GmbH. The company has also sold its key-making business to Kluge, now part of Steinway.

Steinberg says it will not be making the 49" vertical available with a Fandrich action, as mentioned in *The Piano Book*.

The warranty has been changed to five years, parts and labor.

Although not rated in *The Piano Book*, Wilh. Steinberg pianos, both grand and vertical, are well made and would probably be rated in Group 2.

Correction: *The Piano Book* says that the Wilh. Steinberg grand is identical to the Steingraeber grand. Although the Steinberg grand evolved from the Steingraeber, unlike the Steingraeber, the Steinberg has a duplex scale, as well as a different method of rim construction and a different bridge design.

STEINER, BERNHARD

Samick is no longer making pianos under this name.

STEINGRAEBER & SÖHNE

New address for U.S. contact:

Unique Pianos, Inc.
159 Parkhill Blvd.
Melbourne, Florida 32904

Additional web site address: www.steingraeber.de

Steingraeber has a new 8' 11" concert grand, model E-272.

Steingraeber is known for its many innovative technical improvements to the piano. One new one is a cylindrical knuckle (grand piano part) that revolves when played softly. It acts like a normal knuckle during normal and hard playing, but the revolving knuckle makes pianissimo playing easier, smoother, and more accurate. Another is a new action for upright pianos. The "DFM" action, as it is called, contains no springs, but uses a novel method of keeping the jack under the hammer butt for faster repetition. It is now available in the 51" model 130 vertical and will soon be available in the 54" model 138.

The Steingraeber engineering department has designed and manufactured prototypes of new piano models for a number of other European piano manufacturers. These designs are not the same as Steingraeber's own current models.

Steingraeber has entered the high-end loudspeaker manufacturing business in conjunction with a Bayreuth company.

STEINWAY & SONS

In 2006 Steinway reintroduced the model O (5' 10½") to the United States, replacing the model L of the same size. The model O was first produced by the New York factory in 1902 as the "Miniature" Steinway grand. It was the first Steinway to use the spade-shaped legs now standard on all the company's grands. During its early years, the model O was altered slightly from its original design, changing the straight bass bridge to a curved one and the fixed duplex scale to an adjustable one, and the length was increased by one-half inch to its current size. In 1924 it was replaced by the model L, which had a squared-off tail as opposed to the O's round tail. The square tail design allows for more soundboard vibrating area near the bass bridge. The shape of the tail was the only difference between the two models. Although discontinued in New York in 1924, Steinway's Hamburg, Germany factory has continued to produce the model O to this day.

The model L has generally been considered to be slightly superior to the O, so I was curious as to why Steinway chose to have its New York factory switch to the O rather than have the Hamburg factory change to the L. A Steinway dealer explained to me that at the time the model O was discontinued, Steinway had not yet implemented a number of technical innovations, including tapered soundboards. Once these modern innovations (including a thicker rim) were applied, tests showed that pianists actually preferred the modernized model O to the L.

Reintroduction of the model O to New York follows by one year the reintroduction of the legendary model A (6' 2"). Designed by C.F. Theodore Steinway and first offered in 1878, model A revolutionized piano making by featuring for the first time radial bracing and one-piece bent rim construction. Among other things, these features allowed the use of higher string tension and longer strings for greater volume and projection of sound. At the time the model was introduced, it was the smallest grand the company made, but was considered to provide the sound of a larger piano. Over the years, the model A has gone through several makeovers, each of slightly different size and scaling. The version being reintroduced was made from 1896 to 1914 and is the same size as the model A currently made in Steinway's Hamburg plant. The reintroduction of models O and A furthers the company's stated intention to bring its two factories into greater alignment with one another.

Several years ago Steinway launched its new Legendary Collection—one-of-a-kind reproductions of historical art case pianos—with a reproduction of the famous Alma Tadema art case Steinway. Commissioned in the 1880s by Henry Marquand, then president of the Metropolitan Museum of Art in New York, this piano was designed and created by the famous English design firm of Sir Lawrence Alma-Tadema. In 1997, it was purchased at Sotheby's for $1,200,000. Offered at a price of $675,000, the reproduction, like the original, contains just about every possible art case decoration possible, including elaborate carvings, 17 different levels of decorative moldings, medallions, engravings, inlaid mother-of-pearl, marquetry, goatskin parchment, a frieze consisting of more than 6,000 parts, and even an oil painting. It is considered the most expensive piano ever built.

As mentioned in *The Piano Book*, Steinway maintains a restoration facility at its factory for the rebuilding of older Steinway pianos. Taking a cue from other firms that market "certified pre-owned" products, Steinway is now making these "Heirloom Collection Steinways" available through its dealer network. This program is designed to assist Steinway dealers in competing with rebuilders of older Steinways. The restored pianos will be identified by a medallion and will carry the same warranty as a new piano.

Steinway has made small design changes to its models 4510 (45") and 1098 (46½") vertical pianos to make them easier to tune, including shortening the tuning pin length, reducing string bearing angles, correcting alignment problems in the plate, and adding string-stretching operations at the factory. Some technicians report that the vertical pianos now tune with the same ease as other brands. Steinway is also now shipping all ebony, mahogany, and walnut verticals with artist benches.

Steinway recently commemorated its 150th anniversary with numerous events, concerts, publications, and several new art case pianos. Each year brings stunning new instruments in the Art Case Collection. They can be viewed on Steinway's web site, www.steinway.com.

Correction: On page 206 of *The Piano Book*, I wrote that Steinway operated its own plate foundry until about 1930. My sources now tell me that the foundry operated until about 1939 or 1940.

STORY & CLARK

New contact information:

800-247-6557
www.qrsmusic.com

Story & Clark has ceased all its U.S. piano production. Pianos bearing the Story & Clark name are now made in China by the Dongbei piano factory, except for the upright models 120 and 140, which are made by Beijing Heintzman. To maintain quality control, all pianos go to the Story & Clark facility in Pennsylvania for inspection and adjustment before being shipped to U.S. dealers. The majority of Story & Clark grands are outfitted with the QRS Pianomation system in the factory in China, where the pianos are preslotted and modified to accept the player systems without cutting into the keys and key frame.

STRAUSS

This brand improved somewhat before distribution was discontinued.

SUZUKI (new listing)

Suzuki Corporation
P.O. Box 261030
San Diego, California 92196

800-854-1594
858-566-9710
www.suzukimusic.com

Suzuki Corporation, the world's largest producer of musical instruments for education, has entered the acoustic piano business with a line of verticals and grands made in China by Dongbei. The pianos feature solid spruce soundboards, German Delignit pinblocks, and German Roslau strings.

VIVACE

See "Sejung" and "Cristofori"

VOGEL

See "Schimmel"

WALTER, CHARLES R.

New phone number (area code change): 574-266-0615
Web site address: www.walterpiano.com

Walter is changing over to Renner actions in its vertical pianos (they're already in the grands) and to Renner hammers on both verticals and grands.

Walter says he has made some changes to his vertical pianos to better control tuning pin torque (tightness), to reduce the incidence of false beats in the treble, and to smooth out the break between tenor and bass.

The new Walter 5' 9" model W-175 grand was released in 2006. Like the 6' 4" model, it was designed by Del Fandrich, one of the country's most respected piano design engineers, who also designed and built the Fandrich piano (see *The Piano Book*). Fandrich is known for his fearlessness in piano design, and some innovations are present in the new Walter piano. A portion of the inner rim and soundboard at the bass end of the piano are separated from the rest of the rim and allowed to "float." Less restricted in its movement, the soundboard can reproduce the fundamental frequencies of the lower bass notes more like a larger piano can. A special extension of the tenor bridge creates a smoother transition from bass to treble. Eight plate nosebolts increase plate stability, helping to reduce energy loss to the plate and thus increase sustain. Inverted half-agraffes embedded in the capo bar maintain string alignment and reduce unwanted string noise. The piano has Kluge keys, Renner action, and Abel hammers, among other high-quality features, and is available in the same styles and finishes as the 6' 4" grand.

66

WEBER

The Weber Piano Co. described in *The Piano Book* ceased operations in 2004. The company's owner, Samsung, licensed the Weber name from Young Chang and was required by the terms of its contract to purchase all pianos bearing that name from Young Chang. In addition, it only had the rights to sell Weber pianos in North and South America. Given these restrictions, Weber found it impossible to turn a profit in a changing business environment involving the existence of numerous new Chinese companies. Samsung first tried to purchase the Weber name from Young Chang, and then to distance itself from Young Chang by starting up a "Behning" line of pianos made in China by Sejung. These efforts proved unsuccessful, however, resulting in the decision to close Weber rather than continue to lose money.

Now that Samsung's license to use the Weber name has terminated, Young Chang is using it once again on its own line of pianos. See under "Young Chang" for more information.

WEINBACH (new listing)

Geneva International Corporation
29 East Hintz Road
Wheeling, Illinois 60090

800-533-2388
847-520-9970
pianos@geneva-intl.com
www.geneva-intl.com

Pianos made by: Dongbei Piano Co., Dongbei, China

Formerly made by Petrof and for years virtually identical to Petrof pianos, the Weinbach piano line was given a complete makeover in 2006. The pianos are now assembled in the section of the Dongbei Piano Co. in China in which Nordiska pianos are manufactured. The scale designs are modified from the Nordiska, the plate designs are completely new, and the pianos are strung with a combination of loop and single stringing (one loop and one single-tied string per unison), with bass strings made in the U.S. by Mapes. Like the Nordiska, the Weinbach grands have maple rims, solid spruce soundboards, Abel hammers, and an advanced leg plate design, among other features. The action is Petrof's new "Petrof Original" action (see "Petrof" for details). Fully-assembled actions, keys, and key frames are shipped from

Petrof to Dongbei and added to the Chinese-made strung back and cabinet. At press time, only grand models exist, but two vertical models (118 and 125) will follow in mid-2006.

WEINBERGER (new listing)

Cathy Harl
Harl Pianos
318 Montgomery Street
Alexandria, Virginia 22314

703-739-2220
800-440-HARL (4275)
cathy@harlpianos.com

Pianos made by: Klavierhaus Weinberger, Brucknerstrasse 21, A 4470 Enns, Austria; phone 43-7223-86084-0, fax 43-7223-86084-20; klavierhaus@weinberger.net, www.weinberger-pianos.com

Bruno Weinberger is an Austrian piano technician who markets his own line of pianos. Distribution in the U.S. is very limited. For the most part, the pianos are manufactured by Thüringer Pianoforte GmbH, the maker of Wilh. Steinberg pianos, with Mr. Weinberger providing the musical finishing work. Mr. Weinberger says that the verticals are similar to the Wilh. Steinberg line, but that the grands are built to his own design. The grands have a couple of unique cabinet design features. The closed lid is supported on short posts so that even in the closed position there is a small space for sound to escape. The music desk folds down into the front part of the lid.

WHELPDALE, MAXWELL & CODD

This company was renamed The British Piano Manufacturing Company Ltd. See under that name for more information. The company ceased operations in April 2003.

WOODCHESTER

Woodchester was purchased by Whelpdale, Maxwell & Codd, later called The British Piano Manufacturing Company Ltd., which ceased operations in April 2003. See under "British" for more information.

WYMAN (new listing)

Wyman Piano Company
P.O. Box 218802
Nashville, Tennessee 37221

615-356-9143
info@wymanpiano.com
www.wymanpiano.com

Wyman Piano Company is a new venture created by experienced former Baldwin executives. The Wyman line consists of six vertical piano sizes and four grand sizes in a variety of cabinet styles and finishes. All are manufactured in China by the Beijing Hsinghai Piano Group (see "Beijing Hsinghai"). Wyman says that its executives make frequent trips to Beijing to monitor manufacturing and inspect finished instruments. The pianos come with a ten-year transferable parts and labor warranty.

Wyman now offers a CD player piano system by Pianoforce, a new entrant into the field of player piano systems. The optional CD systems are installed at the Beijing factory and add about $4,200 to the retail price of the piano.

XINGHAI

See "Beijing Hsinghai"

YAMAHA
including Cable-Nelson and Disklavier

Yamaha has replaced its 4' 11" model GA1 and GA1E grands and corresponding Disklavier models with model GB1 (and Disklaviers) of the same size. The GB1 has a new scale design and some plate changes for better tuning stability. It is made at a Yamaha facility in Indonesia.

Perhaps in response to criticisms of the tone of its 5' 3" GH1B series of grands (or perhaps because the introduction of an inexpensive piano from Indonesia has made the low-priced 5' 3" pianos redundant), Yamaha has replaced the GH1B series, and the less-expensive variant model GP1, with a new 5' 3" GC1 series. The new models feature the same scale design, duplex scaling, and tone collector construction as the more expensive C1 series, but with a bass sustain pedal instead of a sostenuto, and with less expensive cabinetry and plate finish. The price of the GC1 is about the same as the GH1B and it is available in most of the same furniture styles and finishes. A

Disklavier version of the GC1 replaces the corresponding Disklavier versions of the GH1B and GP1 pianos being discontinued.

New versions of advanced grand models S4 and S6 – the S4B and S6B – have been introduced. Scale changes in the mid-range area of the piano, along with changes in hammer shape and voicing, have resulted in a more mellow tone. The laminations for the rim are now from quarter-sawn dimensional lumber instead of rotary-cut veneers. The stiffer, more stable rim contributes to the production of a more powerful sound. The keybed has undergone a similar change in method of construction.

In the verticals, model M475 is a new 44" console with cabinetry sophistication halfway between models M450 and M500. Model M425 is an entry-level version of the M450 with simpler cabinetry and finish. Model P600 is a fancy furniture version of the popular P22 studio. A few of the furniture-style models are now available in high polish. Satin ebony versions of models P22 and T116 have been added. The polished ebony T116S is a special limited edition with silver hardware.

Upright models U1 and U3 now sport a longer music desk—a very welcome addition. Model U3 joins model U5 in the use of a "floating" soundboard support system—the soundboard is not completely attached to the back at the top, allowing it to vibrate a little more freely for enhanced tonal performance. A new "Super U" series of uprights (YUS1, YUS3, YUS5) (available Summer 2006) get additional tuning and voicing at the factory, including voicing by machine to create a more consistent, more mellow tone. Model YUS5 uses Roslau music wire instead of Yamaha wire, also for a more mellow tone. Cosmetically, the Super U series pianos come with brass casters and the lids have rounded edges. (Prices for the Super U series were not available at press time.)

The Chinese-made Eterna model was discontinued a few years ago. In 2006, Yamaha introduced a 45" Cable-Nelson studio. The Cable-Nelson is made in Yamaha's factory in Hangzhou, China (southwest of Shanghai), where the company also makes guitars. It is identical in quality and musical specifications to Yamaha's U.S.-made model T116 studio except that the Cable-Nelson has a laminated soundboard, whereas the T116, like all other Yamaha pianos sold in the United States, has a solid spruce soundboard. This same model Cable-Nelson is sold in Canada under the Yamaha name. Cable-Nelson comes with a ten-year Yamaha warranty, but not the service bond. Cable-Nelson is the name of an old American piano maker that traces its roots back to 1903. Yamaha acquired the name when it bought the

Everett Piano Company in 1973, and used the name in conjunction with Everett pianos until 1981.

The "A" at the end of some Disklavier model designations refers to the CD (audio) function in these instruments, one of the Mark III (i.e., third generation) Disklavier features. Disklavier grands are no longer available without the CD function. Most Disklavier verticals don't have the CD function; however, it can be added. DCD1 is an add-on CD drive that can be added to any Disklavier grand or vertical, new or old.

The model DU1A is a new Disklavier version of the 48" U1 upright. It is the only Disklavier upright with Mark III features. It replaces both the MX1Z Disklavier and the MPX1Z Disklavier with Silent Feature. The DU1A contains the Silent Feature; a version of this model without the Silent Feature is no longer offered. The 48" MIDIPiano model MP1Z will become the MPU1.

In late 2004, Yamaha released the Mark IV version of the Disklavier. It contains: an 80 gigabyte hard drive capable of holding all the Disklavier software ever written (and then some!); a tablet or pocket remote control to communicate wirelessly with the Disklavier (pocket on the GC1, C1 and C2 models, both tablet and pocket on C3 and above); built-in ethernet for connecting to your network and downloading MIDI files; the ability to play much softer as a result of a higher-speed CPU, greater MIDI resolution, and improved solenoids; more sensitive recording capabilities due to the use of greyscale (continuous) hammershank and key sensors; karaoke capability, with pitch correction when your singing is off key; an improved speaker system; and more. The performance level of the Mark IV Disklavier is the same as formerly found in the Mark III Pro series. A limited-edition Elton John Signature model is available in several sizes of Mark IV Disklavier. Playback-only versions of models DGB1 and DGC1 will continue to use the Mark III system.

PianoSmart technology is a new feature of all Mark III and Mark IV Disklavier pianos. Yamaha has prepared a piano track in MIDI format on a floppy disk to go along with each of a number of popular audio CDs available on the general market. When the owner plays both the floppy and the CD at the same time, PianoSmart links them together, enabling the Disklavier to accurately play along with the CD. One can also record a piano accompaniment to a favorite audio CD. Pop the CD and a blank floppy into a Mark III or Mark IV Disklavier and record yourself playing along. The two will then be linked together for future playback. PianoSmart is available as a free software upgrade from Yamaha. The "smart" MIDI files will be added to the library of Disklavier musical offerings available from Yamaha. Customers with older Disklavier versions can retrofit PianoSmart into their system by buying the DCD1 Disklavier CD player and a software upgrade, although it may require a memory upgrade as well.

Similar in concept to PianoSmart is Disklavier's videosynch function. Plug a camcorder into the Mark IV Disklavier while videotaping a piano performance, and the Disklavier will play the performance back perfectly on the piano whenever you play back the video of the performance through the camcorder.

In 2006, the Disklavier received the Frances Clark Keyboard Pedagogy Award from the Music Teachers National Association. Typically awarded to a music educator who has made significant contributions to the field of keyboard pedagogy, this marks the first time the award has been given to a music product.

To help its dealers overcome competition from "grey market" pianos, Yamaha has begun an "Heirloom Assurance" program that provides a five-year warranty on a used Yamaha piano less than twenty-five years old purchased from an authorized Yamaha dealer. Obviously, the instrument must be a Yamaha originally manufactured for the U.S. market. For the piano to be eligible for the warranty, the dealer must first submit technical information about the piano's condition to Yamaha and gain the company's approval.

YOUNG CHANG
including Bergmann, Pramberger, and Weber

New U.S. distributor information:

AND Music Corporation
10107 S. Tacoma Way A-3
Lakewood, Washington 98499

253-589-3580

Young Chang America has changed its corporate name to AND Music Corporation.

In *The Piano Book*, it was stated that Young Chang was retiring its "Gold" series in favor of its Pramberger Signature series. The Gold series has now been resurrected as Young Chang's upper-level Chinese line from its factory in Tianjin, China. Model numbers begin with "G." It differs from the company's Bergmann line (also made in China) as follows: Warranty (twelve years on Young Chang Gold, ten years on Bergmann); cosmetic differences in legs, casters, plate color, inner rim color, lid, other cabinetry; tapered soundboard and upgraded hammers on Young Chang Gold grands; laminated soundboard on Bergmann verticals, solid spruce soundboard on Young Chang Gold verticals.

All Bergmann model numbers now begin with "B," the grands with "BTG." A new 5' 9" model BTG-175 and 6' 1" model BTG-185, both made in China, are based on the scales of the corresponding Young Chang Gold series pianos.

Young Chang says it has changed the front duplex scale on all its grand models to a new configuration for a cleaner sound.

In March 2004, Young Chang's Korean rival, Samick, acquired a controlling interest in Young Chang. Under Samick's control, the company then entered into an agreement with Samick's U.S. distributor, SMC, to handle all U.S. distribution and administration of Young Chang products from SMC headquarters in the Los Angeles area. The existing inventory of Young Chang pianos and piano parts held by AND Music Corporation (Young Chang America) was controlled by SMC as well.

In September 2004, however, the Korean Fair Trade Commission ruled that Samick's purchase of Young Chang violated Korean anti-monopoly laws and ordered Samick to sell its interest in Young Chang within a year. Naturally, Samick stopped making payments to creditors on Young Chang's behalf, forcing Young Chang into bankruptcy. In December 2005, the court-appointed receiver for the Korean bankruptcy court cancelled the SMC/Young Chang distribution agreement and reconstituted AND Music Corporation as the exclusive U.S. distributor for Young Chang products. For a time, both SMC and AND were claiming to be the "real" Young Chang distributor, both providing Young Chang and Bergmann pianos to dealers. In March 2005, a U.S. court ruled that the inventory SMC had taken from AND should be returned, ending SMC's distribution of these products. This decision was re-affirmed by an arbitration panel in April 2006, permanently ending SMC's claims. Both companies have said they will honor the warranty of any pianos they supplied to dealers. Young Chang says it has been discharged from bankruptcy, has received an influx of new capital, and is in the process of negotiating with bidders for purchase of the company.

Concerning Young Chang's Pramberger line of pianos, Pramberger was a name used by Young Chang under license from piano engineer Joseph Pramberger. When Mr. Pramberger died in 2003, his estate had the opportunity to terminate its relationship with Young Chang and did so. Samick quickly licensed the rights to the Pramberger name. However, Young Chang still holds the rights to the original designs, and will be making them under different names. The Young Chang Pramberger Signature series (P) has been renamed the Young Chang Premier (P) series. The Pramberger Platinum (JP) series has been renamed the Young Chang Platinum (YP) series. The name on the fallboard will read "Young Chang" instead of "Pramberger."

Prior to the name change, Young Chang had added a 52" vertical and 7' 6" grand to the Pramberger Platinum line. Beginning in 2003, all Pramberger Platinum grands came with a Pramberger/Renner action (Renner parts on a Pramberger action frame), including the damper action. These actions can be identified by their wooden action rail and the Renner label. Please see under "Samick" for more information on current Pramberger pianos.

Following the demise of the Samsung-owned Weber Piano Co. (see "Weber"), Young Chang took back the Weber name, which it owns, and brought out a line of Weber pianos patterned after existing Young Chang and Bergmann pianos and the former Pramberger line. The Weber "Legend" series is like the Bergmann, "Dynasty" like Young Chang Gold, "Sovereign" like the Young Chang Premier series (formerly Pramberger Signature), and "Albert Weber" like Young Chang Platinum (formerly Pramberger Platinum).

The Kurzweil Player System (KPS) is similar to the QRS Ancho system when installed in Young Chang pianos. When installed in Bergmann pianos, the KPS is only available as the QRS 2000 CD+ system.

OTHER ITEMS OF INTEREST

MOOG PIANO BAR

Moog Music Inc.
2004-E Riverside Drive
Asheville, North Carolina 28804

828-251-0090
info@moogmusic.com
www.moogmusic.com

Moog Music Inc., founded by electronic music pioneer Robert Moog, has introduced an amazingly simple and elegant way of turning any acoustic piano into a MIDI controller without modifying the piano in any way. The system consists of three parts: A *scanner bar* sits on the cheek blocks, spanning the keyboard immediately in front of the fallboard and slightly above the keys. Optical sensors in the scanner bar measure the movement of the keys and translate it into note and velocity information. A *pedal sensor* rests beneath the pedals and detects their motion. A *control module* sits on the piano, receiving the data from the scanner bar and pedal sensor, turning it into MIDI information that can trigger over 300 built-in sounds. The control module can hold up to 100 setups, twenty of which can be stored on a portable "library card," twenty that are factory-supplied, and sixty that are user-determined. The control module also contains a headphone jack, audio outputs, and MIDI in and out ports. The Moog Piano Bar is completely portable and comes with a carrying case. It sells for about $1,495 from piano dealers, selected piano technicians, and musical instrument dealers.

MODEL and PRICING GUIDE

This guide contains the "list price" for nearly every brand, model, style, and finish of new piano that has regular distribution in the United States and, for the most part, Canada. Some marginal, local, or "stencil" brands are omitted. Except where indicated, prices are in U.S. dollars and the pianos are assumed to be for sale in the U.S. (Canadians will find the information useful after translation into Canadian dollars, but there may be differences in import duties and sales practices that will affect retail prices.) Prices and specifications are, of course, subject to change. Most manufacturers revise their prices at least once a year; two or three times a year is not uncommon when currency exchange rates are unstable. The prices in this edition were compiled in the spring of 2006.

Note that prices of most European pianos vary with the value of the dollar against the Euro. For this *Supplement*, the exchange rate used was Euro = $1.20. All prices are "landed" prices, i.e., including import duties and estimated costs of freight to the U.S. warehouse or port of entry. However, such costs will vary depending on the shipping method employed, the port of entry, and other variables.

Some terms used in this guide require special explanation and disclaimers:

List Price

The list price is usually a starting point for negotiation, not a final sales price. The term "list price," as used in this *Supplement*, is a "standard" or "normalized" list price computed from the published wholesale price according to a formula commonly used in the industry. Some manufacturers use a different formula, however, for their own suggested retail prices, usually one that raises the prices above "standard" list by ten to fifty percent so that their dealers can advertise a larger "discount" without losing profit. For this reason, price-shopping by comparing discounts from the manufacturers' own suggested retail prices may result in a faulty price comparison. To provide a level playing field for comparing prices, all prices in this guide are computed according to a uniform "standard" formula, *even though it may differ from the manufacturers' own suggested retail prices.* Where my list prices and those of a manufacturer differ, then, no dishonesty should be inferred; we simply employ different formulas. For most brands, but not all, the price includes a bench and the standard manufacturer's warranty for that brand (see *The Piano Book* for details). Prices for some European brands do not include a bench. Most dealers will also include moving and one or two tunings in the home, but these are optional and a matter of agreement between you and the dealer.

Style and Finish

Unless otherwise indicated, the cabinet style is assumed to be "traditional" and is not stated. Exactly what "traditional" means varies from brand to brand. In general, it is a "classic" styling with minimal embellishment and straight legs. The vertical pianos have front legs, which are free-standing on smaller verticals and attached to the cabinet with toe blocks on larger verticals. "Continental" or European styling refers to vertical pianos without decorative trim and usually without front legs. Other furniture styles (Chippendale, French Provincial, Queen Anne, etc.) are as noted. The manufacturer's own trademarked style name is used when an appropriate generic name could not be determined.

Unless otherwise stated, all finishes are assumed to be "satin," which reflects light but not images. "Polished" finishes, also known as "high-gloss" or "high-polish," are mirror-like. "Oiled" finishes are usually matte (not shiny). "Open-pore" finishes, common on some European pianos, are slightly grainier satin finishes due to the wood pores not being filled in prior to finishing. In fact, many finishes labeled "satin" on European pianos are actually open-pore. "Ebony" is a black finish.

Special-order–only styles and finishes are in italics.

Some descriptions of style and finish may be slightly different from the manufacturer's own for the purpose of clarity, consistency, saving space, or other reason.

Size

The height of a vertical piano is measured from the floor to the top of the piano. The length of a grand piano is measured from the very front (keyboard end) to the very back (tail end).

About Actual Selling or "Street" Prices

Buying a piano is something like buying a car—the list price is deliberately set high in anticipation of negotiating.[*] But sometimes this is carried to extremes, as when the salesperson reduces the price three times in the first fifteen minutes to barely half the sticker price. In situations like this, the customer, understandably confused, is bound to ask in exasperation, "What is the *real* price of this piano?"

Unfortunately, there *is* no "real" price. In theory, the dealer pays a wholesale price and then marks it up by an amount sufficient to cover the overhead and produce a profit. In practice, however, the markup can vary considerably from sale to sale depending on such factors as:

- how long the inventory has been sitting around, racking up finance charges for the dealer

- how much of a discount the dealer received at the wholesale level for buying in quantity or for paying cash

- the dealer's cash flow situation

- the competition in that particular geographic area for a particular brand or type of piano

- special piano sales events taking place in the area

- how the salesperson sizes up your situation and your willingness to pay

- the level of pre- and post-sale service the dealer seeks to provide

- the dealer's other overhead expenses

It's not unusual for one person to pay fifty percent more than another for the same brand and model of piano—sometimes even from the same dealer on the same day! It may seem as if pricing is so chaotic that no advice can be given, but in truth, enough piano sales do fall within a certain range of typical profit margins that some guidance is possible as long as the reader understands the limitations inherent in this kind of advice.

Historically, discounts from "standard" list price have averaged ten or fifteen percent in the piano business. In recent years, however, conditions

---

[*] A relatively small number of dealers have non-negotiable prices.

have changed such that, according to some industry sources, the average discount from list has increased to twenty or twenty-five percent. Essentially, due to growing competition from used pianos and digital pianos, and a decrease in the cultural importance attached to having a piano in the home, there are too many dealers of new pianos chasing after too few consumer dollars. In addition, higher labor costs in some parts of the world and unfavorable international currency values make some brands so expensive in the U.S. that they can only be sold at very large discounts. I think, too, that consumers are becoming more savvy and are shopping around. Unfortunately, the overhead costs of running a traditional piano store are so high that most dealers cannot stay in business if they sell at an average discount from "standard" list price of more than about twenty percent. To survive, dealers are evolving multiple new approaches: becoming more efficient, instituting low-price/high volume strategies, cutting their overhead—sometimes including service—or subsidizing their meager sales of new pianos with used pianos (which command higher profit margins), rentals, rebuilding, and other products and services.

Although the average discount has increased, it is by no means uniform. Some brands dependably bring top dollar; others languish or the price is highly situational. I did consider giving a typical range of "street" prices for each brand and model listed in this volume, but concluded that the task would be too daunting due to the extreme variation that can exist from one situation to another, and because of the political fallout that would likely result from dealers and manufacturers who fear the loss of what little power they still have over aggressive, price-shopping customers. So, for now, I've decided just to give general advice in print. (For those who desire more specific information on "street" prices, I offer additional services, such as private telephone consultations and a Pricing Guide Service on the internet. See my web site, **www.pianobook.com**, for more information.)

One way some manufacturers assist dealers in overcoming downward price pressure is to publish wholesale price lists that are less than honest. That is, dealers are routinely offered large discounts (ten to thirty percent) from the published wholesale price if they buy in sufficient quantity, or for certain models, or for any other reason the manufacturer can think of. Since the prices in this *Supplement* are calculated from the published wholesale prices, this practice results in over-inflated list prices in this book for those particular companies, allowing dealers of those brands to advertise larger "discounts" without losing profit. This practice is especially common among some Chinese and Korean companies, but has also spread to some high-end makers, too. (Most manufacturers offer small discounts from the published wholesale price list from time to time or for paying cash, but lately some manufacturers seem to be carrying this practice to greater heights.) The problem for the consumer is that these wholesale discounts are not given out uniformly by manufacturers or among dealers, another reason why an appropriate "street" price figured from the price information presented here will have to remain a rough estimate.

It should be clearly understood that the advice given here is based on my own observations, subjective judgment, and general understanding of the piano market, *not* on statistical sales data or scientific analysis. (Brand-by-brand statistical sales data are virtually nonexistent.) This knowledge is the product of discussions with hundreds of customers, dealers, technicians, and industry executives over the years. Other industry observers may come to different conclusions. This rundown of "street" prices won't cover every brand, but should give a rough idea of what to expect and the ability to predict prices for some of the brands not specifically covered. I can't emphasize enough, however, that pricing can be highly situational, dependent on the mix of available products and the ease of comparison shopping in any particular geographic area, as well as on the financial situation of dealer and customer. The following generalizations should prove useful to you, but expect almost anything.

As a general rule of thumb:

• the more expensive the piano, the higher the possible discount

• the more "exclusive" a brand is perceived to be, the less likely head-to-head competition, and therefore the lower the possible discount

• the longer a piano remains unsold, the higher the possible discount

• the more service-intensive the piano, the lower the possible discount

Discounts from "standard" list price for Yamaha grands and Disklavier grands may be limited by company policy, although how well this new policy will be adhered to by dealers is not yet known. Don't expect more than about twenty percent in most cases. Discounts on verticals may be about the same, or a little higher on expensive verticals. Kawai dealers tend to discount a little more than Yamaha; twenty-five to thirty percent off is not uncommon in a competitive environment. Inexpensive Chinese pianos tend to be service intensive and it's not cost-effective to sell them at a steep discount. On the other hand, the wholesale (and therefore retail) prices are sometimes vastly inflated. Therefore, discounts can vary a lot — from ten to thirty percent. Some dealers just use them as "loss leaders," that is, just to get people into the store, whereupon the customer is sold on a more expensive piano. Discounts on other Asian pianos vary a lot, too, from twenty to perhaps thirty percent.

The Boston piano, although manufactured in Asia, is generally viewed as being a little more "exclusive" due to its association with Steinway, so deep discounting is much less likely. Discounts in the range of ten to fifteen percent or so are common. Selling-price information is scarce on Baldwin products because of the company's recent bankruptcy and the sharp trimming of its dealerships, but fifteen to twenty-five percent would probably be a safe bet, with larger discounts possible on some of the more expensive U.S.-made Baldwin products.

Western European instruments tend to be extremely expensive here due to their high quality, the high European cost of doing business, additional middlemen/importers and, recently, unfavorable exchange rates. There appear to be two types of dealers of these pianos. One type, specializing in selling higher-quality instruments to a demanding clientele, manages to get top dollar for them despite their high price, with discounts averaging only twenty percent or so. They are not particularly into negotiating. The other type of dealer, more numerous, depends for his or her "bread and butter" on consumer-grade pianos and is pleased to make a relatively small profit on the occasional sale of a luxury instrument. Discounts here may well approach thirty to forty percent at times, especially if the piano has gone unsold for an extended period of time. Eastern European brands like Petrof and Estonia are already seen as being a good deal for the money, so expect moderate discounts—perhaps fifteen to twenty percent on Petrof and twenty to twenty-five percent on Estonia.

Steinway pianos have always been in a class by themselves, historically the only expensive piano to continually command high profit margins. Except for older Steinways and the occasional Mason & Hamlin, Steinway has little competition and only about seventy-five dealers in the United States. Service requirements can be quite high, at least in part because of the higher standards often required to satisfy a fussier clientele. Historically, Steinway pianos have sold at or near full list price. (Some dealers even sell *above* list!) This is still true in some places, but in recent years I have seen a little more discounting than in the past. Five percent is most common in the largest metropolitan areas (except New York, where there is no discounting). Ten to fifteen percent is not unusual in some less populated areas. As much as twenty percent would be rare, and is usually limited to institutional purchases of larger instruments. Mason & Hamlin pianos are typically sold at discounts of twenty-five percent or more.

For brands not mentioned or implied in the above discussion, it's usually a safe bet to figure a discount of fifteen to twenty-five percent from the prices in this *Supplement*, with greater discounts possible in selected situations.

There is no "fair" price for a piano except the one the buyer and seller agree on. The dealer is no more obligated to sell you a piano at a deep discount than you are obligated to pay the list price. Many dealers are simply not able to sell at the low end of the range consistently and still stay in business. It's understandable that you would like to pay the lowest price possible, and there's no harm in asking, but remember that piano shopping is not just about chasing the lowest price. Be sure you are getting the instrument that best suits your needs and preferences and that the dealer is committed to providing the proper pre- and post-sale service.

(Note: Remember that the "street" price discounts suggested above should be subtracted from the "standard" list prices in this *Supplement*, not from the manufacturer's suggested retail price.)

For more information on shopping for a new piano and on how to save money, please see pages 60–75 in *The Piano Book* (fourth edition).

Model	Size	Style and Finish	Price*

Altenburg

Grands

Model	Size	Style and Finish	Price*
AG160	5' 3"	Polished Ebony	9,560.
AG160	5' 3"	Wood Finish	9,960.
AG170	5' 7"	Polished Ebony	10,360.
AG170	5' 7"	Wood Finish	10,760.
AG185	6' 1"	Polished Ebony	12,360.
AG185	6' 1"	Wood Finish	12,760.
All models		With Round or Curved Legs, add'l	200.

Astin-Weight

Verticals

Model	Size	Style and Finish	Price*
U-500	50"	Oiled Oak	13,380.

Model	Size	Style and Finish	Price*
U-500	50"	Santa Fe Oiled Oak	14,780.
U-500	50"	Lacquer Oak	13,780.
U-500	50"	Oiled Walnut	13,980.
U-500	50"	Lacquer Walnut	14,380.
Grands			
———	5' 9"	Ebony	35,700.

Baldwin

Verticals

660E	43½"	Mahogany	4,598.
662E	43½"	French Provincial Cherry	4,598.
667E	43½"	Country French Oak	4,598.
2090E	43½"	Mahogany	5,320.
2095E	43½"	Oak	5,320.
2096W	43½"	French Provincial Cherry	5,320.
243E	45"	Ebony/Oak/Walnut	5,512.
243Elvis	45"	Elvis Presley Signature	11,334.
BBK 243	45"	BB King Polished Ebony	14,020.
GSV10	45"	Gibson Les Paul Signature	16,360.
5050E	45"	Mahogany	11,230.
5052E	45"	Cherry	11,230.
5057E	45"	Oak	11,230.
5062E	45"	Queen Anne Distressed Cherry	11,890.
248E	48"	Walnut	8,390.
6000E	52"	Ebony/Mahogany	15,620.
6000E	52"	Cherry with Gold Trim	17,150.

Grands

M1	5' 2"	Ebony and Polished Ebony	41,340.
M1	5' 2"	Mahogany/Walnut	42,540.
M1	5' 2"	Polished Mahogany/Walnut/Cherry	45,140.
225E	5' 2"	French Provincial Cherry	50,940.
R1	5' 8"	Ebony and Polished Ebony	46,540.
R1	5' 8"	Mahogany/Walnut/Cherry	48,214.
R1	5' 8"	Polished Mahogany/Walnut	51,030.
226E	5' 8"	French Provincial Cherry and Pol. Cherry	56,840.
227E	5' 8"	Louis XVI Mahogany	56,840.
BBK 58L	5' 8"	BB King (includes Lucille Guitar)	48,000.
L1	6' 3"	Ebony and Polished Ebony	52,460.
L1	6' 3"	Mahogany/Walnut	54,420.

*For explanation of terms and prices, please see pages 76–82.

Model	Size	Style and Finish	Price*

Baldwin (continued)

L1	6' 3"	Polished Mahogany/Walnut/Cherry	57,480.
SF10E	7'	Ebony	73,580.
SF10E	7'	Polished Ebony	74,760.
SD10	9'	Ebony	115,780.
SD10	9'	Polished Ebony	123,900.

ConcertMaster (approximate, including installation by factory or dealer)

Grands		ConcertMaster CD	5,406.
		ConcertMaster with Playback only	7,024.
		ConcertMaster with Performance Option	8,058.
		With stop rail, add $314	

Note: Discounts may apply, especially as an incentive to purchase the piano.

Baldwin, D.H.

Verticals

561	43½"	Lyptus Wood Clear Finish	2,900.
562	43½"	Red Cherry/Brown Cherry	2,900.
562	43½"	Distressed Red Cherry/Brown Cherry	2,900.
569	43½"	Lyptus Wood Ebony	2,900.
570	43½"	Lyptus Wood Mahogany	4,198.
572	43½"	Red Cherry	4,198.

Bechstein, (C.)

Models beginning with "A" say only "Bechstein" on the fallboard. Others say "C. Bechstein." See article in Manufacturer and Product Update section of this Supplement for details.

Bechstein Verticals

A-3	45½"	Polished Ebony	14,980.
A-3	45½"	Mahogany/Walnut/Cherry	15,160.
A-3	45½"	Polished Mahogany/Walnut/Cherry/White	15,600.
A-2	47"	Polished Ebony	16,400.
A-2	47"	Mahogany/Walnut/Cherry	15,800.
A-2	47"	Polished Mahogany/Walnut/Cherry	17,200.
A-1	49"	Polished Ebony	17,500.
A-1	49"	Mahogany/Walnut/Cherry	17,200.
A-1	49"	Polished Mahogany/Walnut/Cherry	18,600.

Model	Size	Style and Finish	Price*
C. Bechstein Verticals			
Balance	45½"	Polished Ebony	25,200.
Avance	46½"	Polished Ebony	30,000.
Ars Nova	49"	Polished Ebony	33,600.
Elegance	49"	Polished Ebony	29,000.
Concert 8	51½"	Polished Ebony	39,000.
Concert 8	51½"	Polished Mahogany/Walnut/Cherry	40,000.
Concert 8	51½"	Special Woods	49,000.
Bechstein Grands			
A-160	5' 3"	Polished Ebony	41,800.
A-160	5' 3"	Polished Mahogany	43,600.
A-160	5' 3"	Polished White	48,400.
A-160	5' 3"	Special Woods	49,000.
A-190	6' 3"	Polished Ebony	48,600.
A-190	6' 3"	Polished Mahogany	50,200.
A-190	6' 3"	Special Woods	55,800.
A-208	6' 10"	Polished Ebony	56,000.
A-208	6' 10"	Polished Mahogany	57,400.
A-208	6' 10"	Special Woods	62,000.
C. Bechstein Grands			
L-167	5' 6"	Polished Ebony	72,000.
L-167	5' 6"	Mahogany/Walnut	72,000.
L-167	5' 6"	Polished Mahogany/Walnut	75,800.
L-167	5' 6"	Special Woods	86,000.
M/P 192	6' 4"	Ebony and Polished Ebony	89,000.
M/P 192	6' 4"	Mahogany/Walnut/Cherry	88,000.
M/P 192	6' 4"	Polished Mahogany/Walnut/Cherry	90,000.
M/P 192	6' 4"	Special Woods	104,000.
B-210	6' 11"	Ebony and Polished Ebony	100,000.
C-232	7' 7"	Polished Ebony	106,000.
C-234	7' 8"	Polished Ebony	123,000.
D-280	9' 2"	Polished Ebony	164,000.

Bergmann

Model	Size	Style and Finish	Price*
Verticals			
BE-109	43"	Continental Polished Ebony	3,645.
BE-109	43"	Continental Polished Mahogany	3,745.
BE-109	43"	Continental Polished Ivory	3,645.

*For explanation of terms and prices, please see pages 76–82.

Model	Size	Style and Finish	Price*

Bergmann (continued)

BAF-108	43"	Mahogany	4,245.
BAF-108	43"	Queen Anne Oak/Cherry	4,245.
BAF-108	43"	Mediterranean Oak	4,245.
BAF-108	43"	French Provincial Cherry	4,245.
BAF-118	47"	Cherry	4,495.
BE-118	47"	Polished Ebony	4,745.
BE-118	47"	Polished Mahogany	4,895.
BE-120C	47"	Chippendale Polished Mahogany	4,795.
BE-120CD	47"	Polished Mahogany	4,895.
BE-121	48"	Polished Ebony	4,445.
BE-121	48"	Polished Mahogany/Walnut/Bubinga	4,595.
BE-131	52"	Polished Ebony	4,745.
BE-131	52"	Polished Mahogany/Bubinga	4,895.

Grands

BTG-150	4' 11"	Polished Ebony/Ivory	11,045.
BTG-150	4' 11"	Polished Mahogany	11,295.
BTG-157	5' 2"	Polished Ebony/Ivory	12,345.
BTG-157	5' 2"	Polished Mahogany	12,495.
BTG-175	5' 9"	Polished Ebony	13,895.
BTG-175	5' 9"	Polished Mahogany	14,145.
BTG-185	6' 1"	Polished Ebony	14,995.
BTG-185	6' 1"	Polished Mahogany	15,395.

Blüthner

Prices do not include bench.

Verticals

I	45"	Ebony and Polished Ebony	22,530.
I	45"	Walnut and Polished Walnut	23,720.
I	45"	Mahogany and Polished Mahogany	23,596.
I	45"	Cherry and Polished Cherry	23,596.
I	45"	White and Polished White	23,720.
C	46"	Ebony and Polished Ebony	23,786.
C	46"	Walnut and Polished Walnut	25,198.
C	46"	Mahogany and Polished Mahogany	24,956.
C	46"	Cherry and Polished Cherry	25,078.
C	46"	White and Polished White	25,198.
C	46"	Polished Bubinga/Yew/Macassar Ebony	26,592.
C	46"	Saxony Polished Pyramid Mahogany	31,426.

Model	Size	Style and Finish	Price*
C	46"	Saxony Pol. Burl Walnut Inlay/Camphor	31,728.
A	49"	Ebony and Polished Ebony	30,338.
A	49"	Walnut and Polished Walnut	32,090.
A	49"	Mahogany and Polished Mahogany	31,784.
A	49"	Cherry and Polished Cherry	31,940.
A	49"	White and Polished White	32,090.
A	49"	Polished Bubinga/Yew/Macassar Ebony	33,870.
A	49"	Saxony Polished Pyramid Mahogany	40,026.
A	49"	Saxony Pol. Burl Walnut Inlay/Camphor	40,412.
B	52"	Ebony and Polished Ebony	34,638.
B	52"	Walnut and Polished Walnut	36,640.
B	52"	Mahogany and Polished Mahogany	36,292.
B	52"	Cherry and Polished Cherry	36,464.
B	52"	White and Polished White	36,640.
B	52"	Polished Bubinga/Yew/Macassar Ebony	38,668.
B	52"	Saxony Polished Pyramid Mahogany	45,700.
B	52"	Saxony Pol. Burl Walnut Inlay/Camphor	46,140.
—	—	*Sostenuto pedal on vertical piano, add'l*	2,160.

Grands

Model	Size	Style and Finish	Price*
11	5' 1"	Ebony and Polished Ebony	61,424.
11	5' 1"	Walnut and Polished Walnut	64,978.
11	5' 1"	Mahogany and Polished Mahogany	64,358.
11	5' 1"	Cherry and Polished Cherry	64,668.
11	5' 1"	White and Polished White	64,978.
11	5' 1"	Polished Bubinga/Yew/Macassar Ebony	68,578.
11	5' 1"	Saxony Polished Pyramid Mahogany	81,046.
11	5' 1"	Saxony Pol. Burl Walnut Inlay/Camphor	81,824.
11	5' 1"	"President" Polished Ebony	68,578.
11	5' 1"	"President" Polished Mahogany	71,320.
11	5' 1"	"President" Polished Walnut	72,004.
11	5' 1"	"President" Polished Bubinga	75,436.
11	5' 1"	Louis XV Ebony and Polished Ebony	71,692.
11	5' 1"	Louis XV Mahogany and Pol. Mahogany	75,278.
11	5' 1"	Louis XV Walnut and Polished Walnut	74,560.
11	5' 1"	"Kaiser Wilhelm II" Polished Ebony	72,316.
11	5' 1"	"Kaiser Wilhelm II" Polished Mahogany	75,208.
11	5' 1"	"Kaiser Wilhelm II" Polished Walnut	75,930.
11	5' 1"	"Kaiser Wilhelm II" Polished Cherry	75,570.
11	5' 1"	"Ambassador" East Indian Rosewood	84,160.
11	5' 1"	"Ambassador" Walnut	77,928.

*For explanation of terms and prices, please see pages 76–82.

Model	Size	Style and Finish	Price*
Blüthner (continued)			
11	5' 1"	"Nicolas II" Walnut with Burl Inlay	84,160.
11	5' 1"	Louis XVI Rococo White with Gold	90,396.
11	5' 1"	"Classic Alexandra" Polished Ebony	69,824.
11	5' 1"	"Classic Alexandra" Polished Mahogany	73,313.
11	5' 1"	"Classic Alexandra" Polished Walnut	72,616.
10	5' 5"	Ebony and Polished Ebony	70,808.
10	5' 5"	Walnut and Polished Walnut	74,904.
10	5' 5"	Mahogany and Polished Mahogany	74,190.
10	5' 5"	Cherry and Polished Cherry	74,548.
10	5' 5"	White and Polished White	74,904.
10	5' 5"	Polished Bubinga/Yew/Macassar Ebony	79,052.
10	5' 5"	Saxony Polished Pyramid Mahogany	93,426.
10	5' 5"	Saxony Pol. Burl Walnut Inlay/Camphor	94,322.
10	5' 5"	"President" Polished Ebony	79,052.
10	5' 5"	"President" Polished Mahogany	82,216.
10	5' 5"	"President" Polished Walnut	83,004.
10	5' 5"	"President" Polished Bubinga	86,958.
10	5' 5"	"Senator" French Walnut with Leather	86,240.
10	5' 5"	"Senator" Jacaranda Rosewd w/Leather	91,990.
10	5' 5"	Louis XV Ebony and Polished Ebony	82,646.
10	5' 5"	Louis XV Mahogany and Pol. Mahogany	86,778.
10	5' 5"	Louis XV Walnut and Polished Walnut	85,952.
10	5' 5"	"Kaiser Wilhelm II" Polished Ebony	83,364.
10	5' 5"	"Kaiser Wilhelm II" Polished Mahogany	86,698.
10	5' 5"	"Kaiser Wilhelm II" Polished Walnut	87,532.
10	5' 5"	"Kaiser Wilhelm II" Polished Cherry	87,114.
10	5' 5"	"Ambassador" East Indian Rosewood	97,016.
10	5' 5"	"Ambassador" Walnut	89,834.
10	5' 5"	"Nicolas II" Walnut with Burl Inlay	97,016.
10	5' 5"	Louis XVI Rococo White with Gold	104,204.
10	5' 5"	"Classic Alexandra" Polished Ebony	80,490.
10	5' 5"	"Classic Alexandra" Polished Mahogany	84,514.
10	5' 5"	"Classic Alexandra" Polished Walnut	83,708.
6	6' 3"	Ebony and Polished Ebony	77,230.
6	6' 3"	Walnut and Polished Walnut	81,698.
6	6' 3"	Mahogany and Polished Mahogany	80,918.
6	6' 3"	Cherry and Polished Cherry	81,308.
6	6' 3"	White and Polished White	81,698.
6	6' 3"	Polished Bubinga/Yew/Macassar Ebony	86,222.

Model	Size	Style and Finish	Price*
6	6' 3"	Saxony Polished Pyramid Mahogany	101,898.
6	6' 3"	Saxony Pol. Burl Walnut Inlay/Camphor	102,878.
6	6' 3"	"President" Polished Ebony	86,222.
6	6' 3"	"President" Polished Mahogany	89,670.
6	6' 3"	"President" Polished Walnut	90,532.
6	6' 3"	"President" Polished Bubinga	94,844.
6	6' 3"	"Senator" French Walnut with Leather	94,058.
6	6' 3"	"Senator" Jacaranda Rosewd w/Leather	100,330.
6	6' 3"	Louis XV Ebony and Polished Ebony	90,138.
6	6' 3"	Louis XV Mahogany and Pol. Mahogany	94,644.
6	6' 3"	Louis XV Walnut and Polished Walnut	93,746.
6	6' 3"	"Kaiser Wilhelm II" Polished Ebony	90,924.
6	6' 3"	"Kaiser Wilhelm II" Polished Mahogany	94,558.
6	6' 3"	"Kaiser Wilhelm II" Polished Walnut	95,468.
6	6' 3"	"Kaiser Wilhelm II" Polished Cherry	95,014.
6	6' 3"	"Ambassador" East Indian Rosewood	105,818.
6	6' 3"	"Ambassador" Walnut	97,978.
6	6' 3"	"Nicolas II" Walnut with Burl Inlay	105,818.
6	6' 3"	Louis XVI Rococo White with Gold	113,656.
6	6' 3"	"Classic Alexandra" Polished Ebony	87,788.
6	6' 3"	"Classic Alexandra" Polished Mahogany	92,176.
6	6' 3"	"Classic Alexandra" Polished Walnut	91,298.
6	6' 3"	*Jubilee Edition Plate, add'l*	5,980.
4	6' 10"	Ebony and Polished Ebony	91,598.
4	6' 10"	Walnut and Polished Walnut	96,896.
4	6' 10"	Mahogany and Polished Mahogany	95,972.
4	6' 10"	Cherry and Polished Cherry	96,434.
4	6' 10"	White and Polished White	96,896.
4	6' 10"	Polished Bubinga/Yew/Macassar Ebony	102,262.
4	6' 10"	Saxony Polished Pyramid Mahogany	120,856.
4	6' 10"	Saxony Pol. Burl Walnut Inlay/Camphor	122,016.
4	6' 10"	"President" Polished Ebony	102,262.
4	6' 10"	"President" Polished Mahogany	106,354.
4	6' 10"	"President" Polished Walnut	107,374.
4	6' 10"	"President" Polished Bubinga	112,488.
4	6' 10"	"Kaiser Wilhelm II" Polished Ebony	107,840.
4	6' 10"	"Kaiser Wilhelm II" Polished Mahogany	112,152.
4	6' 10"	"Kaiser Wilhelm II" Polished Walnut	113,232.
4	6' 10"	"Kaiser Wilhelm II" Polished Cherry	112,694.
4	6' 10"	"Ambassador" East Indian Rosewood	125,502.
4	6' 10"	"Ambassador" Walnut	116,208.

*For explanation of terms and prices, please see pages 76–82.

Blüthner (continued)

Model	Size	Style and Finish	Price*
4	6' 10"	"Classic Alexandra" Polished Ebony	104,120.
4	6' 10"	"Classic Alexandra" Polished Mahogany	109,326.
4	6' 10"	"Classic Alexandra" Polished Walnut	108,286.
2	7' 8"	Ebony and Polished Ebony	102,374.
2	7' 8"	Walnut and Polished Walnut	108,294.
2	7' 8"	Mahogany and Polished Mahogany	107,264.
2	7' 8"	Cherry and Polished Cherry	107,780.
2	7' 8"	White and Polished White	108,294.
2	7' 8"	Polished Bubinga/Yew/Macassar Ebony	114,294.
2	7' 8"	Saxony Polished Pyramid Mahogany	135,074.
2	7' 8"	Saxony Pol. Burl Walnut Inlay/Camphor	136,372.
2	7' 8"	"President" Polished Ebony	114,294.
2	7' 8"	"President" Polished Mahogany	118,864.
2	7' 8"	"President" Polished Walnut	120,006.
2	7' 8"	"President" Polished Bubinga	125,720.
2	7' 8"	"Kaiser Wilhelm II" Polished Ebony	120,526.
2	7' 8"	"Kaiser Wilhelm II" Polished Mahogany	125,350.
2	7' 8"	"Kaiser Wilhelm II" Polished Walnut	126,554.
2	7' 8"	"Kaiser Wilhelm II" Polished Cherry	125,950.
2	7' 8"	"Ambassador" East Indian Rosewood	140,268.
2	7' 8"	"Ambassador" Walnut	129,876.
1	9' 2"	Ebony and Polished Ebony	133,400.
1	9' 2"	Walnut and Polished Walnut	141,118.
1	9' 2"	Mahogany and Polished Mahogany	139,772.
1	9' 2"	Cherry and Polished Cherry	140,448.
1	9' 2"	White and Polished White	141,118.
1	9' 2"	"President" Polished Ebony	148,924.
1	9' 2"	"President" Polished Mahogany	154,894.
1	9' 2"	"President" Polished Walnut	156,376.
1	9' 2"	"President" Polished Bubinga	163,830.

Bohemia

Adjustable Artist Bench included with all pianos.

Verticals

Model	Size	Style and Finish	Price*
111	43"	Ebony and Polished Ebony	5,000.
111	43"	Open-pore Mahogany/Walnut/Oak	4,780.
111	43"	Polished Mahogany/Walnut	5,180.
111	43"	Polished White	5,260.

Model	Size	Style and Finish	Price*
113	45"	Ebony and Polished Ebony	5,200.
113	45"	Open-pore Mahogany/Walnut/Oak	5,000.
113	45"	Polished Mahogany/Walnut	5,380.
113	45"	Polished White	5,500.
121A	48"	Ebony and Polished Ebony	5,980.
122A	48"	Demi-Chippendale Ebony and Pol. Ebony	6,460.
122A	48"	Demi-Chippendale Polished Walnut/Mahog.	6,640.
122A	48"	Demi-Chippendale Polished Pomele	6,960.
122A	48"	Chippendale Ebony and Polished Ebony	7,100.
122A	48"	Chippendale Polished Walnut/Mahogany	7,320.
122A	48"	"Romance" Ebony with Mahogany Oval	7,480.
123A	48"	Ebony and Polished Ebony	6,400.
123A	48"	Open-pore Walnut/Mahogany/Oak	6,120.
123A	48"	Polished Walnut/Mahogany	6,560.
123A	48"	Open-pore Cherry	6,380.
123A	48"	Polished Pomele	6,760.
123A	48"	Polished White	6,680.
123A	48"	"Exclusive" Ebony with Mahogany Oval	6,760.
122A-123A	48"	With Bohemia/Renner Action, add'l	1,000.
125A	49"	Ebony and Polished Ebony	6,960.
125A	49"	Polished Walnut/Mahogany	7,160.
125A	49"	Open-pore Cherry	6,960.
125A	49"	Polished Pomele	7,480.
125A	49"	Polished White	7,240.
125A-BR	49"	125A with Bohemia/Renner Action, add'l	1,200
132	52"	Ebony and Polished Ebony	7,900.
132	52"	Polished Mahogany	8,700.
132BR	52"	Ebony and Pol. Ebony w/Bohemia/Renner	9,180.
132BR	52"	Pol. Mahogany w/Bohemia/Renner Action	10,160.

Grands

Model	Size	Style and Finish	Price*
150-B	4' 11"	Ebony and Polished Ebony	19,800.
150-B	4' 11"	Walnut and Polished Walnut	21,800.
150-B	4' 11"	Mahogany and Polished Mahogany	21,800.
150-B	4' 11"	Polished White	21,800.
156A-B	5' 2"	Ebony and Polished Ebony	20,400.
156A-B	5' 2"	Walnut and Polished Walnut	22,400.
156A-B	5' 2"	Mahogany and Polished Mahogany	22,400.
156A-B	5' 2"	Polished Pomele	26,400.
156A-B	5' 2"	Polished White	22,400.
156A-B	5' 2"	Demi-Chip. Mahogany and Pol. Mahogany	24,940.

*For explanation of terms and prices, please see pages 76–82.

Bohemia (continued)

Model	Size	Style and Finish	Price*
156A-B	5' 2"	Demi-Chip. Walnut and Polished Walnut	24,940.
156A-B	5' 2"	Chippendale Mahog. and Pol. Mahogany	25,720.
156A-B	5' 2"	Chippendale Walnut and Polished Walnut	25,720.
156A-BR	5' 2"	156A-B with Bohemia/Renner Action, add'l	2,100.
170-B	5' 7"	Ebony and Polished Ebony	22,200.
170-B	5' 7"	Walnut and Polished Walnut	24,400.
170-B	5' 7"	Mahogany and Polished Mahogany	24,400.
170-B	5' 7"	Polished White	24,400.
185A-B	6' 1"	Ebony and Polished Ebony	27,200.
185A-B	6' 1"	Walnut and Polished Walnut	27,340.
185A-B	6' 1"	Mahogany and Polished Mahogany	27,340.
185A-B	6' 1"	*Polished Vavone/Pyramid Mahogany*	35,780.
185A-B	6' 1"	Polished White	27,340.
185A-BR	6' 1"	185A-B with Bohemia/Renner Action, add'l	2,100.
185AE-B	6' 1"	Empire Polished Ebony	26,340.
185AE-B	6' 1"	Empire Walnut and Polished Walnut	28,980.
185AE-B	6' 1"	Empire Mahogany and Pol. Mahogany	28,980.
185AE-BR	6' 1"	185AE-B w/ Bohemia/Renner Action, add'l	2,100.
225R	7' 4"	Ebony and Polished Ebony (Full Renner)	39,740.
272R	8' 11"	Ebony and Polished Ebony (Full Renner)	50,200.
		Upgrade to Full Renner Action from B/R	900.

Bösendorfer

Verticals

Model	Size	Style and Finish	Price*
130CL	*52"*	*Polished Ebony*	45,334.

Grands

Model	Size	Style and Finish	Price*
170	5' 8"	Polished Ebony	88,170.
170	5' 8"	Polished, Satin, Open-pore: Walnut, Mahogany, Pomele, Cherry, Bubinga, Wenge, White	97,240.
170	5' 8"	Polished, Satin, Open-pore: Pyramid Mahogany, Amboyna, Rio Rosewood, Burl Walnut, Birdseye Maple, Yew, Macassar	102,960.
170	5' 8"	"Johann Strauss" Polished Ebony	93,704.
170	5' 8"	"Johann Strauss," other finish	109,138.
170	5' 8"	"Franz Schubert" Polished Ebony	93,704.
170	5' 8"	"Franz Schubert," other finish	109,138.
170	5' 8"	"Classic" Polished Ebony	93,704.

Model	Size	Style and Finish	Price*
170	5' 8"	"Classic" other finish	109,138.
170	5' 8"	"Senator," any finish	105,480.
170	5' 8"	"Chopin," any finish	128,980.
170	5' 8"	"Yacht"	115,434.
170	5' 8"	"Artisan"	165,264.
185	6' 1"	Polished Ebony	90,422.
185	6' 1"	Polished, Satin, Open-pore: Walnut, Mahogany, Pomele, Cherry, Bubinga, Wenge, White	101,762.
185	6' 1"	Polished, Satin, Open-pore: Pyramid Mahogany, Amboyna, Rio Rosewood, Burl Walnut, Birdseye Maple, Yew, Macassar	107,828.
185	6' 1"	"Johann Strauss" Polished Ebony	99,878.
185	6' 1"	"Johann Strauss" other finish	114,216.
185	6' 1"	"Franz Schubert" Polished Ebony	99,878.
185	6' 1"	"Franz Schubert" other finish	114,216.
185	6' 1"	"Classic" Polished Ebony	99,878.
185	6' 1"	"Classic" other finish	114,216.
185	6' 1"	"Senator," any finish	111,236.
185	6' 1"	"Chopin," any finish	132,068.
185	6' 1"	"Porsche Design" Polished Ebony	128,186.
185	6' 1"	"Porsche Design" Colored	137,052.
185	6' 1"	"Liszt" (2006)	126,510.
185	6' 1"	"Artisan"	172,354.
200CS	6' 7"	"Conservatory" Ebony	73,154.
200	6' 7"	Polished Ebony	99,724.
200	6' 7"	Polished, Satin, Open-pore: Walnut, Mahogany, Pomele, Cherry, Bubinga, Wenge, White	108,808.
200	6' 7"	Polished, Satin, Open-pore: Pyramid Mahogany, Amboyna, Rio Rosewood, Burl Walnut, Birdseye Maple, Yew, Macassar	113,784.
200	6' 7"	"Johann Strauss" Polished Ebony	108,808.
200	6' 7"	"Johann Strauss" other finish	127,658.
200	6' 7"	"Franz Schubert" Polished Ebony	108,808.
200	6' 7"	"Franz Schubert" other finish	127,658.
200	6' 7"	"Classic" Polished Ebony	108,808.
200	6' 7"	"Classic" other finish	127,658.
200	6' 7"	"Vienna," any finish	143,280.
200	6' 7"	"Senator," any finish	119,280.
200	6' 7"	"Chopin," any finish	143,312.

*For explanation of terms and prices, please see pages 76–82.

Model	Size	Style and Finish	Price*

Bösendorfer (continued)

Model	Size	Style and Finish	Price*
200	6' 7"	"Yacht"	135,022.
200	6' 7"	"Artisan"	176,790.
214CS	7'	"Conservatory" Ebony	79,770.
214	7'	Polished Ebony	116,164.
214	7'	Polished, Satin, Open-pore: Walnut, Mahogany, Pomele, Cherry, Bubinga, Wenge, White	128,044.
214	7'	Polished, Satin, Open-pore: Pyramid Mahogany, Amboyna, Rio Rosewood, Burl Walnut, Birdseye Maple, Yew, Macassar	132,538.
214	7'	"Johann Strauss" Polished Ebony	125,674.
214	7'	"Johann Strauss" other finish	140,608.
214	7'	"Franz Schubert" Polished Ebony	125,674.
214	7'	"Franz Schubert" other finish	140,608.
214	7'	"Classic" Polished Ebony	125,674.
214	7'	"Classic" other finish	140,608.
214	7'	"Vienna," any finish	160,264.
214	7'	"Senator," any finish	129,616.
214	7'	"Chopin," any finish	158,526.
214	7'	"Porsche Design," Polished Ebony	149,552.
214	7'	"Porsche Design," Colored	164,508.
214	7'	"Mozart" (2006)	125,484.
214	7'	"Artisan"	201,832.
225	7' 4"	Polished Ebony	121,788.
225	7' 4"	Polished, Satin, Open-pore: Walnut, Mahogany, Pomele, Cherry, Bubinga, Wenge, White	132,604.
225	7' 4"	Polished, Satin, Open-pore: Pyramid Mahogany, Amboyna, Rio Rosewood, Burl Walnut, Birdseye Maple, Yew, Macassar	138,228.
225	7' 4"	"Johann Strauss" Polished Ebony	132,604.
225	7' 4"	"Johann Strauss" other finish	154,998.
225	7' 4"	"Franz Schubert" Polished Ebony	132,604.
225	7' 4"	"Franz Schubert" other finish	154,998.
225	7' 4"	"Classic" Polished Ebony	132,604.
225	7' 4"	"Classic" other finish	154,998.
225	7' 4"	"Vienna," any finish	172,224.
225	7' 4"	"Senator," any finish	136,240.
225	7' 4"	"Chopin," any finish	165,140.
225	7' 4"	"Artisan"	217,066.

Model	Size	Style and Finish	Price*
280	9' 2"	Polished Ebony	157,914.
280	9' 2"	Polished, Satin, Open-pore: Walnut, Mahogany, Pomele, Cherry, Bubinga, Wenge, White	175,894.
280	9' 2"	Polished, Satin, Open-pore: Pyramid Mahogany, Amboyna, Rio Rosewood, Burl Walnut, Birdseye Maple, Yew, Macassar	182,632.
280	9' 2"	"Johann Strauss" Polished Ebony	172,636.
280	9' 2"	"Johann Strauss" other finish	196,228.
280	9' 2"	"Franz Schubert" Polished Ebony	172,636.
280	9' 2"	"Franz Schubert" other finish	196,228.
280	9' 2"	"Classic" Polished Ebony	172,636.
280	9' 2"	"Classic" other finish	196,228.
280	9' 2"	"Vienna," any finish	217,672.
280	9' 2"	"Senator," any finish	177,390.
280	9' 2"	"Chopin," any finish	211,220.
280	9' 2"	"Porsche Design," Polished Ebony	198,640.
280	9' 2"	"Porsche Design," Colored	218,504.
280	9' 2"	"Artisan"	250,406.
290	9' 6"	Polished Ebony	179,546.
290	9' 6"	Polished, Satin, Open-pore: Walnut, Mahogany, Pomele, Cherry, Bubinga, Wenge, White	198,806.
290	9' 6"	Polished, Satin, Open-pore: Pyramid Mahogany, Amboyna, Rio Rosewood, Burl Walnut, Birdseye Maple, Yew, Macassar	205,994.
290	9' 6"	"Johann Strauss" Polished Ebony	195,124.
290	9' 6"	"Johann Strauss" other finish	218,276.
290	9' 6"	"Franz Schubert" Polished Ebony	195,124.
290	9' 6"	"Franz Schubert" other finish	218,276.
290	9' 6"	"Classic" Polished Ebony	195,124.
290	9' 6"	"Classic" other finish	218,276.
290	9' 6"	"Vienna," any finish	241,592.
290	9' 6"	"Senator," any finish	199,672.
290	9' 6"	"Chopin," any finish	238,118.
290	9' 6"	"Artisan"	264,436.
170-225	5' 8"-7' 4"	Louis XVI, any finish, add'l	21,200.
280-290	9' 2"-9' 6"	Louis XVI, any finish, add'l	25,440.
170-225	5' 8"-7' 4"	Baroque, any finish, add'l	21,200.
280-290	9' 2"-9' 6"	Baroque, any finish, add'l	25,440.
170-280	5' 8"-9' 2"	"CEUS" Computer Grand, add'l	61,402.
290	9' 6"	"CEUS" Computer Grand, add'l	67,682.

*For explanation of terms and prices, please see pages 76–82.

Model	Size	Style and Finish	Price*

Boston

Verticals

Model	Size	Style and Finish	Price*
UP-118E	46"	Ebony and Polished Ebony	9,820.
UP-118E	46"	Walnut	10,990.
UP-118E	46"	Polished Walnut/Mahogany	11,220.
UP-118E	46"	Polished White	11,060.
UP-118A	46"	Art Deco Aniegre	7,990.
UP-118S	46"	Open-Pore Honey Oak/Black Oak/Red Oak	6,140.
UP-118S	46"	Mahogany	7,600.
UP-126E	50"	Ebony and Polished Ebony	11,920.
UP-126E	50"	Polished Mahogany	13,760.
UP-132E	52"	Polished Ebony	13,100.

Grands

Model	Size	Style and Finish	Price*
GP-156	5' 1"	Ebony and Polished Ebony	17,190.
GP-163	5' 4"	Ebony	20,540.
GP-163	5' 4"	Polished Ebony	21,100.
GP-163	5' 4"	Mahogany	22,480.
GP-163	5' 4"	Polished Mahogany	23,100.
GP-163	5' 4"	Walnut	22,680.
GP-163	5' 4"	Polished Walnut	23,360.
GP-163	5' 4"	Polished White/Ivory	21,680.
GP-178	5' 10"	Ebony	23,700.
GP-178	5' 10"	Polished Ebony	24,300.
GP-178	5' 10"	Mahogany	25,340.
GP-178	5' 10"	Polished Mahogany	26,040.
GP-178	5' 10"	Walnut	25,640.
GP-178	5' 10"	Polished Walnut	26,520.
GP-178	5' 10"	Polished White/Ivory	24,820.
GP-193	6' 4"	Ebony	30,120.
GP-193	6' 4"	Polished Ebony	30,900.
GP-193	6' 4"	Walnut	33,560.
GP-193	6' 4"	Polished Mahogany	33,800.
GP-193	6' 4"	Polished White	32,520.
GP-215	7' 1"	Ebony	38,920.
GP-215	7' 1"	Polished Ebony	39,900.

Breitmann

Verticals

Model	Size	Style and Finish	Price*
B110	44"	Polished Ebony	3,420.

Model	Size	Style and Finish	Price*
B110	44"	Polished Mahogany/Walnut	3,480.
B120	47¼"	Polished Ebony	3,710.
B120	47¼"	Polished Mahogany/Walnut	3,780.
B122	48"	Polished Ebony	4,050.
B122	48"	Polished Mahogany/Walnut	4,140.
B130	52"	Polished Ebony	4,390.
B130	52"	Polished Mahogany/Walnut	4,730.
B130	52"	Polished White	4,680.
Grands			
B16	5' 2"	Polished Ebony	9,750.
B16	5' 2"	Polished White	9,900.
B17	5' 8"	Polished Ebony	10,650.

Brodmann

Verticals

BU 116	45"	Polished Ebony	5,190.
BU 121	47"	Polished Ebony	5,720.
BU 123C	48"	Italian Provincial Cherry	6,750.
BU 123M	48"	French Provincial Mahogany	6,750.
BU 123W	48"	Walnut	6,750.
BU 125	49"	Polished Ebony	6,630.
BU 132	52"	Polished Ebony	8,800.

"European Premium" Verticals

SB 121	47"	Polished Ebony	15,060.
SB 121	47"	Polished Mahogany/Walnut	15,590.
VE 125	48"	Polished Ebony	15,200.
VE 125	48"	Polished Mahogany	16,370.
VE 125	48"	Polished Pyramid Mahogany	19,360.
VE 125	48"	Polished Bubinga/Pommele	17,540.
VE 125	48"	Polished Rosewood	18,840.

Grands

BG 150	4' 11"	Polished Ebony	14,430.
BG 162	5' 4"	Polished Ebony	15,860.
BG 187	6' 2"	Polished Ebony	17,160.
BG 212	7'	Polished Ebony *(available 2007)*	
BG 228	7' 5"	Polished Ebony	36,140.
BG 275	9'	Polished Ebony *(available 2008)*	

*For explanation of terms and prices, please see pages 76–82.

Model	Size	Style and Finish	Price*

Cable, Hobart M.

Model numbers ending in "D" indicate slow-close fallboard.

Verticals

Model	Size	Style and Finish	Price*
UH 09	43"	Continental Polished Ebony	2,870.
UH 09	43"	Continental Cherry/Mahogany	2,930.
UH 09	43"	Continental Polished Mahogany/Walnut	2,990.
UH 09	43"	Continental Polished Ivory/White	2,990.
UH 09A	43"	Continental Polished Ebony (no back posts)	2,680.
UH 09A	43"	Continental Pol. Mahogany (no back posts)	2,800.
UH 09L	43"	Continental (w/legs) Polished Ebony	2,950.
UH 09L	43"	Continental (w/legs) Pol, Mahogany/Walnut	3,070.
UH 09L	43"	Continental (w/legs) Polished White	3,070.
CH 12F	43"	French Provincial Cherry/Brown Oak	3,370.
CH 12F1	44"	French Provincial Cherry/Brown Oak	3,190.
CH 12FD	44"	French Provincial Cherry/Brown Oak	3,490.
CH 12IP	44"	Italian Provincial Walnut	3,570.
CH 12M	44"	Mediterranean Cherry/Brown Oak	3,370.
CH 12M1	44"	Mediterranean Cherry/Brown Oak	3,190.
CH 12MD	44"	Mediterranean Cherry/Brown Oak	3,490.
UH 12F	44"	Cherry/Mahogany	3,260.
UH 12T	44"	Polished Ebony	3,080.
UH 12T	44"	Mahogany/Walnut/Cherry	3,140.
UH 12T	44"	Polished Mahogany/Walnut	3,200.
UH 12T	44"	Polished Ivory and White	3,200.
CH 13F1D	44½"	French Designer Cherry/Brown Oak	3,790.
CH 13MD	44½"	Designer Cherry/Dark Cherry/Mahogany	3,590.
CH 13M1D	44½"	Designer Cherry/Brown Oak	3,790.
CH 16ATD	45½"	Cherry	3,990.
CH 16FPD	45½"	French Provincial Cherry/Brown Oak	3,790.
CH 16IPD	45½"	Italian Provincial Cherry	3,790.
CH 16QAD	45½"	Queen Anne Cherry	4,090.
UH 16I	46"	Polished Walnut	3,160.
UH 16ST	46"	Brown Oak/Cherry (school)	3,200.
UH 16STL	46"	Brown Oak/Cherry (school with lock)	. 3,500.
CH 19F	46¾"	Country French Cherry/Brown Oak	3,700.
CH 19FD	46¾"	Country French Cherry/Brown Oak	3,820.
CH 19M	46¾"	Mediterranean Brown Oak/Cherry	3,700.
CH 19MD	46¾"	Mediterranean Cherry/Brown Oak	3,820.
CH 19M1D	46¾"	Mediterranean Cherry	3,820.
CH 19QAD	46¾"	Queen Anne Cherry	4,190.

Model	Size	Style and Finish	Price*
UH 19F	46¾"	Demi-Chippendale Polished Ebony	3,320.
UH 19F	46¾"	Demi-Chippendale Mahogany/Cherry	3,380.
UH 19F	46¾"	Demi-Chip. Pol. Mahogany/Walnut/Cherry	3,440.
UH 19F	46¾"	Demi-Chippendale Polished Ivory/White	3,440.
UH 19FC	46¾"	Chippendale Polished Mahogany/Walnut	3,500.
UH 19FD	46¾"	Demi-Chippendale Polished White	3,560.
UH 19ST	46¾"	Polished Ebony	3,200.
UH 19ST	46¾"	Oak/Brown Oak/Cherry/Dark Cherry	3,260.
UH 19ST	46¾"	Polished Mahogany/Walnut/White	3,320.
UH 19T	46¾"	Polished Ebony	3,200.
UH 19T	46¾"	Cherry/Brown Oak	3,260.
UH 19T	46¾"	Polished Mahogany/Walnut/Ivory	3,320.
UH 20T	47"	Designer Polished Ebony	3,490.
UH 22F	48"	French Provincial Polished Ebony	3,490.
UH 22F	48"	French Provincial Pol. Mahogany/Walnut	3,610.
UH 22FD	48"	Fr. Prov. Pol. Mahog./Walnut/Ivory/White	3,730.
UH 22T	48"	Polished Ebony	3,370.
UH 22T	48"	Polished Mahogany/Walnut/White	3,490.
UH 22TD	48"	Polished Ebony	3,490.
UH 22TD	48"	Polished Mahogany/Walnut/White/Ivory	3,610.
UH 23FD	48½"	French Provincial Polished Walnut	3,860.
UH 23TD	48½"	Designer Polished Ebony	3,620.
UH 23TD	48½"	Designer Polished Mahogany/Walnut	3,740.
UH 32F	52"	French Provincial Polished Ebony	3,740.
UH 32F	52"	French Provincial Pol. Mahogany	3,860.
UH 32FD	52"	French Provincial Polished Ebony	3,860.
UH 32FD	52"	French Provincial Pol. Mahogany/Walnut	3,980.
UH 32T	52"	Polished Ebony	3,620.
UH 32T	52"	Polished Mahogany/Walnut	3,740.
UH 32TD	52"	Polished Ebony	3,740.
UH 32TD	52"	Polished Mahogany/Walnut	3,860.

Grands

Some "D" models are available without slow-close fallboard for $120 less.

GH 42D	4' 8"	Ebony	8,740.
GH 42D	4' 8"	Polished Ebony	8,540.
GH 42D	4' 8"	Cherry/Mahogany/Walnut	9,140.
GH 42D	4' 8"	Polished Mahogany/Walnut/Cherry	8,940.
GH 42D	4' 8"	Polished Bubinga	9,540.
GH 42D	4' 8"	Polished Ivory	8,740.
GH 42F	4' 8"	French Provincial Polished Ebony	9,020.

*For explanation of terms and prices, please see pages 76–82.

Model	Size	Style and Finish	Price*

Cable, Hobart M. (continued)

Model	Size	Style and Finish	Price*
GH 42FD	4' 8"	French Prov. Cherry/Walnut/Mahogany	9,740.
GH 42FD	4' 8"	French Prov. Pol. Cherry/Walnut/Mahogany	9,540.
GH 52D	5'	Ebony	9,580.
GH 52D	5'	Polished Ebony	9,380.
GH 52D	5'	Mahogany/Cherry/Walnut	9,980.
GH 52D	5'	Polished Mahogany/Walnut/Cherry	9,780.
GH 52D	5'	Polished Bubinga	10,380.
GH 52FD	5'	French Provincial Mahogany/Cherry	10,580.
GH 52FD	5'	French Provincial Pol. Mahogany/Walnut	10,380.
GH 52FAD	5'	FrenchAnn Polished Cherry	10,580.
GH 62D	5' 4"	Ebony	10,610.
GH 62D	5' 4"	Polished Ebony	10,410.
GH 62D	5' 4"	Cherry/Walnut/Mahogany	11,010.
GH 62D	5' 4"	Polished Mahogany/Walnut	10,810.
GH 62D	5' 4"	Polished Bubinga	11,410.
GH 62F	5' 4"	French Provincial Ebony	11,090.
GH 62F	5' 4"	French Provincial Polished White	11,090.
GH 62FD	5' 4"	French Provincial Cherry	11,610.
GH 62FD	5' 4"	French Provincial Polished Mahogany	11,410.
GH 72D	5' 8"	Ebony	11,640.
GH 72D	5' 8"	Polished Ebony	11,440.
GH 72D	5' 8"	Mahogany/Cherry	12,040.
GH 72D	5' 8"	Polished Mahogany/Walnut	11,840.
GH 72D	5' 8"	Polished Bubinga	12,440.
GH 72FD	5' 8"	French Provincial Polished Mahogany	12,440.
GH 72LD	5' 8"	Louis XVI Polished Ebony	11,920.
GH 72LD	5' 8"	Louis XVI Polished Mahogany	12,320.
GH 72PLD	5' 8"	Polished Mahogany (Octagonal Leg)	12,440.
GH 72QAD	5' 8"	Queen Anne Cherry	12,840.
GH 87D	6' 2"	Ebony	12,660.
GH 87D	6' 2"	Polished Ebony	12,460.
GH 87D	6' 2"	Mahogany/Cherry	13,060.
GH 87D	6' 2"	Polished Mahogany	12,860.
GH 87FD	6' 2"	French Provincial Cherry	13,660.
GH 87FD	6' 2"	French Provincial Polished Mahogany	13,460.
GH 87HLD	6' 2"	Mahogany (Hexagonal Leg)	13,760.
GH 87LD	6' 2"	Louis XVI Ebony	13,140.
GH 87LD	6' 2"	Louis XVI Polished Ebony	12,940.
GH 87LD	6' 2"	Louis XVI Mahogany	13,540.

Model	Size	Style and Finish	Price*
GH 87LD	6' 2"	Louis XVI Polished Mahogany	13,340.
GH 208D	6' 10"	Ebony	15,800.

Cable-Nelson

Verticals

CN 116	45"	Polished Ebony	3,190.

Chase, A. B.

Verticals

EV-112	44"	Continental Polished Ebony	2,580.
EV-112	44"	Continental Polished Mahogany	2,700.
EV-113	45"	Polished Ebony	2,780.
EV-113	45"	Polished Mahogany	2,900.
EV-115CB	45"	Chippendale Polished Mahogany	3,100.
EV-121	48"	Polished Ebony	3,180.
EV-121	48"	Polished Mahogany	3,300.

Grands

EV-152	5'	Polished Ebony	7,780.
EV-152	5'	Polished Mahogany/Walnut	8,280.
EV-152	5'	Polished Sapele	8,480.
EV-152	5'	Polished White	8,280.
EV-165	5' 5"	Polished Ebony	8,780.
EV-165	5' 5"	Polished Mahogany/Walnut	9,280.
EV-185	6' 1"	Polished Ebony	10,780.
EV-185	6' 1"	Polished Mahogany	11,280.

Conover Cable

Verticals

CC-142	42"	Continental Polished Ebony	2,990.
CC-142	42"	Continental Walnut/Cherry	2,990.
CC-142	42"	Continental Pol. Mahogany/Walnut/Ivory	3,090.
CC-043F	43"	French Provincial Cherry	3,890.
CC-043T	43"	Mahogany	3,890.
CC-145	45"	Polished Ebony	3,390.
CC-145	45"	Walnut/Cherry	3,390.
CC-145	45"	Polished Mahogany/Walnut/Ivory	3,490.
CC-247	46½"	Ebony and Polished Ebony	4,990.

*For explanation of terms and prices, please see pages 76–82.

Model	Size	Style and Finish	Price*

Conover Cable (continued)

Model	Size	Style and Finish	Price*
CC-247	46½"	Walnut/Mahogany	4,990.
CC-247	46½"	Polished Walnut/Mahogany	4,990.
CC-121M	48"	Mediterranean Polished Ebony	4,190.
CC-121M	48"	Mediterranean Polished Mahogany	4,390.
CC-131	52"	Polished Ebony	4,790.

Grands
CCIG-50	4' 11½"	Polished Ebony	8,390.
CCIG-50	4' 11½"	Polished Mahogany/Walnut	9,090.
CCIG-54	5' 3"	Polished Ebony	10,090.
CCIG-54	5' 3"	Polished Mahogany/Walnut	10,790.
CCIG-57	5' 7"	Polished Ebony	10,990.
CCIG-57	5' 7"	Polished Mahogany/Walnut	11,590.
CCIG-61	6' 1"	Polished Ebony	11,790.
CCIG-61	6' 1"	Polished Mahogany/Walnut	12,390.

Cristofori

Verticals
CRV430C	43"	Continental Polished Ebony	2,798.
CRV430C	43"	Continental Polished Mahogany/Walnut	2,998.
CRV430C	43"	Continental Walnut/Oak	2,998.
CRV440P	44"	Ebony	3,498.
CRV440P	44"	Polished Ebony	3,398.
CRV440P	44"	Polished Mahogany/Walnut	3,598.
CRV440P	44"	Walnut/Oak	3,598.
CRV445F	44½"	French Provincial Cherry	3,798.
CRV445T	44½"	Cherry	3,798.
CRV445M	44½"	Mediterranean Oak	3,798.
CRV460F	46"	French Provincial Cherry	4,398.
CRV460CF	46"	Country French Oak	4,398.
CRV460R	46"	Regency Cherry	4,598.
CRV460SP	46"	School Ebony	3,798.
CRV460SP	46"	School Walnut/Oak	3,998.
CRV470P	47"	Ebony	4,098.
CRV470P	47"	Polished Ebony	3,998.
CRV470P	47"	Polished Mahogany/Walnut	4,198.
CRV470P	47"	Walnut/Oak	4,198.
CRV480P	48"	Ebony	4,898.
CRV480P	48"	Polished Ebony	4,798.

Model	Size	Style and Finish	Price*
CRV480P	48"	Polished Mahogany/Walnut	4,998.
CRV480P	48"	Walnut/Oak	4,998.

Grands

Model	Size	Style and Finish	Price*
G42/CRG48L	4' 8"	"Vivace" Ebony	6,848.
G42/CRG48L	4' 8"	"Vivace" Polished Ebony	6,598.
G42/CRG48L	4' 8"	"Vivace" Polished Mahogany/Walnut	6,948.
G42/CRG48L	4' 8"	"Vivace" Walnut/Oak	6,948.
G42/CRG48L	4' 8"	"Vivace" French Provincial Cherry	7,298.
G42/CRG48L	4' 8"	"Vivace" Bubinga	7,298.
CRG48	4' 8"	Ebony	7,648.
CRG48	4' 8"	Polished Ebony	7,398.
CRG48	4' 8"	Polished Mahogany/Walnut	7,748.
CRG48	4' 8"	Walnut/Oak	7,748.
CRG48	4' 8"	French Provincial Cherry	8,098.
CRG48	4' 8"	Bubinga	8,098.
CRG50	5'	Ebony	8,248.
CRG50	5'	Polished Ebony	7,998.
CRG50	5'	Polished Mahogany/Walnut	8,348.
CRG50	5'	Walnut/Oak	8,348.
CRG50	5'	French Provincial Cherry	8,698.
CRG50	5'	Bubinga	8,698.
CRG54	5' 4"	Ebony	9,448.
CRG54	5' 4"	Polished Ebony	9,198.
CRG54	5' 4"	Polished Mahogany/Walnut	9,548.
CRG54	5' 4"	Walnut/Oak	9,548.
CRG54	5' 4"	French Provincial Cherry	9,898.
CRG54	5' 4"	Bubinga	9,898.
CRG58	5' 8"	Ebony	10,248.
CRG58	5' 8"	Polished Ebony	9,998.
CRG58	5' 8"	Polished Mahogany/Walnut	10,348.
CRG58	5' 8"	Walnut/Oak	10,348.
CRG58	5' 8"	French Provincial Cherry	10,698.
CRG58	5' 8"	Bubinga	10,698.
CRG62	6' 2"	Ebony	11,648.
CRG62	6' 2"	Polished Ebony	11,398.
CRG62	6' 2"	Polished Mahogany/Walnut	11,748.
CRG62	6' 2"	Walnut/Oak	11,748.
CRG62	6' 2"	French Provincial Cherry	12,098.
CRG62	6' 2"	Bubinga	12,098.

*For explanation of terms and prices, please see pages 76–82.

Model	Size	Style and Finish	Price*

Ebel, Carl

Verticals

115	45"	Polished Ebony	5,040.
115	45"	Polished Mahogany/Walnut/Oak	5,250.
121	48"	Polished Ebony	5,390.
121	48"	Polished Mahogany/Walnut	5,590.

Grands

G-151	4' 11½"	Polished Ebony	10,990.
G-151	4' 11½"	Polished Mahogany/Walnut/Oak/White	11,490.
G-151	4' 11½"	Satin Finishes	11,490.
G-151	4' 11½"	Polished Ebony (round leg)	11,290.
G-151	4' 11½"	Polished Mahogany/Walnut (round leg)	11,790.
G-151	4' 11½"	Satin Finishes (round leg)	11,790.
G-151	4' 11½"	Polished Ebony (curved leg)	11,290.
G-151	4' 11½"	Polished Mahogany/Walnut (curved leg)	11,790.
G-151	4' 11½"	Satin Finishes (curved leg)	11,790.

Essex

Verticals

EUP-107C	42"	Continental Polished Ebony	3,770.
EUP-111E	44"	European Polished Ebony	4,110.
EUP-111E	44"	European Polished Mahogany	4,210.
EUP-111E	44"	European Polished Walnut	4,230.
EUP-111E	44"	European Polished White	4,140.
EUP-111F	44"	French Provincial Cherry	4,250.
EUP-111M	44"	Modern Walnut	4,070.
EUP-111R	44"	English Regency Mahogany	3,970.
EUP-111T	44"	Ash	4,010.

Grands

EGP-161	5' 3"	Ebony	12,390.
EGP-161	5' 3"	Polished Ebony	12,190.
EGP-161	5' 3"	Mahogany	13,390.
EGP-161	5' 3"	Polished Mahogany	13,190.
EGP-161	5' 3"	Walnut	13,790.
EGP-161	5' 3"	Cherry	13,990.
EGP-161	5' 3"	Oak	13,790.
EGP-161	5' 3"	Polished White	12,390.
EGP-161N	5' 3"	Neo-Classic Mahogany	14,990.

Model	Size	Style and Finish	Price*
EGP-161N	5' 3"	Neo-Classic Polished Mahogany	14,790.
EGP-161N	5' 3"	Neo-Classic Cherry	15,590.
EGP-183	6'	Ebony	18,100.
EGP-183	6'	Polished Ebony	17,840.
EGP-183	6'	Polished Mahogany	19,050.
EGP-183	6'	Walnut	19,850.

Estonia

Prices include Jansen adjustable artist bench.

Grands

168	5' 6"	Ebony and Polished Ebony	28,350.
168	5' 6"	Mahogany and Polished Mahogany	30,764.
168	5' 6"	Walnut and Polished Walnut	30,764.
168	5' 6"	Bubinga and Polished Bubinga	33,444.
168	5' 6"	"Hidden Beauty" Pol. Ebony w/Bubinga	31,500.
168	5' 6"	"Hidden Beauty" Pol. Ebony w/Kareelia	33,074.
190	6' 3"	Ebony and Polished Ebony	34,650.
190	6' 3"	Mahogany and Polished Mahogany	37,340.
190	6' 3"	Pyramid Mahogany	44,800.
190	6' 3"	Walnut and Polished Walnut	37,340.
190	6' 3"	Bubinga and Polished Bubinga	40,320.
190	6' 3"	"Hidden Beauty" Pol. Ebony w/Bubinga	36,910.
190	6' 3"	"Hidden Beauty" Pol. Ebony w/Kareelia	37,744.
273	9'	Ebony and Polished Ebony	84,000.

Everett

Verticals

EV-112	44"	Continental Polished Ebony	2,580.
EV-112	44"	Continental Polished Mahogany	2,700.
EV-113	45"	Polished Ebony	2,780.
EV-113	45"	Polished Mahogany	2,900.
EV-115CB	45"	Chippendale Polished Mahogany	3,100.
EV-121	48"	Polished Ebony	3,180.
EV-121	48"	Polished Mahogany	3,300.

Grands

EV-152	5'	Polished Ebony	7,780.
EV-152	5'	Polished Mahogany/Walnut	8,280.
EV-152	5'	Polished Sapele	8,480.
EV-152	5'	Polished White	8,280.

*For explanation of terms and prices, please see pages 76–82.

Everett (continued)

EV-165	5' 5"	Polished Ebony	8,780.
EV-165	5' 5"	Polished Mahogany/Walnut	9,280.
EV-185	6' 1"	Polished Ebony	10,780.
EV-185	6' 1"	Polished Mahogany	11,280.

Falcone

Model numbers ending in "D" indicate slow-close fallboard.

Verticals

UF 09	43"	Continental Polished Ebony	2,870.
UF 09	43"	Continental Cherry/Mahogany	2,930.
UF 09	43"	Continental Polished Mahogany/Walnut	2,990.
UF 09	43"	Continental Polished Ivory	2,990.
UF 09L	43"	Polished Ebony (w/legs)	2,950.
UF 09L	43"	Polished Mahogany/Walnut (w/legs)	3,070.
CF 12MD	44"	Mediterranean Brown Oak/Cherry	3,490.
CF 12IPD	44"	Italian Provincial Cherry/Walnut	3,690.
UF 12F	44"	French Provincial Polished Ebony	3,200.
UF 12F	44"	French Provincial Cherry/Mahogany	3.260.
UF 12F	44"	French Provincial Pol. Mahogany/Walnut	3,320.
UF 12F	44"	French Provincial Polished Ivory	3,320.
UF 12T	44"	Polished Ebony	3,080.
UF 12T	44"	Cherry/Walnut/Mahogany	3,140.
UF 12T	44"	Polished Mahogany/Walnut/Ivory/White	3,200.
CF 13FD	44½"	French Provincial Cherry/Mahogany	3,590.
CF 13F1D	44½"	French Provincial Cherry/Mahogany	3,790.
CF 13MD	44½"	Cherry/Mahogany	3,590.
CF 13M1D	44½"	Cherry/Mahogany	3,790.
CF 16ATD	45½"	Cherry	3,990.
CF 16FD	45½"	French Provincial Cherry/Brown Oak	3,770.
CF 16FPD	45½"	French Provincial Cherry/Brown Oak	3,790.
CF 16IPD	45½"	Italian Provincial Cherry/Walnut	3,790.
CF 16QAD	45½"	Queen Anne Cherry/Brown Oak	4,090.
CF 19FD	46¾"	Country French Cherry/Brown Oak	3,820.
CF 19F1D	46¾"	French Provincial Cherry/Brown Oak	3,820.
CF 19MD	46¾"	Mediterranean Cherry/Oak	3,820.
CF 19M1D	46¾"	Mediterranean Cherry/Oak	3,820.
CF 19QAD	46¾"	Queen Anne Cherry/Brown Oak	4,190.
CF 47FD	46¾"	French Designer Cherry	5,320.

Model	Size	Style and Finish	Price*
CF 47MD	46¾"	Mediterranean Mahogany	5,320.
UF 19F	46¾"	Demi-Chippendale Polished Ebony	3,320.
UF 19F	46¾"	Demi-Chippendale Cherry/Mahogany	3,380.
UF 19F	46¾"	Demi-Chip. Pol. Mahogany/Walnut/Cherry	3,440.
UF 19F	46¾"	Demi-Chippendale Polished Ivory/White	3,440.
UF 19T	46¾"	Polished Ebony	3,200.
UF 19T	46¾"	Polished Mahogany/Ivory/White	3,320.
UF 20T	46¾"	Designer Polished Ebony	3,490.
UF 20T	46¾"	Designer Polished Mahogany/Walnut	3,610.
UF 20T	46¾"	Designer Polished Ivory/Cherry	3,610.
UF 22ITD	48"	Designer Polished Ebony	3,490.
UF 26T	48"	Polished Ebony	3,840.
UF 23FD	48½"	French Provincial Polished Ebony	3,740.
UF 23FD	48½"	French Provincial Cherry/Mahogany	3,800.
UF 23FD	48½"	French Provincial Pol. Mahogany/Walnut	3,860.
UF 23TD	48½"	Designer Polished Ebony	3,620.
UF 23TD	48½"	Designer Polished Mahogany/Walnut/Ivory	3,740.
UF 32FD	52"	Chippendale Polished Ebony	3,860.
UF 32FD	52"	Chippendale Polished Mahogany	3,980.
UF 32TD	52"	Polished Ebony	3,740.
UF 32TD	52"	Polished Mahogany/Walnut	3,860.

Falcone Georgian Verticals

Model	Size	Style and Finish	Price*
FV 12F	44"	French Provincial Polished Walnut	3,320.
FV 12T	44"	Polished Ebony	3,080.
FV 12T	44"	Polished Mahogany/Walnut	3,200.
FV 16STL	46"	Polished Ebony (school, with lock)	3,440.
FV 16STL	46"	Ebony/Oak/Walnut (school, with lock)	3,500.
FV 18M	46½"	Mediterranean Polished Mahogany	3,290.
FV 18MS	46½"	Mediterr. Pol. Mahog. w/Front Panel Inlay	3,360.
FV 19PD	46¾"	Provincial Polished Bubinga	3,720.
FV 19T	46¾"	Polished Ebony	3,200.
FV 47CI	46¾"	Designer Polished Ebony	4,590.
FV 47R	46¾"	Designer Polished Ebony	4,690.
FV 47R	46¾"	Designer Polished Cherry	4,810.
FV 47V	46¾"	Designer Polished Ebony	4,790.
FV 22ITD	48"	Polished Ebony	3,490.
FV 22WTD	48"	Polished Ebony	3,590.
FV 28SD	48"	Polished Bubinga	4,490.
FV 23FD	48½"	French Provincial Polished Ebony	3,740.
FV 23FD	48½"	French Provincial Pol. Mahogany/Walnut	3,860.

*For explanation of terms and prices, please see pages 76–82.

Model	Size	Style and Finish	Price*

Falcone (continued)

Model	Size	Style and Finish	Price*
FV 23TD	48½"	Polished Ebony	3,620.
FV 23TD	48½"	Polished Mahogany	3,740.
FV 25BD	49"	Polished Ebony	3,990.
FV 25S	49"	Polished Ebony	3,790.
FV 25SM	49"	Polished Ebony	3,790.
FV 26T	49"	Ebony	3,900.
FV 26T	49"	Polished Ebony	3,840.
FV 32HD	52"	Polished Bubinga (reinforced hammer)	4,390.
FV 32SSD	52"	Polished Ebony	5,190.
FV 32SSD	52"	Polished Bubinga	5,430.
FV 32TD	52"	Ebony/Cherry/Walnut	3,800.
FV 32TD	52"	Polished Ebony	3,740.
FV 32TD	52"	Polished Mahogany/Walnut	3,860.

Grands

Some models are available without slow-close fallboard for $120 less.

Model	Size	Style and Finish	Price*
GF 42D	4' 8"	Ebony	8,740.
GF 42D	4' 8"	Polished Ebony	8,540.
GF 42D	4' 8"	Cherry	9,140.
GF 42D	4' 8"	Polished Cherry/Mahogany	8,940.
GF 52D	5'	Polished Ebony	9,380.
GF 52D	5'	Polished Mahogany/Walnut	9,780.
GF 52D	5'	Cherry	9,980.
GF 52D	5'	Polished Ivory	9,580.
GF 52FD	5'	French Provincial Polished Ebony	9,980.
GF 52FD	5'	French Provincial Pol. Mahogany/Walnut	10,380.
GF 52FD	5'	French Provincial Cherry/Mahogany	10,580.
GF 52FD	5'	French Provincial Polished Ivory	10,180.
GF 62D	5' 4"	Ebony	10,610.
GF 62D	5' 4"	Polished Ebony	10,410.
GF 62D	5' 4"	Polished Mahogany/Walnut/Brown Oak	10,810.
GF 62D	5' 4"	Cherry/Mahogany	11,010.
GF 62D	5' 4"	Polished Ivory/White	10,610.
GF 62FD	5' 4"	French Provincial Cherry	11,610.
GF 62FD	5' 4"	French Provincial Polished Mahogany	11,410.
GF 72D	5' 8"	Ebony	11,640.
GF 72D	5' 8"	Polished Ebony	11,440.
GF 72D	5' 8"	Polished Mahogany/Walnut	11,840.
GF 72D	5' 8"	Cherry/Mahogany	12,040.
GF 72D	5' 8"	Polished Bubinga	12,440.

Model	Size	Style and Finish	Price*
GF 72D	5' 8"	Polished Ivory	11,640.
GF 72FD	5' 8"	French Provincial Polished Mahogany	12,440.
GF 72FD	5' 8"	French Provincial Polished Ivory	12,240.
GF 72LD	5' 8"	Louis XVI Polished Ebony	11,920.
GF 72LD	5' 8"	Louis XVI Mahogany	12,520.
GF 72LD	5' 8"	Louis XVI Polished Mahogany	12,320.
GF 87D	6' 2"	Ebony	12,660.
GF 87D	6' 2"	Polished Ebony	12,460.
GF 87D	6' 2"	Polished Mahogany/Walnut	12,860.
GF 87D	6' 2"	Polished Bubinga	13,460.
GF 87D	6' 2"	Polished Ivory	12,660.
GF 87FD	6' 2"	French Provincial Polished Ebony	13,060.
GF 87FD	6' 2"	French Provincial Cherry/Mahogany	13,660.
GF 87FD	6' 2"	French Provincial Pol. Cherry/Mahogany	13,460.
GF 87LD	6' 2"	Louis XVI Polished Ebony	12,940.
GF 87LD	6' 2"	Louis XVI Mahogany	13,540.
GF 87LD	6' 2"	Louis XVI Polished Mahogany	13,340.
GF 87LD	6' 2"	Louis XVI Polished Ivory	13,140.
GF 208D	6' 10"	Ebony	15,800.
GF 208D	6' 10"	Polished Ebony	15,600.
GF 228D	7' 6"	Ebony	19,800.
GF 228D	7' 6"	Polished Ebony	19,600.
GF 278D	9' 2"	Ebony	47,800.
GF 278D	9' 2"	Polished Ebony	47,600.

Falcone Georgian Grands

Model	Size	Style and Finish	Price*
FG 42D	4' 8"	Ebony	8,980.
FG 42D	4' 8"	Polished Ebony	8,780.
FG 42D	4' 8"	Polished Ivory/White	8,980.
FG 42D	4' 8"	Cherry/Mahogany/Walnut	9,380.
FG 42D	4' 8"	Polished Cherry/Mahogany/Walnut	9,180.
FG 42D	4' 8"	Polished Bubinga	9,780.
FG 42FD	4' 8"	French Provincial Mahogany/Cherry	9,980.
FG 42FD	4' 8"	French Provincial Pol. Mahogany/Cherry	9,780.
FG 42LD	4' 8"	Louis XVI Polished Ebony	9,260.
FG 52D	5'	Ebony	9,820.
FG 52D	5'	Polished Ebony	9,620.
FG 52D	5'	Cherry/Mahogany/Walnut	10,220.
FG 52D	5'	Polished Mahogany/Walnut	10,020.
FG 52FD	5'	French Provincial Polished Ebony	10,220.
FG 52FD	5'	French Provincial Polished Ivory	10,420.

*For explanation of terms and prices, please see pages 76–82.

Model	Size	Style and Finish	Price*

Falcone (continued)

Model	Size	Style and Finish	Price*
FG 52FD	5'	French Provincial Cherry/Mahogany	10,820.
FG 52FD	5'	French Prov. Pol. Cherry/Mahogany/Walnut	10,620.
FG 52FAD	5'	FrenchAnn Polished Cherry	10,820.
FG 52LD	5'	Louis XVI Polished Ebony	10,100.
FG 62D	5' 4"	Ebony	11,180.
FG 62D	5' 4"	Polished Ebony	10,980.
FG 62D	5' 4"	Cherry/Mahogany/Walnut/Brown Oak	11,580.
FG 62D	5' 4"	Polished Cherry/Mahogany/Walnut	11,380.
FG 62FD	5' 4"	French Provincial Cherry/Mahogany	12,180.
FG 62FD	5' 4"	French Provincial Pol. Cherry/Mahogany	11,980.
FG 62QAD	5' 4"	Queen Anne Cherry	12,380.
FG 72D	5' 8"	Ebony	12,210.
FG 72D	5' 8"	Polished Ebony	12,010.
FG 72D	5' 8"	Polished White	12,210.
FG 72D	5' 8"	Mahogany	12,610.
FG 72D	5' 8"	Polished Cherry/Walnut	12,410.
FG 72D	5' 8"	Polished Bubinga	13,010.
FG 72FD	5' 8"	French Provincial Polished Ivory	12,810.
FG 72FD	5' 8"	French Provincial Pol. Mahogany/Walnut	13,010.
FG 72FD	5' 8"	French Provincial Polished Cherry	13,010.
FG 72LD	5' 8"	Louis XVI Polished Ebony	12,490.
FG 72LD	5' 8"	Louis XVI Mahogany	13,090.
FG 72LD	5' 8"	Louis XVI Polished Mahogany	12,890.
FG 72QAD	5' 8"	Queen Anne Cherry	13,410.
FG 87D	6' 2"	Ebony	13,230.
FG 87D	6' 2"	Polished Ebony	13,030.
FG 87D	6' 2"	Polished Mahogany/Walnut	13,430.
FG 87D	6' 2"	Polished Bubinga	14,030.
FG 87FD	6' 2"	French Provincial Polished Ebony	13,630.
FG 87FD	6' 2"	French Provincial Cherry/Mahogany	14,230.
FG 87FD	6' 2"	French Provincial Pol. Cherry/Mahogany	14,030.
FG 87HLD	6' 2"	Mahogany (Hexagonal Leg)	14,230.
FG 87LD	6' 2"	Louis XVI Ebony	13,710.
FG 87LD	6' 2"	Louis XVI Polished Ebony	13,510.
FG 87PLD	6' 2"	Walnut (Octagonal Leg)	14,230.
FG 87PLD	6' 2"	Polished Bubinga (Octagonal Leg)	14,630.
FG 208D	6' 10"	Ebony	16,180.
FG 208D	6' 10"	Polished Ebony	15,980.
FG 208D	6' 10"	Polished Mahogany	16,380.

Model	Size	Style and Finish	Price*
FG 208BD	6' 10"	Ebony with Rim Band	16,300.
FG 208BD	6' 10"	Polished Ebony with Rim Band	16,100.
FG 208HLD	6' 10"	Mahogany (Hexagonal Leg)	17,180.
FG 208HLBD	6' 10"	Pol. Ebony (Hexagonal Leg) with Rim Band	17,180.
FG 208HLBCD	6' 10"	Cherry (Hexag. Leg) w/Rim &Keybed Band	17,980.
FG 228D	7' 6"	Ebony	20,180.
FG 228D	7' 6"	Polished Ebony	19,980.
FG 278D	9' 2"	Ebony	47,800.
FG 278D	9' 2"	Polished Ebony	47,600.

Fazioli

Fazioli is willing to make custom-designed cases with exotic veneers, marquetry, and other embellishments. Prices on request to Fazioli.

Grands

F156	5' 2"	Ebony and Polished Ebony	84,400.
F156	5' 2"	Walnut	88,400.
F156	5' 2"	Polished Walnut	90,600.
F156	5' 2"	Polished Pyramid Mahogany	93,400.
F156	5' 2"	Cherry	88,400.
F156	5' 2"	Polished Cherry	90,600.
F183	6'	Ebony and Polished Ebony	97,500.
F183	6'	Walnut	102,850.
F183	6'	Polished Walnut	104,920.
F183	6'	Polished Pyramid Mahogany	108,600.
F183	6'	Cherry	102,850.
F183	6'	Polished Cherry	104,920.
F212	6' 11"	Ebony and Polished Ebony	112,360.
F212	6' 11"	Walnut	117,960.
F212	6' 11"	Polished Walnut	120,600.
F212	6' 11"	Polished Pyramid Mahogany	124,660.
F212	6' 11"	Cherry	117,960.
F212	6' 11"	Polished Cherry	120,600.
F228	7' 6"	Ebony and Polished Ebony	128,840.
F228	7' 6"	Walnut	135,200.
F228	7' 6"	Polished Walnut	137,400.
F228	7' 6"	Polished Pyramid Mahogany	143,800.
F228	7' 6"	Cherry	135,200.
F228	7' 6"	Polished Cherry	137,400.
F278	9' 2"	Ebony and Polished Ebony	167,200.
F278	9' 2"	Walnut	175,600.

*For explanation of terms and prices, please see pages 76–82.

Model	Size	Style and Finish	Price*

Fazioli (continued)

Model	Size	Style and Finish	Price*
F278	9' 2"	Polished Walnut	179,600.
F278	9' 2"	Polished Pyramid Mahogany	185,680.
F278	9' 2"	Cherry	175,600.
F278	9' 2"	Polished Cherry	179,600.
F308	10' 2"	Ebony and Polished Ebony	198,400.
F308	10' 2"	Walnut	206,700.
F308	10' 2"	Polished Walnut	208,200.
F308	10' 2"	Polished Pyramid Mahogany	217,400.
F308	10' 2"	Cherry	206,700.
F308	10' 2"	Polished Cherry	208,200.
All models		*Fourth Pedal, add'l*	9,150.
All models		*Third and Fourth Pedals (set), add'l*	10,760.
All models		*Magnetic Balanced Action, add'l*	12,200.

Feurich

Prices do not include bench. Euro=$1.20

Verticals

Model	Size	Style and Finish	Price*
F 123	49"	Polished Ebony	31,534.
F 123	49"	Polished Mahogany	36,196.

Grands

Model	Size	Style and Finish	Price*
F 172	5' 8"	Polished Ebony	79,058.
F 172	5' 8"	Polished Sapeli Mahogany	83,821.
F 172	5' 8"	Rococo	130,214.
F 172 ADF	5' 8"	"Old German Style" Polished Ebony	96,081.
F 172 ADF	5' 8"	"Old German Style" Cherry	96,282.
F 227	7' 5"	Polished Ebony	118,131.
F 227 ADF	7' 5"	"Old German Style" Polished Ebony	135,153.

Förster, August

Prices do not include bench. Euro=$1.20

Verticals

Model	Size	Style and Finish	Price*
116C	46"	Chippendale Polished Ebony	19,375.
116C	46"	Chippendale Walnut and Polished Walnut	20,295.
116C	46"	Chippendale Mahog. And Pol. Mahogany	19,451.
116C	46"	Chippendale Polished White	19,804.
116D	46"	Continental Polished Ebony	16,402.
116D	46"	Continental Walnut and Polished Walnut	17,397.

Model	Size	Style and Finish	Price*
116D	46"	Continental Mahog. and Pol. Mahogany	16,465.
116D	46"	Continental Polished White	16,855.
116E	46"	Polished Ebony	19,375.
116E	46"	Walnut and Polished Walnut	20,295.
116E	46"	Mahogany and Polished Mahogany	19,451.
116E	46"	Polished White	19,804.
125G	49"	Polished Ebony	20,812.
125G	49"	Walnut and Polished Walnut	21,832.
125G	49"	Mahogany and Polished Mahogany	20,875.
125G	49"	Polished White	21,265.

Grands

Model	Size	Style and Finish	Price*
170	5' 8"	Polished Ebony	44,219.
170	5' 8"	Walnut and Polished Walnut	45,807.
170	5' 8"	Mahogany and Polished Mahogany	44,358.
170	5' 8"	Polished White	46,197.
170	5' 8"	*Pyramid Mahogany*	50,305.
170	5' 8"	"Classic" Polished Ebony	49,209.
170	5' 8"	"Classic" Walnut and Polished Walnut	55,799.
170	5' 8"	"Classic" Mahogany and Pol. Mahogany	50,166.
170	5' 8"	"Classic" Polished White	53,052.
170	5' 8"	*Chippendale, additional*	9,979.
190	6' 4"	Polished Ebony	50,166.
190	6' 4"	Walnut and Polished Walnut	51,880.
190	6' 4"	Mahogany and Polished Mahogany	50,305.
190	6' 4"	Polished White	52,157.
190	6' 4"	*Pyramid Mahogany*	56,252.
190	6' 4"	"Classic" Polished Ebony	55,156.
190	6' 4"	"Classic" Walnut and Polished Walnut	61,872.
190	6' 4"	"Classic" Mahogany and Pol.Mahogany	56,114.
190	6' 4"	"Classic" Polished White	59,012.
190	6' 4"	*Chippendale, additional*	9,979.
215	7' 2"	Polished Ebony	55,068.
275	9' 1"	Polished Ebony	105,342.

Grotrian

Prices do not include bench. Other woods available on request. Euro=$1.20

Verticals

Model	Size	Style and Finish	Price*
Fried. Grotrian	43½"	Polished Ebony	13,373.
Cristal	44"	Polished Ebony	16,069.

*For explanation of terms and prices, please see pages 76–82.

Grotrian (continued)

Model	Size	Style and Finish	Price*
Cristal	44"	Open-pore Oak/Walnut	15,704.
Cristal	44"	Polished Walnut/White	17,390.
Carat	45½"	Polished Ebony	19,736.
Carat	45½"	Open-pore Oak/Walnut	19,149.
Carat	45½"	Polished Walnut/White	21,349.
College	48"	Ebony	20,293.
College	48"	Polished Ebony	21,739.
College	48"	Open-pore Beech	20,293.
Classic	49"	Polished Ebony	25,844.
Classic	49"	Open-pore Oak/Walnut	24,012.
Classic	49"	Polished Walnut/White	28,044.
Concertino	52"	Polished Ebony	30,499.
	48"-52"	*Sostenuto pedal, add'l*	932.

Grands

Model	Size	Style and Finish	Price*
Chambre	5' 5"	Ebony	44,852.
Chambre	5' 5"	Polished Ebony	49,544.
Chambre	5' 5"	Open-pore Oak/Walnut	46,318.
Chambre	5' 5"	Polished Walnut/White	53,944.
Cabinet	6' 3"	Ebony	51,011.
Cabinet	6' 3"	Polished Ebony	57,023.
Cabinet	6' 3"	Open-pore Oak/Walnut	53,944.
Cabinet	6' 3"	Polished Walnut/White	61,421.
Charis	6' 10"	Polished Ebony	66,307.
Concert	7' 4"	Ebony	66,340.
Concert	7' 4"	Polished Ebony	70,314.
Concert Royal	9' 1"	Polished Ebony	85,177.
All models		*Chippendale/Empire, add'l*	2,772.
All models		*CS Style, add'l*	3,528.
All models		*Rokoko, add'l*	9,954.

Gulbransen

Verticals

Model	Size	Style and Finish	Price*
87050	45"	Oak	3,390.
87058	45"	Cherry	3,390.
87162	47"	Polished Ebony	3,790.
87170	47"	Polished Mahogany	3,790.

Model	Size	Style and Finish	Price*

Grands

Model	Size	Style and Finish	Price*
80462	4' 7"	Polished Ebony	7,500.
80462PM	4' 7"	Polished Ebony w/Pianomation CD2000+	11,790.
80662	5'	Polished Ebony	8,100.
80662PM	5'	Polished Ebony w/Pianomation CD2000+	12,590.

Haessler

Prices do not include bench.

Verticals

Model	Size	Style and Finish	Price*
115 K	45"	Ebony and Polished Ebony	15,378.
115 K	45"	Beech/Ash/Waxed Alder	15,114.
115 K	45"	White and Polished White	15,972.
118 K	47"	Ebony and Polished Ebony	16,940.
118 K	47"	Ebony with Walnut Accent	18,154.
118 K	47"	Mahogany and Polished Mahogany	17,798.
118 K	47"	Walnut and Polished Walnut	17,798.
118 K	47"	Cherry and Polished Cherry	19,074.
118 K	47"	Cherry with Yew Inlay, Satin and Polish	19,074.
118 K	47"	Oak	16,126.
118 K	47"	White and Polished White	17,578.
118 KM	47"	Ebony and Polished Ebony	17,710.
118 KM	47"	White and Polished White	18,370.
118 CH	47"	Chippendale Mahogany and Pol.Mahogany	19,030.
118 CH	47"	Chippendale Walnut and Polished Walnut	19,030.
124 K	49"	Ebony and Polished Ebony	17,996.
124 K	49"	Ebony with Walnut Accent	18,898.
124 K	49"	Mahogany and Polished Mahogany	19,316.
124 K	49"	Walnut and Polished Walnut	19,316.
124 K	49"	Cherry and Polished Cherry	19,778.
124 K	49"	Cherry with Yew Inlay, Satin and Polish	20,702.
124 K	49"	White and Polished White	18,656.
124 KM	49"	Ebony and Polished Ebony	18,370.
124 KM	49"	White and Polished White	19,030.
132	52"	Ebony and Polished Ebony	24,442.

Grands

Model	Size	Style and Finish	Price*
175	5' 8"	Ebony and Polished Ebony	46,630.
175	5' 8"	Mahogany and Polished Mahogany	48,496.
175	5' 8"	Walnut and Polished Walnut	48,962.

*For explanation of terms and prices, please see pages 76–82.

Haessler (continued)

Model	Size	Style and Finish	Price*
175	5' 8"	Cherry and Polished Cherry	48,728.
175	5' 8"	Polished Bubinga	51,292.
175	5' 8"	White and Polished White	54,856.
175	5' 8"	Saxony Polished Pyramid Mahogany	61,524.
175	5' 8"	Saxony Polished Burl Walnut	62,114.
175	5' 8"	"President" Polished Ebony	52,058.
175	5' 8"	"President" Polished Mahogany	54,140.
175	5' 8"	"President" Polished Walnut	54,662.
175	5' 8"	"President" Polished Bubinga	57,266.
175	5' 8"	Louis XV Ebony, Satin and Polished	54,426.
175	5' 8"	Louis XV Mahogany, Satin and Polished	57,146.
175	5' 8"	Louis XV Walnut, Satin and Polished	56,602.
175	5' 8"	Kaiser Wilhelm II Polished Ebony	54,898.
175	5' 8"	Kaiser Wilhelm II Polished Mahogany	57,094.
175	5' 8"	Kaiser Wilhelm II Polished Walnut	57,644.
175	5' 8"	Kaiser Wilhelm II Polished Cherry	57,370.
175	5' 8"	Ambassador East Indian Rosewood	63,892.
175	5' 8"	Ambassador Walnut	59,160.
175	5' 8"	Nicolas II Walnut w/Burl Inlay	63,892.
175	5' 8"	Louis XVI Rococo White w/Gold	68,624.
175	5' 8"	Classic Alexandra Polished Ebony	53,006.
175	5' 8"	Classic Alexandra Polished Mahogany	55,656.
175	5' 8"	Classic Alexandra Polished Walnut	55,124.
186	6' 1"	Ebony and Polished Ebony	52,536.
186	6' 1"	Mahogany and Polished Mahogany	54,308.
186	6' 1"	Walnut and Polished Walnut	55,164.
186	6' 1"	Cherry and Polished Cherry	54,898.
186	6' 1"	Polished Bubinga	57,800.
186	6' 1"	White and Polished White	55,164.
186	6' 1"	Saxony Polished Pyramid Mahogany	69,318.
186	6' 1"	Saxony Polished Burl Walnut	69,982.
186	6' 1"	"President" Polished Ebony	58,654.
186	6' 1"	"President" Polished Mahogany	61,000.
186	6' 1"	"President" Polished Walnut	61,586.
186	6' 1"	"President" Polished Bubinga	64,518.
186	6' 1"	Louis XV Ebony, Satin and Polished	61,318.
186	6' 1"	Louis XV Mahogany, Satin and Polished	64,382.
186	6' 1"	Louis XV Walnut, Satin and Polished	63,772.
186	6' 1"	Kaiser Wilhelm II Polished Ebony	61,852.

Model	Size	Style and Finish	Price*
186	6' 1"	Kaiser Wilhelm II Polished Mahogany	64,326.
186	6' 1"	Kaiser Wilhelm II Polished Walnut	64,944.
186	6' 1"	Kaiser Wilhelm II Polished Cherry	64,636.
186	6' 1"	Ambassador East Indian Rosewood	71,982.
186	6' 1"	Ambassador Walnut	66,652.
186	6' 1"	Nicolas II Walnut w/Burl Inlay	71,982.
186	6' 1"	Louis XVI Rococo White w/Gold	77,316.
186	6' 1"	Classic Alexandra Polished Ebony	59,720.
186	6' 1"	Classic Alexandra Polished Mahogany	62,706.
186	6' 1"	Classic Alexandra Polished Walnut	62,108.

Hailun

Hailun is new to the U.S. market. This is a temporary, abbreviated price list showing only straight-leg styles. Curved-leg and fancy casework styles are also available at slightly higher prices. "Other Finishes" include polished white, light and dark walnut, dark mahogany, and maple.

Verticals
121	48"	Polished Ebony	4,148.
121	48"	Other Finishes	4,278.
123	50"	Polished Ebony	4,314.
123	50"	Other Finishes	4,448.
125	52"	Polished Ebony	4,526.
125	52"	Other Finishes	4,610.

Grands
151	4' 10"	Polished Ebony	9,208.
151	4' 10"	Other Finishes	9,542.
161	5' 3"	Polished Ebony	10,192.
161	5' 3"	Other Finishes	10,516.
178	5' 9"	Polished Ebony	12,156.
178	5' 9"	Polished Ebony Pro	12,360.
178	5' 9"	Other Finishes	12,478.

Hallet, Davis & Co.

Model numbers ending in "I" use imported veneers from around the world.

Verticals
H-C43F	43"	French Oak/Mahogany/Cherry/Walnut	4,650.
H-C43R	43"	Oak/Cherry (round leg)	4,650.
H-111GD	44"	Continental Polished Ebony	3,930.

*For explanation of terms and prices, please see pages 76–82.

Model	Size	Style and Finish	Price*

Hallett, Davis & Co. (continued)

Model	Size	Style and Finish	Price*
H-111GD	44"	Continental Pol. Mahogany/Walnut/White	4,020.
H-111GD I	44"	Continental Polished American Walnut	4,320.
H-115GC	45"	Chippendale Polished Ebony	4,320.
H-115GC	45"	Chippendale Pol. Mahogany/Walnut/White	4,380.
H-115GC I	45"	Chippendale Polished American Walnut	4,680.
H-115WH	46"	Polished Ebony	4,380.
H-115WH	46"	Polished Mahogany/Walnut	4,455.
H-115WH I	46"	Polished Walnut	4,755.
H-121WH	48"	Polished Ebony	4,875.
H-121WH	48"	Polished Mahogany/Walnut	4,875.
H-121WH I	48"	Polished American Walnut	5,175.
H-126WH	50"	Polished Ebony	6,285.
H-126WH	50"	Polished Mahogany	6,585.
H-131WH	52"	Polished Ebony	7,350.

Grands

Model	Size	Style and Finish	Price*
H-143	4' 8"	Ebony	9,585.
H-143	4' 8"	Polished Ebony	10,185.
H-143	4' 8"	Mahogany and Polished Mahogany	10,785.
H-143	4' 8"	Polished Walnut/White	10,785.
H-143F	4' 8"	Queen Anne Polished Ebony	10,785.
H-143F	4' 8"	Queen Anne Mahogany and Pol. Mahogany	11,385.
H-143F	4' 8"	Queen Anne Polished Walnut/White	11,385.
H-143R	4' 8"	Victorian Polished Mahogany	11,385.
H-152C	5'	Ebony	13,185.
H-152C	5'	Polished Ebony	12,585.
H-152C	5'	Mahogany	13,485.
H-152C	5'	Polished Mahogany/White	13,185.
H-152C	5'	Polished Brown Sapeli Mahogany	13,185.
H-152C I	5'	"Metropolitan" Polished Ebony with Nickel	13,185.
H-152C I	5'	Mahogany/Walnut	14,185.
H-152C I	5'	Polished Mahogany/Walnut	13,785.
H-152D	5'	Victorian Polished Ebony	13,485.
H-152D	5'	Victorian Mahogany	14,385.
H-152D	5'	Victorian Polished Mahogany/Walnut	14,085.
H-152D	5'	Victorian Polished Brown Sapeli Mahogany	14,085.
H-152D I	5'	Victorian Mahogany/Walnut	14,965.
H-152D I	5'	Victorian Polished Mahogany/Walnut	14,685.
H-152S	5'	Queen Anne Polished Ebony	13,485.
H-152S	5'	Queen Anne Mahogany	14,385.

Model	Size	Style and Finish	Price*
H-152S	5'	Queen Anne Polished Mahogany	14,085.
H-152S I	5'	Queen Anne Mahogany/Walnut	14,985.
H-152S I	5'	Queen Anne Polished Mahogany/Walnut	14,685.
H-165C	5' 5"	Ebony	14,385.
H-165C	5' 5"	Polished Ebony	13,650.
H-165C	5' 5"	Mahogany	14,685.
H-165C	5' 5"	Polished Mahogany/Walnut/White	14,550.
H-165C	5' 5"	Polished Brown Sapeli Mahogany	14,550.
H-165C I	5' 5"	Mahogany/Walnut	15,285.
H-165C I	5' 5"	Polished Mahogany/Walnut	14,985.
H-165D	5' 5"	"Period" Polished Ebony	14,685.
H-165D	5' 5"	"Period" Pol. Mahogany/Sapeli Mahogany	15,285.
H-165D I	5' 5"	"Period" Mahogany/Walnut	16,185.
H-165D I	5' 5"	"Period" Polished Mahogany/Walnut	15,885.
H-185C	6' 1"	Polished Ebony	16,785.
H-185C	6' 1"	Polished Mahogany/Sapeli Mahog./Walnut	17,385.
H-185C I	6' 1"	Mahogany/Walnut	18,285.
H-185C I	6' 1"	Polished Mahogany/Walnut	17,985.
H-215C	7' 1"	Polished Ebony	26,985.

Hamilton

Verticals

W-H100	39"	Continental Polished Ebony (73-note)	1,978.
W-H100	39"	Continental Polished Cherry (73-note)	2,098.
W-H350	42½"	Continental Polished Ebony/Mahogany	2,790.
W-H310	44"	Mahogany/Oak/Cherry	2,990.
W-H360	47"	Classic Polished Ebony/Oak/Mahogany	3,390.
W-H370	47"	Deluxe Console Oak/Mahogany/Cherry	3,790.

Grands

W-H391	4' 7"	Polished Ebony/White	7,750.
W-H391	4' 7"	Polished Mahogany	7,950.
W-H396	5' 1"	Ebony and Polished Ebony	8,990.
W-H396	5' 1"	Polished Mahogany/White	9,290.
W-H398	5' 4"	Ebony	10,050.
W-H398	5' 4"	Polished Ebony	9,700.
W-H398	5' 4"	Polished Mahogany	10,050.
W-H399	5' 8"	Ebony	10,798.
W-H399	5' 8"	Polished Ebony	10,398.
W-H399	5' 8"	Polished Mahogany	10,798.

*For explanation of terms and prices, please see pages 76–82.

Model	Size	Style and Finish	Price*

Hamilton (continued)

Model	Size	Style and Finish	Price*
W-H401	6' 2"	Ebony	11,500.
W-H401	6' 2"	Polished Ebony	11,100.
W-H401	6' 2"	Polished Mahogany	11,500.

Ibach

Verticals

Model	Size	Style and Finish	Price*
B-114	45"	"Classic/Tradition" Open-Pore Beech	16,754.
B-114	45"	"Classic/Tradition" Open-Pore Alder	16,754.
B-114	45"	"Classic/Tradition" Open-Pore Oak	16,754.
B-114	45"	"Classic/Tradition" Open-Pore Maple	17,115.
B-114	45"	"Classic/Tradition" Open-Pore Cherry	17,115.
C-118	46½"	"Elegance" Open-Pore Beech	18,054.
C-118	46½"	"Elegance" Open-Pore Oak	18,054.
C-118	46½"	"Elegance" Open-Pore Cherry	18,460.
C-118	46½"	"Elegance" Polished Ebony	18,517.
C-118	46½"	"Elegance" Polished White	19,155.
C-118	46½"	"Elegance" Polished Walnut	19,910.
C-118	46½"	"Elegance" Polished Mahogany	19,910.
C-118	46½"	"Elegance" Polished Cherry	19,910.
C-118	46½"	"Elegance" Polished Burr Walnut	22,057.
C-118	46½"	"Edition (Bruno Paul 1911)" Pol. Ebony	21,651.
C-118	46½"	"Edition (Bruno Paul 1911)" Pol. White	22,436.
C-118	46½"	"Edition (Bruno Paul1911)" Oiled Oak	22,436.
C-118	46½"	"Antik" Polished Ebony	on request
K-125	49"	"Exclusive" Polished Ebony	on request
H-128	50"	"Edition" Swiss Pear-Tree	on request
L-132	52"	"Tradition" Polished Ebony	26,060.

Grands

Model	Size	Style and Finish	Price*
F-II 183	6'	Polished Ebony	53,731.
F-II 183	6'	Polished Mahogany	59,474.
F-II 183	6'	Polished Burr Walnut	60,912.
F-II 183	6'	*"Edition Ibach Design 1913"*	56,318.
F-II 183	6'	*"Eigenentwurf Ibach Design 1908"*	55,680.
F-II 183	6'	*"Ausfuhrung Art Design"*	66,873.
F-III 215	7' 1"	"Richard Strauss" Polished Ebony	68,064.
F-III 215	7' 1"	*"Klassizismus"*	115,767.
F-III 215	7' 1"	*"Richard Meier"*	on request
F-IV 240	7' 10½"	"Richard Wagner" Polished Ebony	74,168.

Irmler

Verticals

Model	Size	Style and Finish	Price*
M113E	44½"	Polished Ebony	7,610.
M113E	44½"	Walnut/Beech/Alder	7,360.
M113E	44½"	Mahogany/Cherry	7,540.
M113E	44½"	Polished Walnut/Mahogany/Cherry	7,730.
M113E	44½"	Polished White	8,090.
M122E	48"	Polished Ebony	8,150.
M122E	48"	Polished Ebony with Burl Oval	8,850.
M122E	48"	Walnut	7,910.
M122E	48"	Polished Walnut	8,090.
M122E	48"	Mahogany/Cherry	8,090.
M122E	48"	Polished Mahogany/Cherry	8,280.
M122E	48"	Polished Cherry with Inlay	8,990.
M122E	48"	Beech/Alder	7,730.
M122E	48"	Polished Bubinga	9,710.
M122E	48"	Polished White	8,640.

Grands

Model	Size	Style and Finish	Price*
F16E	5' 5"	Polished Ebony	27,320.
F16E	5' 5"	Walnut/Mahogany	28,250.
F16E	5' 5"	Cherry	27,370.
F16E	5' 5"	Polished Walnut/Mahogany	28,960.
F16E	5' 5"	Polished Cherry	29,570.
F16E	5' 5"	Polished White	28,010.
F18E	5' 11"	Polished Ebony	33,412.
F22E	7' 3"	Polished Ebony	42,670.
F22E	7' 3"	Polished Walnut/Mahogany	45,810.
F22E	7' 3"	Polished White	44,760.

Kawai

Verticals

Model	Size	Style and Finish	Price*
K-15	44"	Continental Polished Ebony	3,390.
K-15	44"	Continental Polished Mahogany	3,590.
K-18	44½"	Ebony and Polished Ebony	4,730.
K-18	44½"	Polished Mahogany	5,330.
506N	44½"	Mahogany/Oak	3,590.
508	44½"	Mahogany/Oak	4,190.
607	44½"	American Oak	4,590.
607	44½"	French Provincial Cherry	4,690.

*For explanation of terms and prices, please see pages 76–82.

Model	Size	Style and Finish	Price*

Kawai (continued)

Model	Size	Style and Finish	Price*
607	44½"	Queen Anne Mahogany	4,690.
UST-7	46"	Ebony/Oak/Walnut	6,690.
UST-8	46"	Ebony/Oak/Walnut	5,590.
VT-118	46"	Vari-Touch Ebony	6,190.
K-25	48"	Ebony and Polished Ebony	5,990.
K-25	48"	Mahogany and Polished Mahogany	6,590.
K-25	48"	Polished Snow White	6,390.
K-50	49"	Ebony and Polished Ebony	8,190.
K-50	49"	Polished Sapeli Mahogany/Walnut	9,390.
K-50	49"	Walnut	8,990.
K-60	52"	Ebony and Polished Ebony	10,990.
K-80	52"	Ebony and Polished Ebony	13,390.

Grands

Model	Size	Style and Finish	Price*
GM-10K	5'	Polished Ebony	10,190.
GM-12	5'	Ebony and Polished Ebony	12,790.
GM-12	5'	Polished Mahogany/Snow White	13,990.
GE-20	5' 1"	Ebony and Polished Ebony	14,890.
GE-20	5' 1"	Walnut	16,390.
GE-20	5' 1"	Polished Mahogany/Sapeli Mahogany	16,590.
GE-20	5' 1"	Polished Snow White	15,990.
GE-20	5' 1"	French Provincial Polished Mahogany	17,990.
GE-30	5' 5"	Ebony and Polished Ebony	16,990.
GE-30	5' 5"	Mahogany	18,890.
GE-30	5' 5"	Polished Mahogany	18,990.
GE-30	5' 5"	Polished Sapeli Mahogany	18,890.
GE-30	5' 5"	Walnut	18,690.
GE-30	5' 5"	Polished Snow White	18,190.
RX-1	5' 5"	Ebony and Polished Ebony	20,390.
RX-1	5' 5"	Walnut	22,790.
RX-1	5' 5"	Polished Walnut/Sapeli Mahogany	23,590.
RX-1	5' 5"	Polished Snow White	22,790.
RX-2	5' 10"	Ebony and Polished Ebony	22,990.
RX-2	5' 10"	Walnut/Cherry/Oak	25,990.
RX-2	5' 10"	Polished Walnut/Mahogany	26,990.
RX-2	5' 10"	Polished Sapeli Mahogany	26,990.
RX-2	5' 10"	Polished Rosewood	29,990.
RX-2	5' 10"	Polished Snow White	24,990.
RX-2	5' 10"	French Provincial Polished Mahogany	29,990.
RX-3	6' 1"	Ebony and Polished Ebony	29,990.

Model	Size	Style and Finish	Price*
RX-3C	6' 1"	Polished Ebony	29,990.
RX-3	6' 1"	Walnut	33,990.
RX-3	6' 1"	Polished Sapeli Mahogany	35,990.
RX-3	6' 1"	Polished Snow White	31,990.
CR40N	6' 1"	Plexiglass	75,260.
RX-5	6' 6"	Ebony and Polished Ebony	33,990.
RX-5	6' 6"	Walnut	37,990.
RX-5	6' 6"	Polished Sapeli Mahogany	39,990.
RX-5	6' 6"	Polished Snow White	35,990.
RX-6	7'	Ebony and Polished Ebony	37,990.
RX-7	7' 6"	Ebony and Polished Ebony	43,990.
GS-100	9' 1"	Polished Ebony	79,990.
EX	9' 1"	Polished Ebony	109,190.
EX-G	9' 1"	Polished Ebony	115,990.

Kawai, Shigeru

Grands

Model	Size	Style and Finish	Price*
SK2	5' 10"	Polished Ebony	36,700.
SK2	5' 10"	Polished Sapeli Mahogany	38,700.
SK2	5' 10"	Polished Pyramid Mahogany	58,700.
SK2	5' 10"	"Classic Noblesse" w/Burl Walnut Inlay	56,500.
SK3	6' 1"	Polished Ebony	42,900.
SK3	6' 1"	Polished Sapeli Mahogany	45,300.
SK5	6' 6"	Polished Ebony	49,300.
SK5	6' 6"	Polished Sapeli Mahogany	52,300.
SK6	7'	Polished Ebony	55,700.
SK7	7' 6"	Polished Ebony	61,700.
SK7	7' 6"	Polished Pyramid Mahogany	93,300.
SK7	7' 6"	"Classic Noblesse" w/Burl Walnut Inlay	84,900.

Kemble

Verticals

Model	Size	Style and Finish	Price*
Cambridge 10	43"	Polished Ebony	7,040.
Cambridge 10	43"	Mahogany/Walnut	7,040.
Oxford	43"	Walnut	7,240.
Oxford	43"	Mahogany with Inlay	7,660.
Oxford	43"	Polished Mahogany	8,040.
Classic-T	45"	Polished Ebony/Mahogany	8,400.
Classic-T	45"	Polished Ebony and Chrome	8,700.

*For explanation of terms and prices, please see pages 76–82.

Model	Size	Style and Finish	Price*

Kemble (continued)

Empire	46½"	Empire Polished Mahogany	10,240.
Prestige	46½"	Cherry with Yew Inlay	10,240.
K121ZT	48"	Polished Ebony/Mahogany/Walnut	10,240.
K121ZT	48"	Georgian Mahogany Lustre	9,990.
Vermont	48"	Cherry	11,940.
Quantum II	49"	Polished Ebony	11,940.
Conservatoire	49"	Polished Ebony	10,740.
K131	52"	Polished Ebony/Mahogany	13,640.

Grands

KC 173	5' 8"	Polished Ebony	24,990.

Kimball

Verticals

K44	44"	Cherry/Oak	3,790.
K44	44"	French Provincial Cherry/Oak	3,790.

Grands

K1	4' 10"	Polished Ebony	8,590.
K1	4' 10"	Polished Mahogany	8,990.

Knabe, Wm.

Verticals

WKV-118F	46½"	French Provincial Semi-Gloss Cherry	7,190.
WKV-118R	46½"	Renaissance Semi-Gloss Ebony/Walnut	7,190.
WKV-118T	46½"	Semi-Gloss Mahogany	7,190.
WKV-121	48"	Ebony	7,390.
WKV-121	48"	Polished Ebony	7,190.
WKV-121	48"	Polished Mahogany	7,990.
WKV-131	52"	Ebony	7,790.
WKV-131	52"	Polished Ebony	7,590.
WKV-131	52"	Polished Mahogany	8,190.

Grands

WKG-53	5' 3"	Ebony	17,690.
WKG-53	5' 3"	Polished Ebony	16,890.
WKG-53	5' 3"	Semi-Gloss Wood Finishes	18,990.
WKG-58	5' 8"	Ebony	23,400.
WKG-58	5' 8"	Polished Ebony	23,200.
WKG-58	5' 8"	Semi-Gloss Wood Finishes	24,400.

Model	Size	Style and Finish	Price*
WKG-58F	5' 8"	French Prov. Semi-Gloss Wood Finishes	27,400.
WKG-58M	5' 8"	Empire Ebony	24,400.
WKG-58M	5' 8"	Empire Polished Ebony	23,600.
WKG-58M	5' 8"	Empire Semi-Gloss Wood Finishes	25,200.
WKG-64	6' 4"	Ebony	28,200.
WKG-64	6' 4"	Polished Ebony	27,400.
WKG-64	6' 4"	Semi-Gloss Wood Finishes	29,000.
WKG-70	7'	Ebony	30,600.
WKG-70	7'	Polished Ebony	29,400.
WKG-70	7'	Semi-Gloss Wood Finishes	30,600.

Kohler & Campbell

Verticals

Model	Size	Style and Finish	Price
KC-142	42"	Continental Polished Ebony	2,990.
KC-142	42"	Continental Cherry/Walnut	2,990.
KC-142	42"	Continental Pol. Mahogany/Walnut/Ivory	3,090.
KC-043F	43"	French Provincial Cherry	3,290.
KC-043T	43"	Mahogany	3,290.
KC-244F	44"	French Provincial Cherry	3,590.
KC-244M	44"	Mediterranean Brown Oak	3,590.
KC-244T	44"	Mahogany	3,690.
KC-245	45"	Polished Ebony	3,890.
KC-245	45"	Cherry/Walnut	3,890.
KC-245	45"	Polished Mahogany/Walnut/Ivory	3,890.
KC-247	46½"	Ebony and Polished Ebony	4,990.
KC-247	46½"	Mahogany/Walnut	4,990.
KC-247	46½"	Polished Mahogany/Walnut	4,990.
KM-647F	46½"	French Provincial Cherry	4,390.
KM-647R	46½"	Renaissance Walnut	4,390.
KM-647T	46½"	Mahogany	4,390.
KC-121M	48"	Polished Ebony	4,190.
KC-121M	48"	Polished Mahogany	4,390.
KMV-48D	48"	Ebony	7,590.
KMV-48D	48"	Polished Ebony	6,990.
KMV-48D	48"	Polished Mahogany	8,190.
KC-131	52"	Polished Ebony	4,890.
KC-131	52"	Polished Mahogany	4,990.
KMV-52D	52"	Ebony	7,790.
KMV-52D	52"	Polished Ebony	7,390.

*For explanation of terms and prices, please see pages 76–82.

Model	Size	Style and Finish	Price*

Kohler & Campbell (continued)

Model	Size	Style and Finish	Price*
KMV-52D	52"	Polished Mahogany	9,090.

Grands

Model	Size	Style and Finish	Price*
KCG-450	4' 9"	Polished Ebony	8,590.
KCG-450	4' 9"	Polished Mahogany/Walnut	9,290.
KCG-500	5' 1½"	Polished Ebony	10,090.
KCG-500	5' 1½"	Polished Mahogany/Walnut	10,790.
KCG-500KBF	5' 1½"	French Provincial Pol. Mahogany/Cherry	13,090.
KCM-500	5' 1½"	Ebony	13,090.
KCM-500	5' 1½"	Polished Ebony	12,590.
KCM-500	5' 1½"	Mahogany/Walnut Lacquer	13,690.
KCM-500	5' 1½"	Polished Mahogany/Walnut	13,490.
KCG-600	5' 9"	Polished Ebony	11,390.
KCG-600	5' 9"	Polished Mahogany/Walnut	11,990.
KCM-600	5' 9"	Ebony	14,790.
KCM-600	5' 9"	Polished Ebony	14,090.
KCM-600	5' 9"	Mahogany/Walnut Lacquer	14,990.
KCM-600	5' 9"	Polished Mahogany/Walnut	14,790.
KCM-650	6' 1"	Ebony	15,990.
KCM-650	6' 1"	Polished Ebony	15,390.
KCM-650	6' 1"	Mahogany/Walnut Lacquer	16,190.
KCM-650	6' 1"	Polished Mahogany/Walnut	15,990.
KFM-700	6' 8"	Ebony	24,210.
KFM-700	6' 8"	Polished Ebony	28,000.
KFM-700	6' 8"	Mahogany/Walnut Lacquer	24,210.
KFM-700	6' 8"	Polished Mahogany/Walnut	24,210.
KFM-850	7' 4"	Polished Ebony	30,000.

Mason & Hamlin

Verticals

Model	Size	Style and Finish	Price*
50	50"	Ebony and Polished Ebony	17,862.
50	50"	Mahogany	18,168.

Grands

Model	Size	Style and Finish	Price*
A	5' 8"	Ebony	45,368.
A	5' 8"	Polished Ebony	48,516.
A	5' 8"	Mahogany/Walnut	48,780.
A	5' 8"	Polished Pyramid Mahogany	59,298.
A	5' 8"	Rosewood/Bubinga	54,144.
A	5' 8"	Polished Bubinga	56,038.

Model	Size	Style and Finish	Price*
A	5' 8"	Macassar Ebony	57,292.
A	5' 8"	Polished Macassar Ebony	59,298.
A	5' 8"	"Monticello" Polished Ebony	51,682.
A	5' 8"	"Monticello" Mahogany	51,930.
A	5' 8"	"Monticello" Walnut/Rosewood	62,954.
AA	6' 4"	Ebony	52,344.
AA	6' 4"	Polished Ebony	54,042.
AA	6' 4"	Mahogany/Walnut	55,100.
AA	6' 4"	Polished Pyramid Mahogany	63,298.
AA	6' 4"	Rosewood/Bubinga	58,144.
AA	6' 4"	Polished Bubinga	60,038.
AA	6' 4"	Macassar Ebony	61,292.
AA	6' 4"	Polished Macassar Ebony	63,298.
AA	6' 4"	"Monticello" Polished Ebony	57,812.
AA	6' 4"	"Monticello" Mahogany	58,250.
AA	6' 4"	"Monticello" Walnut/Rosewood	71,100.
BB	7'	Ebony	59,322.
BB	7'	Polished Ebony	61,028.
BB	7'	Mahogany/Walnut	61,422.
BB	7'	Polished Pyramid Mahogany	73,130.
BB	7'	Rosewood/Bubinga	68,758.
BB	7'	Polished Bubinga	70,464.
BB	7'	Macassar Ebony	71,360.
BB	7'	Polished Macassar Ebony	73,130.
BB	7'	"Monticello" Polished Ebony	63,942.
BB	7'	"Monticello" Mahogany	64,572.
BB	7'	"Monticello" Walnut/Rosewood	79,246.
CC	9' 4"	Ebony	88,200.
CC	9' 4"	Polished Ebony	92,200.

Meister, Otto

Verticals

U-110	43"	Polished Ebony	2,640.
U-110	43"	Polished Mahogany	2,730.
C-45	45"	Cherry/Oak	2,990.
C-45	45"	French Provincial Cherry/Oak	2,990.
U-115	45"	Polished Ebony	3,040.
U-115	45"	Polished Mahogany	3,130.
U-120	47"	Polished Ebony	3,440.
U-120	47"	Polished Mahogany	3,530.

*For explanation of terms and prices, please see pages 76–82.

Model	Size	Style and Finish	Price*

Otto Meister (continued)

Model	Size	Style and Finish	Price*
U-123K	49"	Polished Ebony	3,980.
U-123K	49"	Polished Mahogany	4,180.
U-131K	52"	Polished Ebony	4,380.
U-131K	52"	Polished Mahogany	4,580.

Grands

G-143	4' 9"	Polished Ebony	6,790.
G-143	4' 9"	Polished Mahogany	6,990.
G-143	4' 9"	Empire Polished Ebony	6,990.
G-143	4' 9"	French Provincial Polished Mahogany	7,190.
G-158	5' 3"	Polished Ebony	7,390.
G-158	5' 3"	Polished Mahogany	7,590.
G-158	5' 3"	Empire Polished Ebony	7,590.
G-158	5' 3"	French Provincial Polished Mahogany	7,790.
G-168	5' 7"	Polished Ebony	7,990.
G-168	5' 7"	Empire Polished Ebony	8,190.
G-185	6' 1"	Ebony	10,390.
G-185	6' 1"	Polished Ebony	9,990.
G-185	6' 1"	Polished Mahogany	10,190.
G-185	6' 1"	Empire Polished Ebony	10,190.

Miller, Henry F.

Verticals

HMV-043	42½"	Continental Polished Ebony	3,300.
HMV-043	42½"	Continental Polished Mahogany	3,400.
HMV-045	43½"	French Provincial Cherry	4,200.
HMV-045	43½"	Italian Provincial Oak	4,220.
HMV-045	43½"	Mediterranean Oak	4,220.
HMV-047	46½"	Ebony	4,032.
HMV-047	46½"	Polished Ebony	3,938.
HMV-047	46½"	Polished Mahogany	4,032.
HMV-048	48"	Cherry	4,720.

Grands

HMG-056	4' 8"	Ebony	9,120.
HMG-056	4' 8"	Polished Ebony	9,070.
HMG-058S	4' 10"	Ebony	9,320.
HMG-058S	4' 10"	Polished Ebony	9,270.
HMG-058S	4' 10"	Polished Mahogany	9,520.
HMG-063S	5' 3"	Ebony	10,730.

Model	Size	Style and Finish	Price*
HMG-063S	5' 3"	Polished Ebony	10,530.
HMG-063S	5' 3"	Polished Mahogany	10,930.

Nordiska

Verticals

Model	Size	Style and Finish	Price*
109-CM	43"	Continental Polished Ebony/Mahogany	2,480.
114-MC	45"	French Walnut/Mahogany	3,580.
114-MCH	45"	Walnut/Mahogany	3,580.
116-CB	46"	Chippendale Pol. Ebony/Walnut/Mahogany	3,580.
116-MC	46"	Ebony/Walnut	3,580.
118-C GT	47"	Polished Ebony	3,480.
118-MC	47"	Walnut/Mahogany/Oak	3,780.
120-CA	47"	Polished Ebony/Mahogany	3,780.
126-PRO	50"	Polished Ebony	4,580.
126-PRO	50"	Walnut	4,580.
131	52"	Polished Ebony	5,180.

Grands

Model	Size	Style and Finish	Price*
B	4' 8"	Polished Ebony	7,780.
B	4' 8"	Polished Walnut/Mahogany	8,180.
D	5'	Ebony and Polished Ebony	8,380.
D	5'	Walnut	8,980.
D	5'	Polished Walnut/Mahogany	8,980.
D	5'	Polished Sapeli Mahogany/White	8,780.
D	5'	Demi-Chippendale Polished Ebony	9,300.
D	5'	Demi-Chippendale Mahogany	9,900.
D	5'	Demi-Chippendale Pol. Mahogany/Walnut	9,900.
D	5'	Demi-Chippendale Pol. Sapeli Mahogany	9,580.
G	5' 5"	Polished Ebony	9,580.
G	5' 5"	Polished Sapeli Mahogany	9,900.
G	5' 5"	Polished Walnut/Mahogany	10,180.
G	5' 5"	Demi-Chippendale Polished Ebony	10,580.
G	5' 5"	Demi-Chippendale Pol. Walnut/Mahogany	11,180.
G	5' 5"	Regency Polished Ebony	10,180.
G	5' 5"	Regency Polished Walnut/Mahogany	10,780.
G	5' 5"	Ebony with Acrylic	23,400.
K	6' 1"	Polished Ebony	11,380.
K	6' 1"	Polished Walnut/Mahogany	11,980.
K	6' 1"	Empire Polished Ebony	12,780.
K	6' 1"	Empire Polished Walnut/Mahogany	13,380.

*For explanation of terms and prices, please see pages 76–82.

Model	Size	Style and Finish	Price*

Nordiska (continued)

Model	Size	Style and Finish	Price
K	6' 1"	Imperial Polished Ebony	11,980.
K	6' 1"	Imperial Polished Walnut/Mahogany	12,580.
K	6' 1"	Polished Ebony (round tapered legs)	11,780.
O	7'	Polished Ebony	19,980.
Y	9'	Polished Ebony	51,800.

Palatino

Verticals

Model	Size	Style and Finish	Price
PUP-110TS	43½"	Polished Ebony	2,490.
PUP-110TS	43½"	Polished Mahogany/Cherry/White	2,640.
PUP-121T	48"	Ebony/Brown Mahogany	3,040.
PUP-121T	48"	Polished Ebony	2,890.
PUP-121T	48"	Polished Dark Walnut	3,040.
PUP-121Y	48"	Cherry	3,140.
PUP-123F	48½"	French Polished Ebony	2,890.
PUP-123F	48½"	French Polished Mahogany/Walnut/White	3,040.
PUP-123JH	48½"	French legs w/ Chysanthemum Engraving	3,140.
PUP-123SXH	48½"	French legs with Elodea Vine Engraving	3,140.
PUP-123T	48½"	Ebony/Brown Mahogany/Cherry	3,040.
PUP-123T	48½"	Polished Ebony	2,890.
PUP-123T	48½"	Polished Mahogany/Dark Walnut	3,040.
PUP-123T	48½"	Polished White/Red	3,040.
PUP-123T	48½"	Polished Wine Red	3,140.
PUP-123TU	48½"	Polished Ebony w/Decorated Wood Panel	2,940.
PUP-123Y	48½"	Polished Ebony	2,890.
PUP-123Y	48½"	Polished Mahogany/Cherry/White/Red	3,040.
PUP-123Y	48½"	Polished Wine Red	3,140.
PUP-126C	50"	French Legs Carved	3,690.
PUP-126T	50"	Ebony	3,490.
PUP-126T	50"	Polished Ebony	3,290.
PUP-126T	50"	Polished Mahogany/Cherry/Dark Walnut	3,490.

Grands

Model	Size	Style and Finish	Price
PGD-46F	4' 6"	French Ebony	7,740.
PGD-46F	4' 6"	French Polished Ebony	7,540.
PGD-46F	4' 6"	French Polished Mahogany/White/Red	7,740.
PGD-46T	4' 6"	Ebony	7,490.
PGD-46T	4' 6"	Polished Ebony	7,290.
PGD-46T	4' 6"	Polished Mahogany/White/Red	7,490.

Model	Size	Style and Finish	Price*
PGD-50F	5'	French Ebony	8,490.
PGD-50F	5'	French Polished Ebony	8,290.
PGD-50F	5'	French Mahogany/White/Red	8,490.
PGD-50T	5'	Ebony	8,290.
PGD-50T	5'	Polished Ebony	8,090.
PGD-50T	5'	Polished Mahogany/White/Red	8,290.
PGD-59F	5' 9"	French Ebony	10,540.
PGD-59F	5' 9"	French Polished Ebony	10,340.
PGD-59F	5' 9"	French Mahogany/White/Red	10,540.
PGD-59T	5' 9"	Ebony	10,290.
PGD-59T	5' 9"	Polished Ebony	10,090.
PGD-59T	5' 9"	Polished Mahogany/White/Red	10,290.

Pearl River

Verticals

Model	Size	Style and Finish	Price
UP-108D3	42½"	Continental Polished Ebony	2,640.
UP-108D3	42½"	Continental Polished Mahogany/Walnut	2,790.
UP-108D3	42½"	Continental Polished White	2,790.
UP-108M2	42½"	Demi-Chippendale Polished Ebony	3,190.
UP-108M2	42½"	Demi-Chippendale Pol. Mahogany/Walnut	3,270.
UP-108T2	42½"	Polished Ebony	3,380.
UP-108T2	42½"	Polished Mahogany/Walnut	3,440.
UP-108T2	42½"	Polished White	3,530.
UP-110P1	43½"	Walnut/Cherry/Oak	3,710.
UP-110P2	43½"	French Provincial Oak	3,890.
UP-110P2	43½"	French Provincial Cherry	3,990.
UP-110P5	43½"	Italian Provincial Walnut/Cherry	4,090.
UP-110P6	43½"	French Classic Cherry	4,160.
UP-115E	45"	Ebony/Oak/Walnut	3,490.
UP-115M	45"	Polished Ebony	3,330.
UP-115M	45"	Polished Dark Mahogany	3,370.
UP-115P1	45"	Walnut/Cherry	4,400.
UP-118E	47"	Polished Ebony	3,550.
UP-118E	47"	Polished Mahogany/Walnut	3,630.
UP-118E	47"	Polished White	3,630.
UP-120S	48"	Polished Ebony	4,270.
UP-120S	48"	Polished Mahogany	4,370.
UP-125M1	49"	Polished Ebony (with Yamaha)	5,290.
UP-130T2	51½"	Polished Mahogany w/Burl Oval Inlay	5,640.

*For explanation of terms and prices, please see pages 76–82.

Model	Size	Style and Finish	Price*

Pearl River (continued)

Grands

Model	Size	Style and Finish	Price*
GP-142	4' 7"	Polished Ebony	7,860.
GP-142	4' 7"	Polished Mahogany/Walnut	8,380.
GP-142	4' 7"	Polished White	8,380.
GP-142D	4' 7"	French Provincial Cherry	9,160.
GP-142P	4' 7"	Walnut	9,530.
GP-150	5'	Ebony/Cherry	8,820.
GP-150	5'	Polished Ebony	8,500.
GP-150D	5'	Walnut	9,540.
GP-159	5' 3"	Ebony	11,690.
GP-159	5' 3"	Polished Ebony	11,350.
GP-159	5' 3"	Mahogany and Polished Mahogany	11,690.
GP-170	5' 7"	Ebony	14,490.
GP-170	5' 7"	Polished Ebony	14,120.
GP-170	5' 7"	Mahogany	14,700.
GP-170	5' 7"	Polished Mahogany	14,320.
GP-170D	5' 7"	Cherry	14,830.
GP-183	6'	Polished Ebony	15,040.
GP-186	6' 1"	Polished Ebony (Silver Plate & Trim)	16,200.
GP-188	6' 4"	Polished Ebony	18,050.
GP-213	7'	Polished Ebony	21,140.
GP-275	9'	Polished Ebony	55,500.

Perzina, Gebr.

Verticals

Model	Size	Style and Finish	Price*
GP-112	44"	Continental Polished Ebony	5,220.
GP-112	44"	Continental Pol. Mahogany/Walnut/Oak	5,390.
GP-112	44"	Continental Polished White	5,390.
GP-112	44"	Continental Satin Finishes	5,390.
GP-112	44"	Polished Ebony	5,390.
GP-112	44"	Polished Mahogany/Walnut/Oak	5,580.
GP-112	44"	Polished White	5,580.
GP-112	44"	Satin Finishes	5,580.
GP-112	44"	Queen Anne Polished Ebony	5,580.
GP-112	44"	Queen Anne Polished Mahogany/Walnut	5,760.
GP-112	44"	Queen Anne Walnut	5,760.
GP-118	46½"	Continental Polished Ebony	6,280.
GP-118	46½"	Continental Pol. Ebony w/Mahog. Center	6,480.

Model	Size	Style and Finish	Price*
GP-118	46½"	Continental Pol. Mahogany/Walnut/Oak	6,670.
GP-118	46½"	Continental Polished White	6,670.
GP-118	46½"	Continental Satin Finishes	6,670.
GP-118	46½"	Walnut/Mahogany/Oak	7,180.
GP-118	46½"	Contemporary Walnut/Mahogany/Oak	7,180.
GP-118	46½"	Queen Anne Walnut/Mahogany/Oak	7,180.
GP-118	46½"	Country French Mahogany/Oak	7,180.
GP-122	48"	Polished Ebony	6,990.
GP-122	48"	Polished Ebony with Pommele Center	7,390.
GP-122	48"	Polished Mahogany/Walnut/Oak/White	7,490.
GP-122	48"	Satin Finishes	7,490.
GP-122	48"	Deco Leg Polished Ebony	7,390.
GP-122	48"	Deco Leg Polished Ebony w/Walnut Trim	7,790.
GP-122	48"	Deco Leg Polished Mahogany/Oak/White	7,790.
GP-122	48"	Queen Anne Polished Ebony	7,390.
GP-122	48"	Queen Anne Polished Mahogany/Walnut	7,790.
GP-122	48"	Queen Anne Walnut	7,790.
GP-122	48"	Queen Anne, above, with molding, add'l	200.
GP-129	51"	Polished Ebony	8,170.
GP-129	51"	Polished Ebony w/Pommele Center	8,390.
GP-129	51"	Polished Mahogany/Walnut/Oak/White	8,690.
GP-129	51"	Satin Finishes	8,690.
GP-129	51"	Queen Anne Polished Ebony	8,420.
GP-129	51"	Queen Anne Polished Mahogany/Walnut	8,950.
GP-129	51"	Queen Anne Walnut	8,950.
GP-129	51"	Queen Anne, above, with molding, add'l	160-240.
All models		With slow-fall fallboard, add'l	270.

Grands

On E-series grands, other leg styles and finishes available by special order.

Model	Size	Style and Finish	Price*
E-160	5' 3"	Polished Ebony	24,750.
E-160	5' 3"	Polished Mahogany/Walnut	26,100.
G-160	5' 3"	Polished Ebony	17,850.
G-160	5' 3"	Polished Mahogany/Walnut/Oak/White	18,540.
G-160	5' 3"	Satin Finishes	18,540.
G-160	5' 3"	Polished Ebony (round leg)	18,210.
G-160	5' 3"	Polished Mahogany/Walnut (round leg)	18,890.
G-160	5' 3"	Walnut (round leg)	18,890.
G-160	5' 3"	Queen Anne Polished Ebony	18,210.
G-160	5' 3"	Queen Anne Polished Mahogany/Walnut	18,890.
G-160	5' 3"	Queen Anne Walnut	18,890.

*For explanation of terms and prices, please see pages 76–82.

Model	Size	Style and Finish	Price*

Perzina, Gebr. (continued)

Model	Size	Style and Finish	Price
G-160	5' 3"	Designer Ebony w/Bubinga Fallboard/Lid	19,230.
G-160	5' 3"	with Renner hammers, add'l	550.
E-187	6' 1"	Polished Ebony	27,330.
E-187	6' 1"	Polished Mahogany/Walnut	28,710.
G-187	6' 1"	Polished Ebony	19,920.
G-187	6' 1"	Polished Mahogany/Walnut/Oak/White	20,960.
G-187	6' 1"	Satin Finishes	20,960.
G-187	6' 1"	Polished Ebony (round leg)	20,270.
G-187	6' 1"	Polished Mahogany/Walnut (round leg)	21,300.
G-187	6' 1"	Walnut (round leg)	21,300.
G-187	6' 1"	Queen Anne Polished Ebony	20,270.
G-187	6' 1"	Queen Anne Polished Mahogany/Walnut	21,300.
G-187	6' 1"	Queen Anne Walnut	21,300.
G-187	6' 1"	Designer Ebony w/Bubinga Fallboard/Lid	21,630.
G-187	6' 1"	with Renner hammers, add'l	550.

Petrof

Note: Prices below do not include bench. Add from $220 to $630 (most are under $400), depending on choice of bench.

Verticals

Model	Size	Style and Finish	Price
P 116 E1	45"	Continental Polished Ebony	6,960.
P 118 C1	46"	Chippendale Polished Walnut/Mahogany	7,980.
P 118 D1	46"	Demi-Chip. Designer Pol. Walnut/Mahog.	7,980.
P 118 G1	46"	Polished Ebony/Walnut/Mahogany	7,580.
P 118 H1	46"	Contemporary Pol. Ebony/Walnut/Mahog.	7,180.
P 118 H1	46"	Polished Walnut with Marquetry	7,580.
P 118 H1	46"	Designer Polished Walnut/Mahogany	7,580.
P 118 H2	46"	Polished Ebony with Brass Trim	7,380.
P 118 P1	46"	Classic Polished Ebony/Walnut/Mahogany	7,780.
P 125 F1	50"	Polished Walnut/Mahogany	8,980.
P 125 F1	50"	Polished Walnut/Mahogany w/Fan Panels	9,180.
P 125 G1	50"	Polished Ebony	9,100.
P 125 H2	50"	Polished Ebony w/Burl Walnut/Brass Trim	9,580.
P 131 E1	52"	Polished Ebony/Walnut/Mahogany	12,380.
P 135 K1	52"	Polished Ebony	16,980.

Grands

Model	Size	Style and Finish	Price
VI	4' 8"	Polished Ebony/Walnut/Mahogany	21,980.
VI DC	4' 8"	Demi-Chip. Pol. Ebony/Walnut/Mahogany	25,200.

Model	Size	Style and Finish	Price*
V	5' 3"	Polished Ebony/Walnut/Mahogany	23,200.
V DC	5' 3"	Demi-Chip. Pol. Ebony/Walnut/Mahogany	25,980.
IV	5' 8"	Polished Ebony/Walnut/Mahogany	25,000.
IV C	5' 8"	Chippendale Pol. Ebony/Walnut/Mahogany	31,000.
IV DC	5' 8"	Demi-Chip. Pol. Ebony/Walnut/Mahogany	27,000.
IV	5' 8"	"Klasik" Polished Ebony/Walnut/Mahogany	29,980.
III	6' 4"	Polished Ebony/Walnut/Mahogany	30,200.
III	6' 4"	"Majestic" Pol. Ebony/Walnut/Mahogany	31,980.
Pasat B	6' 10½"	Polished Ebony	43,000.
II	7' 9"	Polished Ebony/Walnut	47,400.
I	9' 3"	"Mistral" Polished Ebony	71,980.
III, IV, V		With Sterling Original Action, add'l approx.	2,900.

PianoDisc

Prices for PianoDisc and QuietTime systems vary by piano manufacturer and installer. The following are suggested retail prices from PianoDisc. The usual dealer discounts may apply, especially as an incentive to purchase a piano.

Opus7 "Opulence," factory-installed or retrofitted	18,357.
Opus7 "Luxury," factory-installed or retrofitted	14,276.
Opus7 Performance Package option	2,733.
228CFX System, factory-installed or retrofitted:	
Playback only	6,635.
Add for MX (Music Expansion) Platinum	1,758.
Add for MX (Music Expansion) Basic	1,171.
Add for SymphonyPro Sound Module	1,115.
Add for TFT MIDI Record system	1,627.
Add for PianoMute Rail	664.
Add for amplified speakers, pair	735.
PianoCD System	5,995.
QuietTime GT-2 System (Control unit w/ Piano and Organ sounds, MIDI Strip, MIDI interface board, pedal switches, cable, headphones, power supply, PianoMute rail)	2,362.
MIDI Controller (TFT MIDI Strip, MIDI interface board, pedal switches, cable, power supply)	1,816.
AudioForte	2,447.

*For explanation of terms and prices, please see pages 76–82.

Pleyel

Verticals

Model	Size	Style and Finish	Price
P 118	47"	Polished Ebony	11,800.
P 118	47"	Polished Mahogany	13,430.
P 118	47"	Walnut	12,860.
P 118	47"	Cherry with Marquetry	12,990.
P 118	47"	Walnut with Leather	15,630.
P 118	47"	"Romantica Noyer" Walnut	12,620.
P 124	49"	Polished Ebony	14,040.
P 124	49"	*Walnut with Marquetry*	15,400.
P 124	49"	Cherry with Marquetry	15,400.
P 131	51"	Polished Ebony	18,900.
P 131	51"	Polished Mahogany	18,900.
P 131	51"	"Fidelio" all available finishes	21,300.
P 131	51"	*With Sostenuto, add*	900.

Grands

Model	Size	Style and Finish	Price
P 170	5' 7"	Polished Ebony	44,140.
P 170	5' 7"	Polished Mahogany	53,380.
P 170	5' 7"	Walnut	49,100.
P 190	6' 3"	Polished Ebony	53,200.
P 190	6' 3"	Cherry with Marquetry	62,600.
P 190	6' 3"	Polished Mahogany with Marquetry	62,600.
P 190	6' 3"	Poplar Burl	80,200.
P 280	9' 2"	Polished Ebony	149,500.

Pramberger

J. Pramberger Signature Series Verticals

Model	Size	Style and Finish	Price
PV-110F	43"	French Provincial Cherry	4,390.
PV-110R	43"	Renaissance Walnut	4,390.
PV-110T	43"	Mahogany	4,390.
PV-118S	46½"	Ebony and Polished Ebony	4,590.
PV-118S	46½"	Mahogany/Walnut	4,590.
PV-121	48"	Polished Ebony/Mahogany	4,590.
PV-131	52"	Polished Ebony	4,790.
PV-131	52"	Polished Mahogany	4,990.

J.P. Pramberger Platinum Series Verticals

Model	Size	Style and Finish	Price
JP-116	45"	Ebony	8,190.
JP-116	45"	Polished Ebony	7,990.

Model	Size	Style and Finish	Price*
JP-116	45"	Semi-Gloss Mahogany/Walnut	8,790.
JP-125	49"	Ebony	8,590.
JP-125	49"	Polished Ebony	8,390.
JP-125	49"	Semi-Gloss Mahogany/Walnut	9,190.
JP-131	52"	Ebony	8,850.
JP-131	52"	Polished Ebony	8,550.
JP-131	52"	Semi-Gloss Mahogany/Walnut	9,590.

J. Pramberger Signature Series Grands

Model	Size	Style and Finish	Price*
PS-150	5'	Ebony/Mahogany/Walnut	10,390.
PS-150	5'	Polished Ebony	9,990.
PS-150	5'	Polished Mahogany/Walnut	10,390.
PS-157	5' 3"	Ebony	10,790.
PS-157	5' 3"	Polished Ebony	10,390.
PS-157	5' 3"	Mahogany/Walnut	11,390.
PS-157	5' 3"	Polished Mahogany/Walnut	10,990.
PS-175	5' 7"	Ebony	11,590.
PS-175	5' 7"	Polished Ebony	11,190.
PS-175	5' 7"	Mahogany/Walnut	12,390.
PS-175	5' 7"	Polished Mahogany/Walnut	11,790.
PS-185	6' 1"	Ebony	12,190.
PS-185	6' 1"	Polished Ebony	11,790.
PS-185	6' 1"	Mahogany/Walnut	12,790.
PS-185	6' 1"	Polished Mahogany/Walnut	12,390.

J.P. Pramberger Platinum Series Grands

Model	Size	Style and Finish	Price*
JP-160S	5' 3"	Ebony	20,400.
JP-160S	5' 3"	Polished Ebony	20,000.
JP-160S	5' 3"	Semi-Gloss Mahogany/Walnut	21,600.
JP-179F	5' 10"	Ebony	26,400.
JP-179F	5' 10"	French Provincial Polished Ebony	25,600.
JP-179F	5' 10"	French Prov. Semi-Gloss Mahogany/Walnut	28,000.
JP-179L	5' 10"	Ebony	23,400.
JP-179L	5' 10"	Polished Ebony	23,000.
JP-179L	5' 10"	Semi-Gloss Mahogany/Walnut	24,400.
JP-190A	6' 3"	Ebony	27,600.
JP-190A	6' 3"	Polished Ebony	27,200.
JP-190A	6' 3"	Semi-Gloss Mahogany/Walnut	29,200.
JP-208B	6' 10"	Ebony	29,400.
JP-208B	6' 10"	Polished Ebony	29,000.
JP-208B	6' 10"	Semi-Gloss Mahogany/Walnut	30,800.

*For explanation of terms and prices, please see pages 76–82.

QRS / Pianomation

Prices for Pianomation systems vary by piano manufacturer, installer, and accessories. The following are approximate retail prices for installed systems from QRS. The usual dealer discounts may apply, especially as an incentive to purchase a piano.

Pianomation:		2000C Player System	5,320.
		2000CD+ Player System, CD player, speaker	6,300.
		Petine Player System, DVD ROM player, speaker	6,800.
Playola:		With 2000C Player System	6,000.
		With 2000CD+ Player System	6,750.

Remington

Also available in polished ivory, white, walnut, and cherry at same price as mahogany.

Verticals

Model	Size	Style and Finish	Price
RVM-108	42"	Continental Polished Ebony	2,590.
RVM-108	42"	Continental Polished Mahogany/Ivory	2,690.
RV-43F	43"	French Provincial Cherry/Brown Oak	3,190.
RV-43T	43"	Mahogany/Walnut	3,190.
RVM-118	45"	Polished Ebony/Mahogany	2,990.
RVM-121	48"	Polished Ebony ·	2,990.
RVM-121	48"	Polished Mahogany	3,090.
RVM-131	52"	Polished Ebony	4,190.
RVM-131	52"	Polished Mahogany	4,590.

Grands

Model	Size	Style and Finish	Price
RG-150	4' 11½"	Polished Ebony	7,590.
RG-150	4' 11½"	Polished Mahogany	7,990.
RG-157	5' 3"	Polished Ebony	8,590.
RG-157	5' 3"	Polished Mahogany	8,990.
RG-175	5' 7"	Polished Ebony	10,190.
RG-175	5' 7"	Polished Mahogany	10,590.
RG-185	6' 1"	Polished Ebony	11,190.
RG-185	6' 1"	Polished Mahogany	11,590.

Ritmüller

Verticals

Model	Size	Style and Finish	Price
UP-110R2	43½"	Continental Polished Ebony	3,680.
UP-110R2	43½"	Continental Polished Mahogany/Walnut	3,720.

Model	Size	Style and Finish	Price*
UP-110R4	43½"	French Provincial Cherry	3,770.
UP-110R5	43½"	Walnut	3,770.
UP-110R6	43½"	American Country Oak	3,770.
UP-118R2	46½"	"Scandinavian Design" Polished Ebony	4,180.
UP-118R2	46½"	"Scandinavian Design" Polished Mahogany	4,250.
UP-118R3	46½"	Cherry	5,180.
UP-120R	48"	Polished Ebony	4,790.
UP-120R	48"	Polished Mahogany/Walnut	4,870.
UP-120R	48"	Polished White	4,870.
UP-120R1	48"	"European Design" Pol. Ebony w/Mahog.	4,770.
UP-120R2	48"	Chippendale Walnut/Mahogany	5,030.
UP-120R3	48"	"Euro-Modern" Continental Polished Ebony	5,380.
UP-120R4	48"	French Provincial Cherry	5,230.
UP-120R6	48"	Queen Anne Cherry	5,540.
UP-120R7	48"	Italian Provincial Walnut	5,540.
UP-120R8	48"	American Classic Walnut	5,540.
UP-123R	48"	"Classic Euro" Polished Ebony	5,940.
UP-123R	48"	"Classic Euro" Polished Mahogany/Walnut	6,000.
UP-123R1	48"	"Deluxe European" Polished Ebony	5,950.
UP-125R	49"	"European" Polished Ebony w/Mahogany	6,400.
UP-125R2	49"	"Deluxe European" Pol. Ebony w/Mahog.	6,600.
UP-126R	49"	Polished Ebony	6,450.
UP-130R	51"	Polished Ebony (movable front)	6,590.
UP-130R	51"	Walnut (movable front)	6,640.
UP-130R	51"	Polished Mahogany (movable front)	6,640.
UP-130R1	51"	Polished Ebony	6,530.
UP-130R2	51"	Polished Ebony	6,940.

Grands

Model	Size	Style and Finish	Price*
GP-148R	4' 10"	Ebony (round leg, brass trim)	9,670.
GP-148R	4' 10"	Polished Ebony (round leg, brass trim)	9,460.
GP-148R	4' 10"	Polished Mahogany (round leg, brass trim)	9,870.
GP-148R1	4' 10"	Polished Ebony (tapered leg, brass trim)	9,340.
GP-159R	5' 3"	Ebony (round leg, brass trim)	13,240.
GP-159R	5' 3"	Polished Ebony (round leg, brass trim)	12,890.
GP-159R	5' 3"	Mahogany (round leg, brass trim)	13,450.
GP-159R	5' 3"	Pol. Mahog./Walnut (round leg, brass trim)	13,240.
GP-159R1	5' 3"	Ebony (tapered leg, brass trim)	13,290.
GP-159R1	5' 3"	Polished Ebony (tapered leg, brass trim)	12,920.
GP-159R1	5' 3"	Polished Mahogany (tapered leg, brass trim)	13,290.
GP-159R2	5' 3"	Louis XV Cherry	13,500.

*For explanation of terms and prices, please see pages 76–82.

Model	Size	Style and Finish	Price*

Ritmüller (continued)

GP-183R	6'	Ebony (round leg, brass trim)	17,080.
GP-183R	6'	Polished Ebony (round leg, brass trim)	16,600.
GP-183R1	6'	Ebony (tapered leg, brass trim)	16,670.
GP-183R1	6'	Polished Ebony (tapered leg, brass trim)	16,470.
GP-213R1	7'	Polished Ebony	23,280.
GP-275R1	9'	Polished Ebony	73,800.

Samick

Verticals

JS-042	42"	Continental Polished Ebony	2,990.
JS-042	42"	Continental Pol. Mahogany/Walnut/Ivory	2,990.
JS-042	42"	Continental Cherry/Walnut	3,090.
JS-143F	43"	French Provincial Cherry	3,890.
JS-143M	43"	Mediterranean Brown Oak	3,890.
JS-143T	43"	Mahogany	3,890.
JS-115	45"	Ebony/Mahogany/Walnut/Cherry	3,490.
JS-115	45"	Polished Ebony/Mahogany	3,390.
JS-247	46½"	Ebony/Mahogany/Walnut	4,990.
JS-247	46½"	Polished Ebony/Mahogany/Walnut	4,990.
JS-121M	48"	Mediterranean Polished Ebony	4,190.
JS-121M	48"	Mediterranean Polished Mahogany	4,390.
JS-131	52"	Polished Ebony	4,790.

Grands

SIG-50	4' 11½"	Ebony	9,190.
SIG-50	4' 11½"	Polished Ebony	8,390.
SIG-50	4' 11½"	Polished Mahogany	9,190.
SIG-54	5' 3"	Ebony	10,790.
SIG-54	5' 3"	Polished Ebony	10,090.
SIG-54	5' 3"	Polished Mahogany	10,790.
SIG-54 KBF	5' 3"	French Provincial Polished Cherry	13,090.
SIG-57	5' 7"	Ebony	11,590.
SIG-57	5' 7"	Polished Ebony	10,990.
SIG-57	5' 7"	Polished Mahogany	11,590.
SIG-57L	5' 7"	Empire Polished Ebony	11,990.
SIG-57L	5' 7"	Empire Polished Mahogany	12,590.
SIG-61	6' 1"	Ebony	12,390.
SIG-61	6' 1"	Polished Ebony	11,790.
SIG-61	6' 1"	Polished Mahogany	12,390.

Sauter

Prices do not include bench

Verticals

Model	Size	Style and Finish	Price*
122	48"	"Ragazza" Polished Ebony	21,460.
122	48"	"Ragazza" Cherry	21,240.
122	48"	"Ragazza" Polished Cherry/Yew	25,180.
122	48"	"Vista" Polished Ebony	23,400.
122	48"	"Vista" Maple	22,300.
122	48"	"Vista" Cherry	23,280.
122	48"	School Piano Ebony/Beech Bright	18,700.
122	48"	"M-Line M2" Polished Ebony	27,620.
122	48"	Peter Maly "Artes" Polished Ebony	32,300.
122	48"	Peter Maly "Artes" Polished Palisander	33,300.
122	48"	Peter Maly "Artes" Polished White	32,900.
122	48"	Peter Maly "Cura" Walnut	30,420.
122	48"	Peter Maly "Cura" Cherry	31,420.
122	48"	Peter Maly "Imago" Swiss Pearwood &Grey	27,620.
122	48"	Peter Maly "Pure 2000 Noble" Pol. Ebony	29,540.
122	48"	Peter Maly "Pure 2000 Noble" Pol. Ebony & Zebrano	29,540.
122	48"	Peter Maly "Pure 2000 Noble" Pol. White	30,320.
122	48"	Peter Maly "Pure 2000 Noble" Pol. Red	30,320.
122	48"	Peter Maly "Pure 2000 Basic" Ebony & Walnut	23,820.
122	48"	Peter Maly "Pure 2000 Basic" White	23,820.
122	48"	Peter Maly "Pure 2000 Basic" Wht & Maple	23,820.
122	48"	Peter Maly "Rondo" Polished Ebony	25,900.
122	48"	Peter Maly "Rondo" Wenge	23,920.
122	48"	Peter Maly "Onda" Maple & Silver	22,160.
122	48"	Peter Maly "Vitrea" Dark Oak with Glass	24,640.
128	51"	"M-Line M1" Polished Ebony	31,360.
128	51'"	"Competence" Polished Ebony	26,780.
128	51"	"Competence" Walnut	25,380.

Grands

Standard wood finishes are Walnut, Mahogany, Oak, Ash, and Alder.

Model	Size	Style and Finish	Price*
160	5' 3"	"Alpha" Polished Ebony	54,700.
160	5' 3"	"Alpha" Standard Wood Finishes	49,980.
160	5' 3"	Queen Anne Cherry	56,600.
160	5' 3"	Queen Anne Polished Cherry	63,800.

*For explanation of terms and prices, please see pages 76–82.

Model	Size	Style and Finish	Price*

Sauter (continued)

Model	Size	Style and Finish	Price*
160	5' 3"	Chippendale Cherry	56,800.
160	5' 3"	Chippendale Standard Wood Finishes	54,600.
160	5' 3"	"Noblesse" Cherry	61,200.
160	5' 3"	"Noblesse" Polished Cherry	68,600.
160	5' 3"	"Noblesse" Burl Walnut	64,400.
160	5' 3"	"Noblesse" Standard Wood Finishes	59,000.
160	5' 3"	"Noblesse" Pol. Standard Wood Finishes	66,400.
185	6' 1"	"Delta" Polished Ebony	59,580.
185	6' 1"	"Delta" Polished Ebony w/Burl Walnut	61,400.
185	6' 1"	"Delta" Polished Pyramid Mahogany	66,140.
185	6' 1"	"Delta" Polished Bubinga/Rio Palisander	66,140.
185	6' 1"	"Delta" Maple with Silver	56,200.
185	6' 1"	"Delta" Polished White	61,800.
185	6' 1"	"Delta" Standard Wood Finishes	54,520.
185	6' 1"	Chippendale Cherry	61,200.
185	6' 1"	Chippendale Standard Wood Finishes	59,000.
185	6' 1"	"Noblesse" Cherry	65,800.
185	6' 1"	"Noblesse" Polished Cherry	73,960.
185	6' 1"	"Noblesse" Burl Walnut	68,800.
185	6' 1"	"Noblesse" Standard Wood Finishes	63,600.
185	6' 1"	"Noblesse" Pol. Standard Wood Finishes	71,900.
185	6' 1"	"Amadeus" French Walnut	78,920.
210	6' 11"	Peter Maly "Vivace" Polished Ebony	85,100.
210	6' 11"	Peter Maly "Vivace" Maple	79,120.
210	6' 11"	Peter Maly "Vivace" Polished White	86,480.
220	7' 3"	"Omega" Polished Ebony	76,180.
220	7' 3"	"Omega" M-Line Version, Polished Ebony	81,000.
220	7' 3"	"Omega" Polished Pyramid Mahogany	83,720.
220	7' 3"	"Omega" Standard Wood Finishes	71,980.
230	7' 6"	Peter Maly "Ambiente" Polished Ebony	102,340.
275	9'	"Concert" Polished Ebony	119,960.

Schimmel

When not mentioned, satin finish available on special order at same price as high-polish finish.

Verticals

Model	Size	Style and Finish	Price*
C 112 S	44"	Open-Pore Ebony/Oak/Walnut	14,180.
C 116 ST	46"	Polished Ebony	12,980.

Model	Size	Style and Finish	Price*
C 116 ST	46"	Open-Pore Alder/Walnut/Beech	13,980.
C 116 ST	46"	Cherry	14,180.
C 116 ST	46"	Polished Mahogany/White	14,180.
C 120 AE	47"	"Anniversary" Polished Ebony	14,980.
C 120 AE	47"	"Anniversary" Polished Mahogany	15,580.
C 120 I	47"	"International" Polished Ebony	14,980.
C 120 I	47"	"International" Polished Mahogany/White	15,580.
C 120 S	47"	"School" Open-Pore Ebony/Oak	14,780.
C 120 T	47"	Polished Ebony	15,180.
C 120 T	47"	Open-Pore Alder/Beech/Walnut	15,180.
C 120 T	47"	Cherry	15,180.
C 120 T	47"	Polished White	15,780.
C 120 TA	47"	"Akademie" Polished Ebony	14,980.
K 122 AC	48"	"Art Cubus" Polished Ebony	19,980.
K 122 AC	48"	"Art Cubus" Waxed Swiss Pear	19,980.
K 122 AC	48"	"Art Cubus" Polished White	21,980.
K 122 SE	48"	"Salon Exquisit" Polished Ebony	17,580.
K 122 TA	48"	"Akademie" Polished Ebony	17,580.
C 124 R	49"	"Royale" Polished Ebony	16,780.
C 124 R	49"	"Royale" Polished Mahogany	18,780.
C 124 RI	49"	"Royale Intarsia" Polished Mahogany	19,780.
C 124 T	49"	Polished Ebony	15,980.
C 124 T	49"	Polished Ebony w/Oval Decoration	16,580.
C 124 T	49"	Polished Mahogany	17,580.
C 124 T	49"	Polished Mahogany w/Oval Decoration	17,980.
C 124 T	49"	Open-Pore Walnut Antique	15,980.
K 125 DN	49"	"Diamond Noblesse" Polished Ebony	21,180.
K 125 DN	49"	"Diamond Noblesse" Polished Mahogany	21,980.
K 125 DP	49"	"Diamond Prestige" Polished Ebony	21,180.
K 125 DP	49"	"Diamond Prestige" Polished Mahogany	21,980.
C 130 T	51"	Polished Ebony	17,580.
C 130 T	51"	Polished Ebony w/Oval Decoration	17,780.
C 130 T	51"	Polished Mahogany/Walnut	19,180.
C 130 T	51"	Open-Pore Walnut	18,580.
K 132 DT	52"	"Diamond Traditional" Polished Ebony	21,980.
K 132 DT	52"	"Diamond Traditional" Pol. Mahogany	23,980.
K 132 EM	52"	"Edition Manufactum" Mahogany/Walnut	34,980.

Grands

Model	Size	Style and Finish	Price*
K 169 BE	5' 7"	"Belle Epoque" Polished Ebony	44,780.
K 169 DE	5' 7"	"Diamond Edition" Polished Ebony	42,180.

*For explanation of terms and prices, please see pages 76–82.

143

Model	Size	Style and Finish	Price*

Schimmel (continued)

Model	Size	Style and Finish	Price*
K 169 DE	5' 7"	"Diamond Edition" Pol. Flame Mahogany	45,780.
K 169 DE	5' 7"	"Diamond Edition" Polished Bubinga	45,780.
K 169 DE	5' 7"	"Diamond Edition" Pol. Bird's-Eye Maple	45,780.
K 169 DE	5' 7"	"Diamond Edition" Macassar	45,780.
K 169 DE	5' 7"	"Diamond Edition" Polished White	45,780.
K 169 DE	5' 7"	"Diamond Edition" "Red Diamond"	45,780.
K 169 E	5' 7"	"Empire" Mahogany and Pol. Mahogany	50,180.
K 169 T	5' 7"	Polished Ebony	39,180.
K 169 T	5' 7"	Polished Mahogany/White	40,380.
K 169 T	5' 7"	Polished Flame Mahogany/Macassar	45,780.
K 169 T	5' 7"	Polished Bubinga/Bird's-Eye Maple	45,780.
K 169 T	5' 7"	"Hidden Beauty" Pol. Ebony w/Bubinga	41,980.
K 169 TE	5' 7"	"Exquisit" Polished Ebony	41,980.
K 169 TE	5' 7"	"Exquisit" Polished Mahogany/White	43,180.
K 169 TE-I	5' 7"	"Exquisit" Polished Mahogany Intarsia	43,780.
K 169 TI-H	5' 7"	"Intarsia Harp" Polished Ebony	43,780.
K 169 TI-V	5' 7"	"Intarsia Vase" Polished Mahogany	43,780.
K 169 TJ	5' 7"	"Centennial" Polished Ebony	41,580.
K 169 TJ	5' 7"	"Centennial" Polished Mahogany/White	42,780.
K 189 BE	6' 3"	"Belle Epoque" Polished Ebony	47,980.
K 189 DE	6' 3"	"Diamond Edition" Polished Ebony	45,380.
K 189 DE	6' 3"	"Diamond Edition" Pol. Flame Mahogany	48,980.
K 189 DE	6' 3"	"Diamond Edition" Polished Bubinga	48,980.
K 189 DE	6' 3"	"Diamond Edition" Pol. Bird's-Eye Maple	48,980.
K 189 DE	6' 3"	"Diamond Edition" Macassar	48,980.
K 189 DE	6' 3"	"Diamond Edition" Polished White	48,980.
K 189 DE	6' 3"	"Diamond Edition" "Red Diamond"	48,980.
K 189 E	6' 3"	"Empire" Mahogany and Pol. Mahogany	53,180.
K 189 NWS	6' 3"	"Nikolaus W. Schimmel Special Edition"	53,780.
K 189 T	6' 3"	Polished Ebony	42,380.
K 189 T	6' 3"	Polished Walnut/Mahogany/White	43,580.
K 189 T	6' 3"	Polished Flame Mahogany/Macassar	48,980.
K 189 T	6' 3"	Polished Bubinga/Bird's-Eye Maple	48,980.
K 189 T	6' 3"	"Hidden Beauty" Pol. Ebony w/Bubinga	45,380.
K 189 T	6' 3"	Open-Pore Walnut Antique	40,380.
K 189 TA	6' 3"	"Akademie" Polished Ebony	42,380.
K 189 TE	6' 3"	"Exquisit" Polished Ebony	45,180.
K 189 TE	6' 3"	"Exquisit" Polished Mahogany/White	46,380.
K 189 TE-I	6' 3"	"Exquisit" Polished Mahogany Intarsia	46,980.

Model	Size	Style and Finish	Price*
K 189 TI-H	6' 3"	"Intarsia Harp" Polished Ebony	46,980.
K 189 TI-V	6' 3"	"Intarsia Vase" Polished Mahogany	46,980.
K 189 TJ	6' 3"	"Centennial" Polished Ebony	44,780.
K 189 TJ	6' 3"	"Centennial" Polished Mahogany/White	45,980.
K 208 P	7'	"Pegasus" colors on request	200,000.
K 213 ART	7'	"Art Edition" Pol. Ebony w/color motifs	141,000.
K 213 DE	7'	"Diamond Edition" Polished Ebony	48,580.
K 213 DE	7'	"Diamond Edition" Pol. Flame Mahogany	52,180.
K 213 DE	7'	"Diamond Edition" Polished Bubinga	52,180.
K 213 DE	7'	"Diamond Edition" Pol. Bird's-Eye Maple	52,180.
K 213 DE	7'	"Diamond Edition" Macassar	52,180.
K 213 DE	7'	"Diamond Edition" Polished White	52,180.
K 213 DE	7'	"Diamond Edition" "Red Diamond"	52,180.
K 213 G	7'	*"Transparent" Clear Acrylic and White*	119,000.
K 213 NWS	7'	"Nikolaus W. Schimmel Special Edition"	57,980.
K 213 T	7'	Polished Ebony	45,580.
K 213 T	7'	Polished Mahogany/Walnut/White	46,780.
K 213 T	7'	Polished Flame Mahogany/Macassar	52,180.
K 213 T	7'	Polished Bubinga/Bird's-Eye Maple	52,180.
K 213 T	7'	"Hidden Beauty" Pol. Ebony w/Bubinga	48,580.
K 213 TA	7'	"Akademie" Polished Ebony	45,580.
K 213 TE	7'	"Exquisit" Polished Ebony	48,380.
K 213 TE	7'	"Exquisit" Polished Mahogany/White	49,580.
K 213 TJ	7'	"Centennial" Polished Ebony	47,980.
K 213 TJ	7'	"Centennial" Polished Mahogany/White	49,180.
K 256 T	8' 4"	Polished Ebony	73,000.
K 280 T	9' 2"	Polished Ebony	98,000.

Schulze Pollmann

Verticals

114/P4	45"	Polished Ebony	7,190.
114/P4	45"	Polished Mahogany/Walnut	7,390.
114/P4	45"	Polished Peacock Ebony/Walnut/Mahogany	7,790.
118/P8	46"	Polished Ebony	11,190.
118/P8	46"	Polished Briar Walnut	11,990.
118/P8	46"	Polished Feather or Peacock Mahogany	11,990.
126/P6	50"	Polished Ebony	12,790.
126/P6	50"	Polished Peacock Ebony	13,390.
126/P6	50"	Polished Peacock Mahogany/Cherry/Walnut	13,390.
126/P6	50"	Polished Briar Mahogany/Walnut	13,390.

*For explanation of terms and prices, please see pages 76–82.

Schulze Pollmann (continued)

Grands

Model	Size	Style and Finish	Price
160/GK	5' 3"	Polished Ebony (spade leg)	29,390.
160/GK	5' 3"	Polished Ebony (round leg)	30,390.
160/GK	5' 3"	Polished Briar Mahogany (spade leg)	32,390.
160/GK	5' 3"	Polished Briar Mahogany (round leg)	34,390.
160/GK	5' 3"	Peacock Mahogany (spade leg)	34,990.
160/GK	5' 3"	Polished Feather Mahogany (spade leg)	37,990.
190/F	6' 2"	Polished Ebony	39,390.
190/F	6' 2"	Polished Briar Mahogany	43,190.
190/F	6' 2"	Polished Briar Walnut	43,990.
190/F	6' 2"	Polished Feather Mahogany	46,390.
197/G2	6' 7"	Polished Ebony	44,390.
197/G2	6' 7"	Polished Briar Mahogany/Walnut	48,390.

Seidl & Sohn

Prices do not include bench.

Verticals

Model	Size	Style and Finish	Price
SL 109	43"	Continental Polished Ebony	7,504.
SL 109	43"	Continental Polished Walnut/Mahogany	7,605.
SL 109	43"	Continental Polished White	7,704.
SL 113	46"	Polished Ebony	7,704.
SL 113	46"	Polished Walnut/Mahogany	7,809.
SL 113	46"	Polished White	7,874.
SL 120	48"	Polished Ebony	8,107.
SL 120	48"	Polished Walnut/Mahogany	8,220.
SL 120	48"	Polished White	8,273.
SL 120	48"	*Renner Action, add'l*	906.
SL 127	51"	Polished Ebony	9,281.
SL 127	51"	Polished Walnut/Mahogany	9,422.
SL 127	51"	*Renner Action, add'l*	918.

Seiler

Verticals

Model	Size	Style and Finish	Price
116	46"	"Primus" Polished Ebony	14,840.
116	46"	"Mondial" Open-Pore Ebony	16,700.
116	46"	"Mondial" Open-Pore Walnut/Mahog./Oak	16,700.
116	46"	"Mondial" Polished Mahogany	17,480.

Model	Size	Style and Finish	Price*
116	46"	"Mondial" Open-Pore Maple/Alder	16,880.
116	46"	"Mondial" Open-Pore Cherry	17,800.
116	46"	"Mondial" Open-Pore Swiss Pear	17,240.
116	46"	"Mondial" Open-Pore Apple Heartwood	17,800.
116	46"	"Mondial" Polished Burl Rosewood	19,340.
116	46"	"Jubilee" Polished Ebony	17,920.
116	46"	"Jubilee" Polished White	18,220.
116	46"	Chippendale Open-Pore Walnut	16,880.
116	46"	"Escorial" Open-Pore Cherry Intarsia	18,220.
122	48"	"School" Open-Pore Ebony/Walnut/Oak	16,600.
122	48"	"Primus" Polished Ebony	17,700.
122	48"	"Konsole" Open-Pore Ebony	17,380.
122	48"	"Konsole" Polished Ebony	18,560.
122	48"	"Konsole" Open-Pore Walnut/Maple/Oak	17,380.
122	48"	"Konsole" Polished Walnut Rootwood	25,120.
122	48"	"Konsole" Maple Burl	18,100.
122	48"	"Konsole" Open-Pore Cherry	18,240.
122	48"	"Konsole" Polished Burl Rosewood	21,460.
122	48"	"Konsole" Polished Brown Ash	21,460.
122	48"	"Konsole" Polished Mahogany	19,140.
122	48"	"Konsole" Polished Redwood/Myrtle Burl	22,560.
122	48"	"Konsole" Polished White	19,180.
122	48"	"Vienna" Polished Ebony w/Pilaster	19,060.
122	48"	"Vienna" Polished Ebony w/Pilaster & Oval	19,260.
122	48"	"Vienna" Pol. Mahogany w/ Flower Inlays	21,460.
122	48"	"Vienna" Polished Walnut w/ Flower Inlays	21,460.
122	48"	"Vienna" Maple with Pilaster	19,060.
122	48"	"Vienna" Maple with Pilaster & Oval	19,260.
122	48"	with SMR Action, add'l	1,980.
132	52"	"Concert SMR" Polished Ebony	23,660.
132	52"	"Concert SMR" Polished Ebony w/Oval	24,360.
132	52"	"Concert SMR" Polished Ebony w/Candle	24,320.
132	52"	"Concert SMR" Polished Ebony w/Panels	24,480.
132	52"	"Concert SMR" Open-Pore Walnut	22,940.
132	52"	"Concert SMR" Polished Mahogany	24,380.
132	52"	"Concert SMR" Polished Burl Rosewood	26,020.
132	52"	"Concert SMR" Pol. Yew/Ash Rootwood	28,040.
132	52"	"Concert SMR" Polished Burl Maple	29,000.
132	52"	"Limited Edition" Polished Ebony	27,260.
132	52"	"Limited Ed." Pol. Ebony w/Oval or Pilaster	27,820.
132	52"	"Limited Ed." Pol. Ebony w/Oval & Pilaster	28,360.

*For explanation of terms and prices, please see pages 76–82.

Seiler (continued)

Grands

Model	Size	Style and Finish	Price
168	5' 6"	"Virtuoso" Polished Ebony	52,600.
168	5' 6"	"Virtuoso" Polished Mahogany	55,060.
180	5' 11"	"Terrestre"	172,500.
180	5' 11"	"Suspension"	187,420.
186	6' 1"	"Maestro" Polished Ebony	53,900.
186	6' 1"	"Maestro" Open-Pore Walnut/Mahogany	53,900.
186	6' 1"	"Maestro" Polished Walnut/Mahogany	57,500.
186	6' 1"	"Maestro" Polished Pyramid Mahogany	75,440.
186	6' 1"	"Maestro" Polished Burl Rosewood	67,240.
186	6' 1"	"Maestro" Polished Flamed Maple	67,940.
186	6' 1"	"Maestro" Polished Peacock Maple	75,440.
186	6' 1"	"Maestro" Polished Laurel Rootwood	75,440.
186	6' 1"	"Maestro" Polished White	55,080.
186	6' 1"	Chippendale Open-Pore Walnut	58,380.
186	6' 1"	"Westminster" Polished Mahogany, Intarsia	75,980.
186	6' 1"	"Florenz" Polished Walnut/Myrtle, Intarsia	75,980.
186	6' 1"	"Florenz" Polished Mahog./Myrtle, Intarsia	75,980.
186	6' 1"	"Louvre" Polished Ebony	60,940.
186	6' 1"	"Louvre" Polished Cherry, Intarsia	75,980.
186	6' 1"	"Louvre" Polished White	61,540.
186	6' 1"	"Prado" Polished Brown Ash	77,600.
186	6' 1"	"Prado" Polished Burl Redwood	77,600.
186	6' 1"	"Stella" Polished Maple Rootwood, Intarsia	92,660.
186	6' 1"	"Showmaster" Chrome/Brass/Polyester	150,300.
208	6' 10"	Polished Ebony	61,940.
208	6' 10"	"Empire 1897" Open-Pore Blue w/Brass	191,500.
208	6' 10"	"Solitaire" Custom with Painting	215,840.
208	6' 10"	"Solitaire" Custom without Painting	175,280.
242	8'	Polished Ebony	81,980.
278	9' 1"	Polished Ebony	95,980.

Sohmer (Persis International)

Verticals

Model	Size	Style and Finish	Price
S-126	50"	Polished Ebony	7,790.
S-126	50"	Polished Mahogany	7,990.

Grands

Model	Size	Style and Finish	Price
S-160	5' 3"	Polished Ebony	17,790.

Model	Size	Style and Finish	Price*
S-160	5' 3"	Polished Mahogany	18,390.
S-180	5' 10"	Polished Ebony	19,790.
S-180	5' 10"	Polished Mahogany	20,390.
S-218	7' 2"	Polished Ebony	33,990.

Sohmer & Co. (SMC)

Verticals

34F	42"	French Provincial Cherry	4,390.
34R	42"	Renaissance Walnut/Cherry	4,390.
34T	42"	Mahogany/Walnut	4,390.
45F	45"	French Provincial Cherry	6,190.
45R	45"	Renaissance Walnut/Cherry	6,190.
45S	45"	Ebony and Polished Ebony	5,790.
45T	45"	Mahogany/Walnut	6,190.

Grands

50T	5'	Polished Ebony	11,390.
50T	5'	Mahogany/Walnut/Cherry	13,790.
63E	5' 4"	Empire Semi-Gloss Mahog./Walnut/Cherry	19,190.
63F	5' 4"	Fr. Prov. Semi-Gloss Mahog/Walnut/Cherry	18,390.
63H	5' 4"	Hepplewhite S-G Mahog./Walnut/Cherry	16,390.
63T	5' 4"	Ebony	13,590.
63T	5' 4"	Polished Ebony	12,990.
63T	5' 4"	Semi-Gloss Mahogany/Walnut/Cherry	14,390.
77E	5' 9"	Empire Semi-Gloss Mahog./Walnut/Cherry	19,390.
77F	5' 9"	Fr. Prov. Semi-Gloss Mahog/Walnut/Cherry	18,590.
77H	5' 9"	Hepplewhite S-G Mahog./Walnut/Cherry	16,390.
77T	5' 9"	Ebony	14,590.
77T	5' 9"	Polished Ebony	13,990.
77T	5' 9"	Semi-Gloss Mahogany/Walnut/Cherry	14,390.
90H	6' 2"	Hepplewhite S-G Mahog./Walnut/Cherry	18,390.
90T	6' 2"	Ebony	15,390.
90T	6' 2"	Polished Ebony	14,790.
90T	6' 2"	Semi-Gloss Mahogany	16,190.
95T	6' 8"	Ebony	21,800.
95T	6' 8"	Polished Ebony	21,000.
95T	6' 8"	Semi-Gloss Mahogany/Walnut/Cherry	22,600.

*For explanation of terms and prices, please see pages 76–82.

Steck, Geo.

Model numbers ending in "D" indicate slow-close fallboard.

Verticals

Model	Size	Style and Finish	Price*
US 09	43"	Continental Polished Ebony	2,870.
US 09	43"	Continental Cherry/Mahogany	2,930.
US 09	43"	Continental Pol. Beech/Mahogany/Walnut	2,990.
US 09	43"	Continental Polished Ivory/White	2,990.
US 09L	43"	Continental (w/legs) Polished Ebony	2,950.
US 09L	43"	Continental (w/legs) Pol. Mahogany/Walnut	3,070.
US 09L	43"	Continental (w/legs) Polished White	3,070.
CS 12FD	44"	French Provincial Brown Oak/Cherry	3,490.
CS 12MD	44"	Mediterranean Brown Oak/Cherry	3,490.
US 12F	44"	French Provincial Cherry/Mahogany	3,260.
US 12T	44"	Polished Ebony	3,080.
US 12T	44"	Walnut/Cherry/Mahogany	3,140.
US 12T	44"	Polished Mahogany/Walnut/White	3,200.
CS 13FD	44½"	French Provincial Oak	3,590.
CS 13M1D	44½"	Brown Oak/Mahogany	3,790.
CS 16AT	45½"	Brown Oak/Cherry	3,870.
CS 16ATD	45½"	Brown Oak/Cherry	3,990.
CS 16F	45½"	French Provincial Cherry/Brown Oak	3,650.
CS 16FD	45½"	French Provincial Cherry/Brown Oak	3,770.
CS 16FPD	45½"	French Provincial Cherry/Brown Oak	3,790.
CS 16IP	45½"	Italian Provincial Walnut/Cherry	3,670.
CS 16IPD	45½"	Italian Provincial Cherry	3,790.
CS 16QA	45½"	Queen Anne Cherry/Brown Oak/Mahogany	3,970.
CS 16QAD	45½"	Queen Anne Cherry/Brown Oak	4,090.
CS 16T	45½"	Cherry/Brown Oak/Walnut	3,870.
US 16IC	46"	Polished Ebony w/Front Panel Decoration	3,200.
US 16IC	46"	Polished Brown Oak w/Front Panel Decor.	3,320.
US 16ST	46"	Brown Oak/Cherry (school)	3,200.
US 16STL	46"	Ebony (school w/lock)	3,500.*
US 16STL	46"	Brown Oak/Cherry/Walnut (school w/lock)	3,500.
US 16TC	46"	Polished Ebony w/Front Panel Decoration	3,240.
US 16TC	46"	Pol. Mahog./Walnut w/Front Panel Decor.	3,360.
US 18MS	46½"	Mediterranean Polished Mahogany	3,360.
CS 19F	46¾"	French Provincial Brown Oak/Cherry	3,700.
CS 19FD	46¾"	Country French Brown Oak/Cherry/Mahog.	3,820.
CS 19MD	46¾"	Brown Oak/Cherry	3,820.
CS 19M1D	46¾"	Mediterranean Cherry	3,820.

Model	Size	Style and Finish	Price*
CS 19QAD	46¾"	Queen Anne Cherry	4,190.
CS 47FD	46¾"	French Provincial Designer Cherry	5,320.
CS 47MD	46¾"	Mediterranean Mahogany	5,320.
US 19F	46¾"	Demi-Chippendale Polished Ebony	3,320.
US 19F	46¾"	Demi-Chippendale Cherry/Mahogany	3,380.
US 19F	46¾"	Demi-Chip. Pol. Cherry/Mahog./Walnut	3,440.
US 19F	46¾"	Demi-Chippendale Polished Ivory/White	3,440.
US 19PD	46¾"	Provincial Mahogany	3,590.
US 19T	46¾"	Polished Ebony	3,200.
US 19T	46¾"	Cherry	3,260.
US 19T	46¾"	Polished Mahogany/Brown Oak/Walnut	3,320.
US 47IC	46¾"	Designer Polished Ebony	4,590.
US 47R	46¾"	Designer Polished Cherry	4,790.
US 47V	46¾"	Designer Polished Ebony	4,790.
US 20T	47"	Designer Polished Ivory	3,610.
US 22F	48"	French Provincial Polished Ebony	3,490.
US 22F	48"	French Provincial Pol. Mahogany/Walnut	3,610.
US 22T	48"	Ebony	3,430.
US 22T	48"	Polished Ebony	3,370.
US 22T	48"	Polished Mahogany/Walnut/White	3,490.
US 22WTD	48"	Polished Ebony	3,590.
US 28SD	48"	Designer Special Polished Bubinga	4,490.
US 23FD	48½"	Cherry/Mahogany	3,800.
US 23FD	48½"	Polished Walnut/Mahogany/White	3,860.
US 23TD	48½"	Polished Ebony	3,620.
US 23TD	48½"	Polished Mahogany/Walnut	3,740.
US 25BD	49"	Designer Special Ebony	4,050.
US 25BD	49"	Designer Special Polished Ebony	3,990.
US 32FD	52"	French Provincial Polished Ebony	3,860.
US 32FD	52"	French Provincial Polished Mahogany	3,980.
US 32HD	52"	Polished Bubinga (reinforced hammer)	4,390.
US 32T	52"	Ebony	3,680.
US 32T	52"	Polished Ebony	3,620.
US 32TD	52"	Polished Ebony	3,740.
US 32TD	52"	Polished Mahogany/Walnut	3,860.

Grands

Some "D" models are also available without slow-close fallboard for $120 less.

GS 42D	4' 8"	Ebony	8,740.
GS 42D	4' 8"	Polished Ebony	8,540.
GS 42D	4' 8"	Cherry/Mahogany/Walnut	9,140.

*For explanation of terms and prices, please see pages 76–82.

Model	Size	Style and Finish	Price*

Steck, Geo. (continued)

Model	Size	Style and Finish	Price*
GS 42D	4' 8"	Polished Cherry/Mahogany/Walnut	8,940.
GS 42D	4' 8"	Polished White	8,740.
GS 42FD	4' 8"	French Provincial Polished Ebony	9,140.
GS 42FD	4' 8"	French Provincial Cherry/Mahogany	9,740.
GS 42FD	4' 8"	French Prov. Pol. Cherry/Mahog./Walnut	9,540.
GS 52D	5'	Ebony	9,580.
GS 52D	5'	Polished Ebony	9,380.
GS 52D	5'	Cherry/Mahogany/Walnut	9,980.
GS 52D	5'	Polished Cherry/Mahogany/Walnut	9,780.
GS 52F	5'	French Provincial Cherry	10,460.
GS 52F	5'	French Provincial Polished Mahogany	10,260.
GS 52FAD	5'	FrenchAnn Polished Cherry	10,580.
GS 52FD	5'	French Provincial Cherry/Mahogany	10,580.
GS 52FD	5'	French Prov. Pol. Cherry/Mahog./Walnut	10,380.
GS 52LD	5'	Louis XVI Polished Ebony	9,860.
GS 62D	5' 4"	Ebony	10,610.
GS 62D	5' 4"	Polished Ebony	10,410.
GS 62D	5' 4"	Cherry/Mahogany	11,010.
GS 62D	5' 4"	Polished Mahogany/Walnut	10,810.
GS 62D	5' 4"	Polished White	10,610.
GS 62FD	5' 4"	French Provincial Pol. Mahogany/Walnut	11,410.
GS 62FD	5' 4"	French Provincial Cherry	11,610.
GS 62FD	5' 4"	French Provincial Polished White	11,210:
GS 62HLED	5' 4"	Polished Ebony w/Hexagonal Leg	11,130.
GS 62QAD	5' 4"	Queen Anne Polished Mahogany	11,610.
GS 72D	5' 8"	Ebony	11,640.
GS 72D	5' 8"	Polished Ebony	11,440.
GS 72D	5' 8"	Cherry/Mahogany	12,040.
GS 72D	5' 8"	Pol. Cherry/Mahogany/Walnut	11,840.
GS 72D	5' 8"	Polished Bubinga	12,440.
GS 72F	5' 8"	French Provincial Polished Ebony	11,920.
GS 72F	5' 8"	French Provincial Cherry	12,520.
GS 72FD	5' 8"	French Provincial Polished Mahogany	12,440.
GS 72HLD	5' 8"	Mahogany w/Hexagonal Leg	12,640.
GS 72LD	5' 8"	Louis XVI Polished Ebony	11,920.
GS 72LD	5' 8"	Louis XVI Polished Mahogany	12,320.
GS 72LD	5' 8"	Louis XVI Walnut	12,520.
GS 72PLSD	5' 8"	Polished Walnut w/Octagonal Leg & Inlay	12,920.
GS 72QAD	5' 8"	Queen Anne Cherry	12,840.

Model	Size	Style and Finish	Price*
GS 87D	6' 2"	Ebony	12,660.
GS 87D	6' 2"	Polished Ebony	12,460.
GS 87D	6' 2"	Mahogany/Cherry	13,060.
GS 87D	6' 2"	Polished Mahogany/Walnut	12,860.
GS 87D	6' 2"	Polished Ivory	12,660.
GS 87FD	6' 2"	French Provincial Polished Mahogany	13,460.
GS 87FFBD	6' 2"	Rococo Ebony w/Rim Band	14,180.
GS 87FFBD	6' 2"	Rococo Polished Ebony w/Rim Band	13,990.
GS 87HLD	6' 2"	Mahogany w/Hexagonal Leg	13,660.
GS 87LD	6' 2"	Louis XVI Ebony	13,140.
GS 87LD	6' 2"	Louis XVI Polished Ebony	12,940.
GS 87LD	6' 2"	Louis XVI Mahogany	13,540.
GS 87LD	6' 2"	Louis XVI Polished Mahogany	13,340.
GS 87PLD	6' 2"	Walnut w/Octagonal Leg	13,660.
GS 87PLSD	6' 2"	Cherry w/Octagonal Leg & Inlay	14,140.
GS 208D	6' 10"	Polished Ebony	15,600.
GS 208CD	6' 10"	Polished Bubinga w/Bevelled Lid	16,800.
GS 208HLD	6' 10"	Mahogany w/Hexagonal Leg	16,800.
GS 208HLBD	6' 10"	Pol. Ebony w/Hexagonal Leg & Rim Band	16,920.
GS 208HLBCD	6' 10"	Cherry w/Hexag. Leg, Rim & Keybed Band	17,720.
GS 208HLBCD	6' 10"	Pol. Mahog. w/Hexag. Leg, Rim & Keybed Band	17,520.
GS 228D	7' 6"	Polished Ebony	19,600.
GS 278D	9' 2"	Polished Ebony	47,600.

Steigerman

Verticals

Model	Size	Style and Finish	Price*
108SM	42"	Continental Polished Ebony	3,000.
108SM	42"	Continental Pol. Dark Walnut/Mahogany	3,100.
C43	43"	American Furniture, Oak/Cherry/Walnut/Mahogany	3,500.
XU110S	43"	Polished Ebony, w/toe blocks	3,300.
XU110S	43"	Polished Mahogany/Walnut, w/toe blocks	3,400.
C45	45"	American Furniture, Oak/Cherry/Walnut/Mahogany	3,700.
115LS	45"	Polished Ebony	3,300.
115LS	45"	Polished Mahogany/Walnut	3,400.
P116	45"	Light Walnut, institutional	3,600.
117XK	46"	Polished Mahogany, curved leg	3,400.
118H	46½"	Polished Ebony/Dark Walnut	2,950.
B120LS	47"	Polished Ebony	3,500.

*For explanation of terms and prices, please see pages 76–82.

Model	Size	Style and Finish	Price*

Steigerman (continued)

Model	Size	Style and Finish	Price
B120LS	47"	Polished Dark Mahogany	3,600.
XU132HA	52"	Polished Ebony	3,792.
All models		Color instead of Polished Ebony, add'l	150.

Grands

Model	Size	Style and Finish	Price
XG143S	4' 8"	Polished Ebony	8,800.
XG148S	4' 10"	Polished Ebony	10,600.
XG158S	5' 2"	Polished Ebony	10,600.
XG168S	5' 6"	Polished Ebony	11,600.
XG185S	6'	Polished Ebony	12,600.
All models		Color instead of Polished Ebony, add'l	300.
All models		Slow-Close Fallboard, add'l	110.

Steinberg, Gerh.

Verticals

Model	Size	Style and Finish	Price
HM-109	43"	Continental Polished Ebony	4,680.
HM-109	43"	Continental Pol. Mahog./Walnut/Oak/White	4,860.
HM-109	43"	Continental Satin Finish	4,860.
HM-109	43"	Polished Ebony	4,860.
HM-109	43"	Polished Mahogany/Walnut/Oak/White	5,040.
HM-109	43"	Satin Finish	5,040.
HM-109	43"	Queen Anne Polished Ebony	5,040.
HM-109	43"	Queen Anne Polished Mahogany/Walnut	5,300.
HM-109	43"	Queen Anne Walnut	5,300.
HM-115	45"	Walnut/Mahogany/Oak	6,060.
HM-115	45"	Contemporary Walnut/Mahogany/Oak	6,060.
HM-115	45"	Queen Anne Walnut/Mahogany/Oak	6,060.
HM-115	45"	Country French Mahogany/Oak	6,060.
HM-116	46"	Deco Leg Polished Ebony	5,250.
HM-116	46"	Deco Leg Polished Ebony w/Walnut Trim	5,390.
HM-116	46"	Deco Leg Polished Mahogany/Oak/White	5,610.
HM-116	46"	Queen Anne Polished Ebony	5,390.
HM-116	46"	Queen Anne Polished Mahogany/Walnut	5,690.
EV-123	48"	Polished Ebony	5,590.
EV-123	48"	Polished Ebony w/Pommele Center	5,690.
EV-123	48"	Polished Mahogany/Walnut/Oak/White	5,760.
EV-123	48"	Satin Finish	5,760.
EV-123	48"	Queen Anne Polished Ebony	5,760.
EV-123	48"	Queen Anne Polished Mahogany/Walnut	5,960.

Model	Size	Style and Finish	Price*
EV-125	49"	Polished Ebony	5,990.
EV-125	49"	Polished Ebony w/Pommele Center	6,120.
EV-125	49"	Polished Mahogany/Walnut/White	6,290.
EV-125	49"	Queen Anne Polished Ebony	6,180.
EV-125	49"	Queen Anne Polished Mahogany/Walnut	6,360.

Grands

Model	Size	Style and Finish	Price*
S-159	5' 3"	Polished Ebony	17,520.
S-159	5' 3"	Polished Mahogany/Walnut/Oak/White	18,200.
S-159	5' 3"	Satin Finish	18,200.
S-159	5' 3"	Polished Ebony (round leg)	17,850.
S-159	5' 3"	Polished Mahogany/Walnut (round leg)	18,540.
S-159	5' 3"	Satin Finish (round leg)	18,540.
S-159	5' 3"	Queen Anne Polished Ebony	17,850.
S-159	5' 3"	Queen Anne Polished Mahogany/Walnut	18,540.
S-159	5' 3"	Queen Anne Satin Finish	18,540.
S-159	5' 3"	Designer Ebony w/Bubinga Fallboard/Lid	18,890.
S-186	6' 1"	Polished Ebony	19,580.
S-186	6' 1"	Polished Mahogany/Walnut/Oak/White	20,460.
S-186	6' 1"	Satin Finish	20,460.
S-186	6' 1"	Polished Ebony (round leg)	19,920.
S-186	6' 1"	Polished Mahogany/Walnut (round leg)	20,790.
S-186	6' 1"	Satin Finish (round leg)	20,790.
S-186	6' 1"	Queen Anne Polished Ebony	19,920.
S-186	6' 1"	Queen Anne Polished Mahogany/Walnut	20,790.
S-186	6' 1"	Queen Anne Satin Finish	20,790.
S-186	6' 1"	Designer Ebony w/Bubinga Fallboard/Lid	20,960.

Steinberg, Wilh.

Verticals

Model	Size	Style and Finish	Price*
IQ 22	49"	Polished Ebony	14,422.
IQ 22	49"	Beech/Oak/Alder	14,422.
IQ 22	49"	Walnut/Mahogany	14,695.
IQ 22	49"	Cherry	15,322.
IQ 22	49"	Cherry with Yew	16,223.
IQ 22	49"	"Amadeus" Polished Ebony	15,909.
IQ 22	49"	"Amadeus" Mahogany/Walnut	16,223.
IQ 28	52"	Polished Ebony	18,011.
IQ 28	52"	Mahogany/Walnut	18,148.
IQ 28	52"	Cherry	18,435.

*For explanation of terms and prices, please see pages 76–82.

Model	Size	Style and Finish	Price*

Steinberg, Wilh. (continued)

Model	Size	Style and Finish	Price*
IQ 28	52"	Cherry with Yew	18,885.
IQ 28	52"	"Amadeus" Polished Ebony	18,885.
IQ 28	52"	"Amadeus" Cherry	19,308.
IQ 28	52"	"Passione" Polished Ebony	20,455.
IQ 28	52"	"Passione" Mahogany/Walnut	20,974.
Grands			
IQ 77	5' 9"	Polished Ebony	45,906.
IQ 77	5' 9"	Mahogany/Walnut	47,271.
IQ 77	5' 9"	Cherry	48,158.
IQ 99	6' 3"	Polished Ebony	53,072.
IQ 99	6' 3"	Mahogany/Walnut	59,228.
IQ 99	6' 3"	Cherry	60,648.

Steingraeber & Söhne

This list includes only those models most likely to be offered to U.S. customers. Other models, styles, and finishes are available.

Verticals

Model	Size	Style and Finish	Price*
130 PS/S	51"	Polished Ebony	37,194.
130 PS/S	51"	Polished Ebony w/Twist & Change Panels	40,458.
130 PS/S	51"	Polished Sapeli Mahogany	37,974.
130 PS/S	51"	Special Veneers	35,316.
130 PS/S	51"	Polished Special Veneers	38,880.
130 PS/R	51"	Polished Ebony with DFM Action	42,508.
130 PS/R	51"	Polished Special Veneers with DFM Action	45,936.
130 K	51"	"Classic" Polished Ebony	37,194.
130 K	51"	"Classic" Pol. Ebony w/Twist & Change	40,458.
130 K	51"	"Classic" Polished Sapeli Mahogany	37,974.
130 K	51"	"Classic" Special Veneers	35,316.
130 K	51"	"Classic" Polished Special Veneers	44,190.
138 K	54"	"Classic" Polished Ebony	41,356.
138 K	54"	"Classic" Pol. Ebony w/Twist & Change	44,620.
Grands			
168 N	5' 6"	Polished Ebony	70,410.
168 N	5' 6"	Polished Ebony with Wood Accents	78,576.
168 N	5' 6"	Polished Sapeli Mahogany	80,932.
168 N	5' 6"	Special Veneers	82,948.
168 N	5' 6"	Polished Special Veneers	93,392.
168 K	5' 6"	"Classicism" Polished Ebony	81,980.

Model	Size	Style and Finish	Price*
168 K	5' 6"	"Classicism" Pol. Ebony w/Wood Accents	90,068.
168 K	5' 6"	"Classicism" Polished Sapeli Mahogany	92,554.
168 K	5' 6"	"Classicism" Special Veneers	94,464.
168 K	5' 6"	"Classicism" Polished Special Veneers	104,986.
168 S	5' 6"	"Studio" Polished Ebony	66,562.
205 N	6' 9"	Polished Ebony	94,046.
205 N	6' 9"	Polished Ebony with Wood Accents	102,186.
205 N	6' 9"	Polished Sapeli Mahogany	104,490.
205 N	6' 9"	Special Veneers	106,610.
205 N	6' 9"	Polished Special Veneers	117,844.
205 K	6' 9"	"Classicism" Polished Ebony	104,700.
205 K	6' 9"	"Classicism" Pol. Ebony w/Wood Accents	112,734.
205 K	6' 9"	"Classicism" Polished Sapeli Mahogany	115,038.
205 K	6' 9"	"Classicism" Special Veneers	117,054.
205 K	6' 9"	"Classicism" Polished Special Veneers	127,498.
205 S	6' 9"	"Studio" Polished Ebony	91,088.
E-272	8' 11"	Polished Ebony	183,120.

Steinway & Sons

Verticals

4510	45"	Sheraton Ebony	21,300.
4510	45"	Sheraton Mahogany	23,400.
4510	45"	Sheraton Walnut	24,200.
4510	45"	Sheraton Dark Cherry	25,000.
4510	45"	Marbelized	29,100.
1098	46½"	Ebony	20,200.
1098	46½"	Mahogany	21,700.
1098	46½"	Walnut	22,500.
1098	46½"	Dark Cherry	23,300.
1098	46½"	Marbelized	27,400.
K-52	52"	Ebony	26,400.
K-52	52"	Mahogany	29,700.
K-52	52"	Walnut	30,600.
K-52	52"	Marbelized	35,600.

Grands

S	5' 1"	Ebony	43,800.
S	5' 1"	Mahogany	48,800.
S	5' 1"	Walnut	50,300.
S	5' 1"	Figured Sapele	53,100.

*For explanation of terms and prices, please see pages 76–82.

Model	Size	Style and Finish	Price*

Steinway & Sons (continued)

Model	Size	Style and Finish	Price*
S	5' 1"	Dark Cherry	53,400.
S	5' 1"	Kewazinga Bubinga	54,500.
S	5' 1"	Santos Rosewood	56,500.
S	5' 1"	East Indian Rosewood	61,900.
S	5' 1"	African Pommele	62,300.
S	5' 1"	Macassar Ebony	68,300.
S	5' 1"	Marbelized	60,800.
M	5' 7"	Ebony	46,900.
M	5' 7"	Mahogany	52,600.
M	5' 7"	Walnut	54,000.
M	5' 7"	Figured Sapele	56,200.
M	5' 7"	Dark Cherry	56,600.
M	5' 7"	Kewazinga Bubinga	59,000.
M	5' 7"	Santos Rosewood	59,700.
M	5' 7"	East Indian Rosewood	65,900.
M	5' 7"	African Pommele	66,300.
M	5' 7"	Macassar Ebony	72,500.
M	5' 7"	Marbelized	65,600.
M	5' 7"	Hepplewhite Dark Cherry	59,200.
M 1014A	5' 7"	Chippendale Mahogany	64,200.
M 1014A	5' 7"	Chippendale Walnut	65,700.
M 501A	5' 7"	Louis XV Walnut	83,800.
M 501A	5' 7"	Louis XV East Indian Rosewood	97,200.
O/L	5' 10½"	Ebony	52,400.
O/L	5' 10½"	Mahogany	59,000.
O/L	5' 10½"	Walnut	60,200.
O/L	5' 10½"	Figured Sapele	62,700.
O/L	5' 10½"	Dark Cherry	63,700.
O/L	5' 10½"	Kewazinga Bubinga	65,900.
O/L	5' 10½"	Santos Rosewood	67,300.
O/L	5' 10½"	East Indian Rosewood	74,500.
O/L	5' 10½"	African Pommele	74,800.
O/L	5' 10½"	Macassar Ebony	81,400.
O/L	5' 10½"	Marbelized	72,500.
O/L	5' 10½"	Hepplewhite Dark Cherry	66,300.
A	6' 2"	Ebony	59,400.
A	6' 2"	Mahogany	66,800.
A	6' 2"	Walnut	68,200.
A	6' 2"	Figured Sapele	71,200.

Model	Size	Style and Finish	Price*
A	6' 2"	Dark Cherry	72,500.
A	6' 2"	Kewazinga Bubinga	74,700.
A	6' 2"	Santos Rosewood	75,500.
A	6' 2"	East Indian Rosewood	84,200.
A	6' 2"	African Pommele	84,600.
A	6' 2"	Macassar Ebony	92,000.
A	6' 2"	Marbelized	80,400.
B	6' 10½"	Ebony	66,300.
B	6' 10½"	Mahogany	74,500.
B	6' 10½"	Walnut	76,200.
B	6' 10½"	Figured Sapele	79,700.
B	6' 10½"	Dark Cherry	81,100.
B	6' 10½"	Kewazinga Bubinga	83,400.
B	6' 10½"	Santos Rosewood	83,800.
B	6' 10½"	East Indian Rosewood	93,900.
B	6' 10½"	African Pommele	94,300.
B	6' 10½"	Macassar Ebony	102,500.
B	6' 10½"	Marbelized	88,200.
D	8' 11¾"	Ebony	98,800.
D	8' 11¾"	Mahogany	108,200.
D	8' 11¾"	Walnut	110,000.
D	8' 11¾"	Figured Sapele	114,900.
D	8' 11¾"	Dark Cherry	117,100.
D	8' 11¾"	Kewazinga Bubinga	119,600.
D	8' 11¾"	Santos Rosewood	122,500.
D	8' 11¾"	East Indian Rosewood	134,100.
D	8' 11¾"	African Pommele	134,500.
D	8' 11¾"	Macassar Ebony	146,800.

Grands (Hamburg)

I frequently get requests for prices of pianos made in Steinway's branch factory in Hamburg, Germany. Officially, these pianos are not sold in North America, but it is possible to order one through an American Steinway dealer, or to go to Europe and purchase one there. The following list shows approximately how much it would cost to purchase a Hamburg Steinway in Europe and have it shipped to the United States. The list was derived by taking the published retail price in Europe, subtracting the value-added tax not applicable to foreign purchasers, converting to U.S. dollars (the rate used here is 1 Euro = $1.20, but is obviously subject to change), and adding approximate charges for duty, air freight, crating, insurance, brokerage fees, and delivery. Only prices for grands in polished ebony are shown here. *Caution:* This list is published for general informational purposes only. The price that Steinway

*For explanation of terms and prices, please see pages 76–82.

Model	Size	Style and Finish	Price*

Steinway & Sons (continued)

would charge for a piano ordered through an American Steinway dealer may be different. (Also, the cost of a trip to Europe to purchase the piano is not included!)

Model	Size	Style and Finish	Price
S-155	5' 1"	Polished Ebony	55,600.
M-170	5' 7"	Polished Ebony	60,800.
O-180	5' 10½"	Polished Ebony	64,400.
A-188	6' 2"	Polished Ebony	68,600.
B-211	6' 11"	Polished Ebony	79,600.
C-227	7' 5½"	Polished Ebony	93,200.
D-274	8' 11¾"	Polished Ebony	120,000.

Story & Clark

Verticals

Model	Size	Style and Finish	Price
111	45"	Continental Polished Ebony/Mahogany	2,590.
112	45"	"Arlington" Fruitwood/Cherry/Oak	3,790.
113	45"	"Charleston" Fruitwood/Cherry/Oak	3,790.
114	45"	Institutional Ebony/Oak/Fruitwood	3,390.
114	45"	Institutional Polished Ebony	3,190.
115	45"	Queen Anne Polished Ebony	2,790.
115	45"	Queen Anne Polished Mahogany	2,990.
120	47"	Polished Ebony/Red and Brown Mahogany	4,190.
123	48"	"Cosmopolitan" Polished Ebony	4,190.
126	49"	Polished Ebony	3,390.
140	53"	Polished Mahogany	5,790.

Grands

Model	Size	Style and Finish	Price
146	4' 9"	"Prelude" Polished Ebony	6,990.
152	5'	"Prelude" Ebony	8,190.
152	5'	"Prelude" Polished Ebony	7,590.
152	5'	"Prelude" Mahogany	8,190.
152	5'	"Prelude" Pol. Red and Brown Mahogany	8,190.
152 I	5'	"Imperial" Ebony/Mahogany	10,590.
152 I	5'	"Imperial" Polished Ebony	10,390.
152 M	5'	"Cosmopolitan" Polished Ebony	8,390.
152 M	5'	"Cosmopolitan" Red and Brown Mahogany	8,790.
152 S	5'	French Provincial Polished Ebony	8,190.
152 S	5'	French Provincial Pol. Red/Brown Mahog.	8,790.
152 S	5'	French Provincial Mahogany	8,790.
152 S	5'	French Provincial Polished White	8,790.
152 V	5'	Victorian Polished Ebony	8,190.

Model	Size	Style and Finish	Price*
152 V	5'	Victorial Red and Brown Mahogany	8,790.
165	5' 5"	"Prelude" Polished Ebony	9,390.
165	5' 5"	"Prelude" Polished Red/Brown Mahogany	9,990.
185	6' 1"	"Prelude" Polished Ebony	11,590.
185	6' 1"	"Prelude" Red and Brown Mahogany	12,190.
215	7'	"Prelude" Polished Ebony	16,990.
All models		With Pianomation CD2000+ Installed, add'l	3,600.
All models		With Pianomation Petine Installed, add'l	4,000.
All models		With Pianomation Ancho Installed, add'l	4,400.

Suzuki

Verticals

Model	Size	Style and Finish	Price*
AU-100	44½"	Continental Polished Ebony	2,498.
AU-100	44½"	Continental Polished Red Mahogany	2,498.
AU-200	46"	Polished Ebony	2,798.
AU-200	46"	Polished Red Mahogany	2,798.
AU-210	46"	French Provincial Polished Ebony	2,998.
AU-210	46"	French Provincial Polished Red Mahogany	2,998.
AU-300	48½"	Polished Ebony	2,998.
AU-300	48½"	Polished Red Mahogany	2,998.
AU-310	48½"	"European Ornate" Polished Ebony	3,198.
AU-310	48½"	"European Ornate" Polished Red Mahogany	3,198.

Grands

Model	Size	Style and Finish	Price*
AGP-500	5'	Polished Ebony	7,980.
AGP-500	5'	Polished Red and Brown Mahogany	8,380.
AGP-550	5' 5"	Polished Ebony	8,980.
AGP-550	5' 5"	Polished Red and Brown Mahogany	9,380.
AGP-600	6'	Polished Ebony	11,580.

Vogel

Verticals

Model	Size	Style and Finish	Price*
V-115 M	45"	Continental Polished Ebony	9,780.
V-115 M	45"	Continental Wood Finish	9,180.
V-115 T	45"	Polished Ebony	9,780.
V-115 T	45"	Polished Mahogany/White	10,580.
V-121 T	48"	Polished Ebony	11,780.

Grands

Model	Size	Style and Finish	Price*
V-160 CH	5' 4"	Chippendale Polished Ebony	25,380.

*For explanation of terms and prices, please see pages 76–82.

Vogel (continued)

Model	Size	Style and Finish	Price*
V-160 CH	5' 4"	Chippendale Pol. Mahogany/Walnut/White	26,580.
V-160 R	5' 4"	"Royal" Polished Ebony	25,380.
V-160 R	5' 4"	"Royal" Pol. Mahogany/Walnut/White	26,580.
V-160 RI	5' 4"	"Royal" Polished Mahogany Intarsia	28,780.
V-160 RI	5' 4"	"Royal" Polished Flame Mahogany Coffer	28,780.
V-160 T	5' 4"	Polished Ebony	22,180.
V-160 T	5' 4"	Polished Mahogany/Walnut/White	23,380.
V-160 TI	5' 4"	Polished Mahogany Intarsia	30,580.
V-177 CH	5' 11"	Chippendale Polished Ebony	26,180.
V-177 CH	5' 11"	Chippendale Pol. Mahogany/Walnut/White	27,380.
V-177 R	5' 11"	"Royal" Polished Ebony	26,180.
V-177 R	5' 11"	"Royal" Polished Mahogany/Walnut/White	27,380.
V-177 RI	5' 11"	"Royal" Polished Mahogany Intarsia	29,580.
V-177 RI	5' 11"	"Royal" Polished Flame Mahogany Coffer	29,580.
V-177 T	5' 11"	Polished Ebony	22,980.
V-177 T	5' 11"	Polished Mahogany/Walnut/White	24,180.
V-177 TI	5' 11"	Polished Mahogany Intarsia	31,380.

Vose & Sons

Verticals

Model	Size	Style and Finish	Price
113	45"	Polished Ebony	2,790.
113	45"	Polished Mahogany	2,890.

Grands

Model	Size	Style and Finish	Price
147	4' 10"	Polished Ebony	7,190.
147	4' 10"	Polished Mahogany	7,590.

Walter, Charles R.

Verticals

Model	Size	Style and Finish	Price
1520	43"	Walnut	8,970.
1520	43"	Cherry	8,950.
1520	43"	Oak	8,660.
1520	43"	Mahogany	9,120.
1520	43"	Italian Provincial Walnut	8,990.
1520	43"	Italian Provincial Mahogany	9,140.
1520	43"	Italian Provincial Oak	8,670.
1520	43"	Country Classic Cherry	8,870.
1520	43"	Country Classic Oak	8,720.

Model	Size	Style and Finish	Price*
1520	43"	French Provincial Oak	8,990.
1520	43"	Fr. Provincial Cherry/Walnut/Mahogany	9,240.
1520	43"	Riviera Oak	8,640.
1520	43"	Queen Anne Oak	9,050.
1520	43"	Queen Anne Mahogany/Cherry	9,240.
1500	45"	Ebony	8,420.
1500	45"	Semi-Gloss Ebony	8,530.
1500	45"	Polished Ebony	8,630.
1500	45"	Oak	8,000.
1500	45"	Walnut	8,460.
1500	45"	Mahogany	8,580.
1500	45"	Gothic Oak/Cherry	8,560.

Grands

Model	Size	Style and Finish	Price*
W-175	5' 9"	Ebony	35,670.
W-175	5' 9"	Semi-Polished and Polished Ebony	36,610.
W-175	5' 9"	Mahogany/Walnut/Cherry	37,290.
W-175	5' 9"	Semi-Pol. & Pol. Mahogany/Walnut/Cherry	38,260.
W-175	5' 9"	Open-Pore Walnut	36,380.
W-175	5' 9"	Oak	34,260.
W-175	5' 9"	Chippendale Mahogany/Cherry	38,490.
W-175	5' 9"	Chip. Semi-Pol. & Pol. Mahogany/Cherry	39,420.
W-190	6' 4"	Ebony	36,670.
W-190	6' 4"	Semi-Polished and Polished Ebony	37,610.
W-190	6' 4"	Mahogany/Walnut/Cherry	38,290.
W-190	6' 4"	Semi-Pol. & Pol. Mahogany/Walnut/Cherry	39,260.
W-190	6' 4"	Open-Pore Walnut	37,380.
W-190	6' 4"	Oak	35,260.
W-190	6' 4"	Chippendale Mahogany/Cherry	39,490.
W-190	6' 4"	Chip. Semi-Pol. & Pol. Mahogany/Cherry	40,420.

Weber

"Legend" Verticals

Model	Size	Style and Finish	Price*
WLE 410	41"	Polished Ebony	3,600.
WLE 410	41"	Polished Mahogany	3,700.
WLE 410	41"	Polished Ivory	3,600.
WLF 430	43"	French Provincial Cherry	4,200.
WLF 430	43"	Mediterranean Oak	4,200.
WLF 430	43"	Queen Anne Cherry/Oak	4,200.
WLF 430	43"	Mahogany	4,200.

*For explanation of terms and prices, please see pages 76–82.

Model	Size	Style and Finish	Price*

Weber (continued)

Model	Size	Style and Finish	Price*
WLE 470	47"	Polished Ebony	4,700.
WLE 470	47"	Polished Mahogany	4,850.
WLF 470	47"	Cherry	4,450.
WLE 475C	47"	Chippendale Polished Mahogany	4,750.
WLE 475CD	47"	Polished Mahogany	4,850.
WLE 480	48"	Polished Ebony	4,400.
WLE 480	48"	Polished Mahogany/Walnut/Bubinga	4,550.
WLE 510	52"	Polished Ebony	4,700.
WLE 510	52"	Polished Mahogany/Bubinga	4,850.

"Dynasty" Verticals

Model	Size	Style and Finish	Price*
WDE 410	43"	Polished Ebony/Ivory	4,450.
WDE 410	43"	Polished Mahogany	4,600.
WDF 440	43½"	French Provincial Cherry	4,950.
WDF 440	43½"	Mediterranean Oak	4,950.
WDF 440	43½"	Queen Anne Cherry/Oak	4,950.
WDF 440	43½"	Mahogany	4,950.
WDE 460S	46½"	Polished Ebony	5,400.
WDE 460S	46½"	Polished Mahogany	5,600.
WDE 480	48"	Polished Ebony	5,450.
WDE 480	48"	Polished Mahogany	5,600.
WDE 510	52"	Polished Ebony	5,950.
WDE 510	52"	Polished Mahogany	6,200.

"Sovereign" Verticals

Model	Size	Style and Finish	Price*
WSF 44	43½"	French Provincial Cherry	6,950.
WSF 44	43½"	Mediterranean Oak	6,700.
WSF 44	43½"	Queen Anne Cherry/Oak	7,200.
WSF 44	43½"	Mahogany	6,700.
WSE 46	46½"	Ebony	6,700.
WSE 46	46½"	American Oak/Walnut	6,950.
WSE 46	46½"	Cherry/Medium Cherry	7,200.
WSF 46	46½"	French Provincial Cherry	7,850.
WSF 46	46½"	Mediterranean Oak	7,550.
WSF 46	46½"	Mahogany	7,550.
WSE 47	47"	Ebony and Polished Ebony	6,450.
WSE 47	47"	Walnut/Oak	6,950.
WSE 47	47"	Polished Mahogany/Oak/Walnut	6,700.
WSE 48	48"	Ebony and Polished Ebony	6,700.
WSE 48	48"	Mahogany/Oak/Walnut	7,200.

Model	Size	Style and Finish	Price*
WSE 48	48"	Polished Mahogany/Oak/Walnut	6,950.
WSE 53	52"	Ebony and Polished Ebony	7,850.

"Albert Weber" Verticals

AW 48	48"	Polished Ebony	9,200.
AW 48	48"	Mahogany/Cherry	9,700.
AW 48	48"	Bubinga/Rosewood	9,950.
AW 49	49"	Mahogany	11,200.
AW 49	49"	Bubinga	11,450.
AW 52	52"	Polished Ebony	11,700.
AW 52	52"	Bubinga/Rosewood	12,450.

"Legend" Grands

WLG 50	4' 11"	Polished Ebony/Ivory	11,000.
WLG 50	4' 11"	Polished Mahogany	11,250.
WLG 51	5' 2"	Polished Ebony/Ivory	12,300.
WLG 51	5' 2"	Polished Mahogany	12,450.
WLG 57	5' 9"	Polished Ebony	13,850.
WLG 57	5' 9"	Polished Mahogany	14,100.
WLG 60	6' 1"	Polished Ebony	14,950.
WLG 60	6' 1"	Polished Mahogany	15,350.

"Dynasty" Grands

WDG 50	4' 11½"	Polished Ebony/Ivory	12,950.
WDG 50	4' 11½"	Polished Mahogany	13,200.
WDG 50	4' 11½"	Polished Walnut	13,450.
WDG 51	5' 1"	Polished Ebony/Ivory	14,450.
WDG 51	5' 1"	Polished Mahogany/Walnut	14,700.
WDG 57	5' 9"	Polished Ebony/Mahogany	15,450.
WDG 57	5' 9"	Polished Walnut	15,700.
WDG 60	6' 1"	Polished Ebony	16,700.
WDG 60	6' 1"	Polished Mahogany/Walnut	16,950.

"Sovereign" Grands

WSG 50	4' 11½"	Ebony and Polished Ebony	16,950.
WSG 50	4' 11½"	Polished Mahogany/Walnut/Oak	17,950.
WSG 50	4' 11½"	Walnut/Oak	18,200.
WSG 50	4' 11½"	Cherry	18,950.
WSG 50	4' 11½"	Polished Ivory/White	17,200.
WSG 50	4' 11½"	Queen Anne Polished Mahogany/Ivory	19,950.
WSG 50	4' 11½"	Queen Anne Polished Cherry	21,200.
WSG 51	5' 1"	Ebony and Polished Ebony	17,950.
WSG 51	5' 1"	Walnut/Oak	18,950.
WSG 51	5' 1"	Polished Mahogany/Walnut/Oak	18,700.

*For explanation of terms and prices, please see pages 76–82.

Weber (continued)

Model	Size	Style and Finish	Price*
WSG 51	5' 1"	Cherry	19,450.
WSG 51	5' 1"	Polished Ivory/White	18,200.
WSG 51	5' 1"	Queen Anne Mahogany	22,450.
WSG 51	5' 1"	Queen Anne Cherry	22,700.
WSG 51	5' 1"	Country French Cherry	22,700.
WSG 51	5' 1"	Empire Brown Mahogany	23,450.
WSG 57	5' 9"	Ebony and Polished Ebony	20,200.
WSG 57	5' 9"	Walnut/Oak	21,200.
WSG 57	5' 9"	Cherry	21,450.
WSG 57	5' 9"	Polished Mahogany/Walnut/Oak	20,950.
WSG 57	5' 9"	Polished Ivory/White	20,450.
WSG 57	5' 9"	Empire Polished Mahogany	25,400.
WSG 60	6' 1"	Ebony and Polished Ebony	22,200.
WSG 60	6' 1"	Walnut/Oak	23,700.
WSG 60	6' 1"	Cherry	24,200.
WSG 60	6' 1"	Polished Mahogany/Walnut/Oak	23,450.
WSG 60	6' 1"	Polished Ivory	22,450.
WSG 69	6' 10"	Ebony	29,200.
WSG 69	6' 10"	Polished Ebony	28,850.

"Albert Weber" Grands

Model	Size	Style and Finish	Price*
AW 51	5' 1"	Ebony	22,700.
AW 51	5' 1"	Polished Ebony	22,450.
AW 51	5' 1"	Polished Ebony with Pommele Inlay	22,950.
AW 51	5' 1"	Polished Mahogany	22,950.
AW 57	5' 9"	Ebony	24,950.
AW 57	5' 9"	Polished Ebony	24,700.
AW 57	5' 9"	Polished Ebony with Pommele Inlay	25,450.
AW 57	5' 9"	Polished Mahogany	25,450.
AW 57	5' 9"	Cherry	25,450.
AW 57	5' 9"	Polished Bubinga	25,700.
AW 60	6' 1"	Ebony	29,200.
AW 60	6' 1"	Polished Ebony	28,950.
AW 60	6' 1"	Polished Ebony with Pommele Inlay	29,950.
AW 60	6' 1"	Polished Mahogany	29,950.
AW 60	6' 1"	Cherry	29,950.
AW 60	6' 1"	Polished Bubinga	32,450.
AW 60	6' 1"	Polished Pommele	32,950.
AW 69	6' 10"	Ebony	37,700.
AW 69	6' 10"	Polished Ebony	37,450.

Model	Size	Style and Finish	Price*
AW 69	6' 10"	Polished Ebony with Pommele Inlay	38,950.
AW 69	6' 10"	Cherry	38,950.
AW 69	6' 10"	Polished Bubinga	42,450.
AW 69	6' 10"	Polished Pommele	42,950.
AW 76	7' 6"	Ebony	45,700.
AW 76	7' 6"	Polished Ebony	45,450.
AW 76	7' 6"	Polished Bubinga	50,700.
AW 76	7' 6"	Polished Pommele	53,450.

Weinbach

Grands

Model	Size	Style and Finish	Price*
Estate 50	5'	Polished Ebony	13,380.
Estate 50	5'	Polished Walnut/Mahogany	13,980.
Estate 50 DC	5'	Demi-Chippendale Polished Ebony	14,380.
Estate 50 DC	5'	Demi-Chippendale Pol. Walnut/Mahogany	14,980.
Manor 55	5' 5"	Polished Ebony	15,380.
Manor 55	5' 5"	Polished Walnut/Mahogany	15,980.
Manor 55 DC	5' 5"	Demi-Chippendale Polished Ebony	16,380.
Manor 55 DC	5' 5"	Demi-Chippendale Pol. Walnut/Mahogany	16,980.
Chateau 60	6'	Polished Ebony	17,380.
Chateau 60	6'	Polished Walnut/Mahogany	17,980.

Weinberger

Prices do not include bench. Euro=$1.20

Verticals

Model	Size	Style and Finish	Price*
Friend	45"	Polished Ebony	13,733.
Friend	45"	Polished Mahogany/Dark Walnut	14,822.
Friend	45"	Walnut	13,836.
Friend	45"	Cherry	14,043.
Friend	45"	Polished Cherry	15,134.
Friend	45"	Cherry Oiled and Waxed	14,356.
Friend	45"	Beech/Alder	13,577.
Friend	45"	Polished White	15,290.
Vision One	47"	Polished Ebony	15,238.
Vision One	47"	Polished Mahogany/Dark Walnut	16,795.
Vision One	47"	Walnut	15,550.
Vision One	47"	Cherry	15,757.
Vision One	47"	Polished Cherry	16,951.
Vision One	47"	Cherry Oiled and Waxed	16,094.

*For explanation of terms and prices, please see pages 76–82.

Weinberger (continued)

Model	Size	Style and Finish	Price*
Vision One	47"	Beech/Alder	15,238.
Vision One	47"	Polished White	16,951.
Concert	51"	Polished Ebony	21,104.
Concert	51"	Polished Mahogany/Dark Walnut	22,740.
Concert	51"	Walnut	21,570.
Concert	51"	Cherry	21,961.
Concert	51"	Polished Cherry	23,128.
Concert	51"	Polished Rosewood	24,141.
Concert	51"	Polished White	22,661.
All models		Other Finishes	on request

Grands

Model	Size	Style and Finish	Price*
Passion	5' 7"	Polished Ebony	57,106.
Passion	5' 7"	Polished Mahogany/Dark Walnut	63,361.
Passion	5' 7"	Polished White	58,664.
Chamber	6' 3"	Polished Ebony	64,666.
All models		Other Finishes	on request

Wurlitzer

Grands

Model	Size	Style and Finish	Price*
C143	4' 7"	Polished Ebony	9,028.
C143	4' 7"	Polished Mahogany/Oak	9,298.
C143	4' 7"	Polished White	9,028.
C153	5' 1"	Ebony and Polished Ebony	10,440.
C153	5' 1"	Polished Mahogany	10,800.
C153	5' 1"	Oak/Walnut	10,800.
C153	5' 1"	Polished Ivory	10,440.
C153QA	5' 1"	Queen Anne Polished Mahogany	12,600.
C153QA	5' 1"	Queen Anne Oak/Cherry	12,600.
C173	5' 8"	Ebony and Polished Ebony	11,520.
C173	5' 8"	Polished Mahogany	11,872.
C173	5' 8"	Polished White	11,520.
C203	6' 9"	Ebony and Polished Ebony	15,710.
C203QA	6' 9"	Queen Anne Polished Cherry	16,710.
C223	7' 5"	Ebony and Polished Ebony	19,744.
C273	9'	Ebony and Polished Ebony	47,978.

Wyman

Verticals

Model	Size	Style and Finish	Price*
WV108	42½"	Continental Polished Ebony	2,790.
WV108	42½"	Continental Polished Mahogany/Cherry	2,850.
WV110	43"	Polished Ebony	3,190.
WV110	43"	Polished Mahogany/Cherry	3,250.
WV110	43"	American Country Gallery Oak	3,790.
WV110	43"	Sable Brown Mahogany	3,790.
WV110	43"	French Provincial Sable Cherry	3,850.
WV110	43"	Country French Oak	3,850.
WV115	45"	Polished Ebony	3,390.
WV115	45"	Polished Mahgoany/Cherry	3,450.
WV118	46½"	Polished Ebony	3,990.
WV118	46½"	Walnut	4,050.
WV120	48"	Polished Ebony	3,790.
WV120	48"	Polished Mahogany	3,850.
WV132	52"	Polished Ebony	4,790.

Grands

Model	Size	Style and Finish	Price*
WG145	4' 9"	Ebony/Mahogany	8,490.
WG145	4' 9"	Polished Ebony	7,590.
WG145	4' 9"	Polished Mahogany/Cherry/Snow White	8,190.
WG145	4' 9"	French Cherry	8,690.
WG145	4' 9"	French Polished Cherry	8,390.
WG160	5' 3"	Ebony/Mahogany	9,890.
WG160	5' 3"	Polished Ebony	9,190.
WG160	5' 3"	Polished Mahogany	9,590.
WG160	5' 3"	French Cherry	10,090.
WG160	5' 3"	French Polished Mahogany	9,790.
WG170	5' 7"	Ebony/Mahogany	10,890.
WG170	5' 7"	Polished Ebony	9,990.
WG170	5' 7"	Polished Mahogany	10,590.
WG185	6' 1"	Polished Ebony	11,990.
WG185	6' 1"	Polished Mahogany	12,590.
All models		CD Player System, add'l	4,200.

Yamaha

Verticals

Model	Size	Style and Finish	Price*
M112	44"	Continental Ebony	5,090.
M112	44"	Continental Polished Ebony	5,190.

*For explanation of terms and prices, please see pages 76–82.

Model	Size	Style and Finish	Price*

Yamaha (continued)

Model	Size	Style and Finish	Price*
M112	44"	Continental American Walnut	5,290.
M112	44"	Continental Polished Mahogany	6,390.
M112	44"	Continental Polished Ivory/White	6,290.
M425	44"	Mahogany	3,390.
M450	44"	Cherry	3,790.
M450	44"	Brown Cherry	3,900.
M475	44"	Mahogany	4,290.
M475	44"	Italian Provincial Dark Cherry	4,290.
M500	44"	Chippendale Brown Mahogany	5,990.
M500	44"	Florentine Light Oak	4,890.
M500	44"	Georgian Mahogany	5,990.
M500	44"	Hancock Brown Cherry	4,290.
M500	44"	Milano Dark Oak	4,890.
M500	44"	Parisian Cherry/Dark Cherry	6,190.
M500	44"	Queen Anne Cherry/Dark Cherry	5,090.
M500	44"	Sheraton Mahogany	4,290.
P22	45"	Ebony/Walnut/Oak	5,190.
T116	45"	Ebony	3,990.
T116	45"	Polished Ebony	5,390.
T116S	45"	Polished Ebony with Silver Hardware	5,790.
T116	45"	Polished Mahogany	6,390.
P600	45"	Sheraton Brown Mahogany	5,990.
P600	45"	Queen Anne Brown Cherry	5,990.
P600	45"	Tuscan Ash	6,190.
T121	48"	Polished Ebony	6,590.
U1	48"	Ebony	8,450.
U1	48"	Polished Ebony	8,190.
U1	48"	American Walnut	8,990.
U1	48"	Polished American Walnut/Mahogany	9,590.
U1	48"	Polished White	9,690.
U3	52"	Polished Ebony	11,690.
U3	52"	American Walnut	11,890.
U3	52"	Polished Mahogany	12,890.
U5	52"	Polished Ebony	13,490.

Disklavier Verticals

Model	Size	Style and Finish	Price*
MX500	44"	Chippendale Brown Mahogany	10,990.
MX500	44"	Florentine Light Oak	9,790
MX500	44"	Georgian Mahogany	10,790.
MX500	44"	Milano Dark Oak	9,790

Model	Size	Style and Finish	Price*
MX500	44"	Parisian Cherry and Dark Cherry	10,990.
MX500	44"	Queen Anne Cherry and Dark Cherry	9,990.
MX22	45"	American Walnut/Oak	10,190.
MX116	45"	Polished Ebony	10,390.
MX116	45"	Polished Mahogany	11,390
MX600	45"	Sheraton Brown Mahogany	10,990.
MX600	45"	Queen Anne Dark Cherry	10,990.
MX600	45"	Tuscan Ash	11,190.

MIDIPiano (Silent) Verticals

MP500	44"	Florentine Light Oak	7,590.
MP500	44"	Georgian Mahogany	8,590.
MP500	44"	Hancock Brown Cherry	7,090.
MP500	44"	Milano Dark Oak	7,590.
MP500	44"	Parisian Cherry	8,790.
MP500	44"	Queen Anne Cherry and Dark Cherry	7,790.
MP500	44"	Sheraton Mahogany	7,090.
MP22	45"	American Walnut	7,790.
MPU1	48"	Polished Ebony	10,900.

Disklavier Verticals with Silent Feature

DU1A	48"	Polished Ebony	15,990.
DU1A	48"	American Walnut	16,790.
DU1A	48"	Polished Mahogany	17,390.
DU1A	48"	Polished White	17,490.

Grands

GB1	4' 11"	Polished Ebony	10,500.
GB1	4' 11"	Polished American Walnut/Mahogany	12,100.
GC1	5' 3"	Ebony	16,500.
GC1	5' 3"	Polished Ebony	15,990.
GC1	5' 3"	American Walnut	17,990.
GC1	5' 3"	Polished Mahogany/American Walnut	17,990.
GC1	5' 3"	Polished Ivory/White	17,590.
GC1FP	5' 3"	French Provincial Brown Cherry	19,100.
GC1G	5' 3"	Georgian Brown Mahogany	19,100.
C1	5' 3"	Ebony	21,390.
C1	5' 3"	Polished Ebony	20,990.
C1	5' 3"	American Walnut	23,790.
C1	5' 3"	Polished American Walnut	24,700.
C1	5' 3"	Mahogany and Polished Mahogany	24,700.
C1	5' 3"	Polished White	23,790.
C2	5' 8"	Ebony	24,190.

*For explanation of terms and prices, please see pages 76–82.

Model	Size	Style and Finish	Price*

Yamaha (continued)

Model	Size	Style and Finish	Price*
C2	5' 8"	Polished Ebony	23,700.
C2	5' 8"	American Walnut	27,190.
C2	5' 8"	Polished American Walnut/Mahogany	27,990.
C2	5' 8"	Light American Oak	27,190.
C2	5' 8"	Polished White	25,590.
C3	6' 1"	Ebony	32,990.
C3	6' 1"	Polished Ebony	32,190.
C3	6' 1"	American Walnut	35,790.
C3	6' 1"	Polished Mahogany/American Walnut	37,790.
C3	6' 1"	Polished White	36,500.
S4B	6' 3"	Polished Ebony	58,390.
C5	6' 7"	Ebony	35,590.
C5	6' 7"	Polished Ebony	34,990.
C5	6' 7"	Polished Mahogany	44,790.
C6	6' 11"	Ebony	39,700.
C6	6' 11"	Polished Ebony	38,990.
C6	6' 11"	Polished Mahogany	46,990.
S6B	6' 11"	Polished Ebony	66,190.
C7	7' 6"	Ebony	45,190.
C7	7' 6"	Polished Ebony	44,790.
C7	7' 6"	Polished Mahogany	51,390.
CFIIIS	9'	Ebony	120,990.
CFIIIS	9'	Polished Ebony	119,500.

Disklavier Grands

Model	Size	Style and Finish	Price*
DGB1CD	4' 11"	Polished Ebony (playback only)	19,070.
DGB1CD	4' 11"	Polished Mahogany/Walnut (playback only)	20,670.
DGC1	5' 3"	Polished Ebony (playback only)	24,560.
DGC1	5' 3"	Polished Mahogany/Walnut (playback only)	26,560.
DGC1M4	5' 3"	Ebony	33,642.
DGC1M4	5' 3"	Polished Ebony	33,132.
DGC1M4	5' 3"	American Walnut	35,132.
DGC1M4	5' 3"	Polished American Walnut/Mahogany	35,132.
DGC1M4	5' 3"	Polished Ivory/White	34,732.
DC1M4	5' 3"	Ebony	38,532.
DC1M4	5' 3"	Polished Ebony	38,132.
DC1M4	5' 3"	American Walnut	40,932.
DC1M4	5' 3"	Polished American Walnut	41,842.
DC1M4	5' 3"	Mahogany and Polished Mahogany	41,842.
DC1M4	5' 3"	Polished White	40,932.

Model	Size	Style and Finish	Price*
DC2M4	5' 8"	Ebony	41,332.
DC2M4	5' 8"	Polished Ebony	40,842.
DC2M4	5' 8"	American Walnut	44,332.
DC2M4	5' 8"	Polished American Walnut/Mahogany	45,132.
DC2M4	5' 8"	Polished White	42,732.
DC3M4T	6' 1"	Ebony	58,690.
DC3M4T	6' 1"	Polished Ebony	57,890.
DC3M4T	6' 1"	American Walnut	61,490.
DC3M4T	6' 1"	Polished Mahogany	63,490.
DC3M4T	6' 1"	Polished White	62,200.
DC5M4T	6' 7"	Ebony	61,290.
DC5M4T	6' 7"	Polished Ebony	60,090.
DC5M4T	6' 7"	Polished Mahogany	70,490.
DC6M4T	6' 11"	Ebony	65,400.
DC6M4T	6' 11"	Polished Ebony	64,690.
DC6M4T	6' 11"	Polished Mahogany	72,690.
DC7M4T	7' 6"	Ebony	70,890.
DC7M4T	7' 6"	Polished Ebony	70,490.

Disklavier Pro Grands

Model	Size	Style and Finish	Price*
DC3M4PRO	6' 1"	Polished Ebony	58,190.
DS4M4PROB	6' 3"	Polished Ebony	84,390.
DC5M4PRO	6' 7"	Polished Ebony	60,990.
DC6M4PRO	6' 11"	Polished Ebony	64,990.
DS6M4PROB	6' 11"	Polished Ebony	92,190.
DC7M4PRO	7' 6"	Polished Ebony	70,790.
DCFIIISM4PRO	9'	Polished Ebony	149,500.

MIDIPiano (Silent) Grands

Model	Size	Style and Finish	Price*
MPC1	5' 3"	Polished Ebony	25,300.
MPC2	5' 8"	Polished Ebony	27,900.
MPC3	6' 1"	Polished Ebony	35,990.
MPC6	6' 11"	Polished Ebony	42,100.
MPC7	7' 6"	Polished Ebony	47,390.

Young Chang

See also under "Bergmann" and "Weber."

Verticals

Model	Size	Style and Finish	Price*
GE-102	43"	Continental Polished Ebony/Ivory	4,495.
GE-102	43"	Continental Polished Mahogany	4,695.
PF-110	43½"	Mahogany	6,745.

*For explanation of terms and prices, please see pages 76–82.

Model	Size	Style and Finish	Price*

Young Chang (continued)

Model	Size	Style and Finish	Price*
PF-110	43½"	Queen Anne Oak/Cherry	7,245.
PF-110	43½"	Mediterranean Oak	6,745.
PF-110	43½"	French Provincial Cherry	6,995.
GE-116	46½"	Polished Ebony	5,445.
GE-116	46½"	Polished Mahogany	5,645.
PE-116S	46½"	Ebony	6,745.
PE-116S	46½"	American Walnut/Oak	6,995.
PE-116S	46½"	American Cherry	7,245.
PF-116	46½"	Mahogany	7,595.
PF-116	46½"	Mediterranean Oak	7,595.
PF-116	46½"	French Provincial Cherry	7,895.
PE-118	47"	Ebony and Polished Ebony	6,495.
PE-118	47"	Walnut/Oak	6,995.
PE-118	47"	Polished Mahogany/Walnut/Oak	6,745.
GE-121	48"	Polished Ebony	5,495.
GE-121	48"	Polished Mahogany/Birch Burl	5,645.
PE-121	48"	Ebony and Polished Ebony	6,745.
PE-121	48"	Mahogany/Walnut/Oak	7,245.
PE-121	48"	Polished Mahogany/Walnut/Oak	6,995.
YP-48	48"	Polished Ebony	9,245.
YP-48	48"	Mahogany/Cherry	9,745.
YP-48	48"	Bubinga/Rosewood	9,995.
YP-49	49"	Mahogany	11,245.
YP-49	49"	Bubinga	11,495.
GE-131	52"	Polished Ebony	5,995.
GE-131	52"	Polished Mahogany	6,245.
PE-131	52"	Ebony and Polished Ebony	7,895.
YP-52	52"	Polished Ebony	11,745.
YP-52	52"	Bubinga/Rosewood	12,495.

Grands

Model	Size	Style and Finish	Price*
GS-150	4' 11½"	Polished Ebony/Ivory	12,995.
GS-150	4' 11½"	Polished Mahogany	13,245.
GS-150	4' 11½"	Polished Walnut	13,495.
PG-150	4' 11½"	Ebony and Polished Ebony	16,995.
PG-150	4' 11½"	Walnut/Oak	18,245.
PG-150	4' 11½"	Cherry	18,995.
PG-150	4' 11½"	Polished Mahogany/Walnut/Oak	17,995.
PG-150	4' 11½"	Polished Ivory/White	17,245.
PG-150	4' 11½"	Queen Anne Polished Mahogany/Ivory	19,995.

Model	Size	Style and Finish	Price*
PG-150	4' 11½"	Queen Anne Polished Cherry	21,245.
GS-157	5' 1"	Polished Ebony/Ivory	14,495.
GS-157	5' 1"	Polished Mahogany/Walnut	14,745.
PG-157	5' 1"	Ebony and Polished Ebony	17,995.
PG-157	5' 1"	Walnut/Oak	18,995.
PG-157	5' 1"	Cherry	19,495.
PG-157	5' 1"	Polished Mahogany/Walnut/Oak	18,745.
PG-157	5' 1"	Polished Ivory/White	18,245.
PG-157	5' 1"	Country French Cherry	22,745.
PG-157	5' 1"	Queen Anne Mahogany	22,495.
PG-157	5' 1"	Queen Anne Cherry	22,745.
PG-157	5' 1"	Empire Polished Mahogany	23,495.
YP-157	5' 1"	Ebony	22,745.
YP-157	5' 1"	Polished Ebony	22,495.
YP-157	5' 1"	Polished Ebony with Pommele Inlay	22,995.
YP-157	5' 1"	Polished Mahogany	22,995.
GS-175	5' 9"	Polished Ebony/Mahogany	15,495.
GS-175	5' 9"	Polished Walnut	15,745.
PG-175	5' 9"	Ebony and Polished Ebony	20,245.
PG-175	5' 9"	Walnut/Oak	21,245.
PG-175	5' 9"	Cherry	21,495.
PG-175	5' 9"	Polished Mahogany/Walnut/Oak	20,995.
PG-175	5' 9"	Polished Ivory/White	20,495.
PG-175	5' 9"	Empire Polished Mahogany	25,445.
YP-175	5' 9"	Ebony	24,995.
YP-175	5' 9"	Polished Ebony	24,745.
YP-175	5' 9"	Polished Ebony with Pommele Inlay	25,495.
YP-175	5' 9"	Cherry	25,495.
YP-175	5' 9"	Polished Mahogany	25,495.
YP-175	5' 9"	Polished Bubinga	25,745.
GS-185	6' 1"	Polished Ebony	16,745.
GS-185	6' 1"	Polished Mahogany/Walnut	16,995.
PG-185	6' 1"	Ebony and Polished Ebony	22,245.
PG-185	6' 1"	Walnut/Oak	23,745.
PG-185	6' 1"	Cherry	24,245.
PG-185	6' 1"	Polished Mahogany/Walnut/Oak	23,495.
PG-185	6' 1"	Polished Ivory	22,495.
YP-185	6' 1"	Ebony	29,245.
YP-185	6' 1"	Polished Ebony	28,995.
YP-185	6' 1"	Polished Ebony with Pommele Inlay	29,995.
YP-185	6' 1"	Cherry	29,995.

*For explanation of terms and prices, please see pages 76–82.

Young Chang (continued)

Model	Size	Style and Finish	Price*
YP-185	6' 1"	Polished Mahogany	29,995.
YP-185	6' 1"	Polished Bubinga	32,495.
YP-185	6' 1"	Polished Pommele	32,995.
PG-208	6' 10"	Ebony	29,245.
PG-208	6' 10"	Polished Ebony	28,895.
YP-208	6' 10"	Ebony	37,745.
YP-208	6' 10"	Polished Ebony	37,495.
YP-208	6' 10"	Polished Ebony with Pommele Inlay	38,995.
YP 208	6' 10"	Cherry	38,995.
YP-208	6' 10"	Polished Bubinga	42,495.
YP-208	6' 10"	Polished Pommele	42,995.
YP-228	7' 6"	Ebony	45,745.
YP-228	7' 6"	Polished Ebony	45,495.
YP-228	7' 6"	Polished Bubinga	50,745.
YP-228	7' 6"	Polished Pommele	53,495.
YP-275	9'	Polished Ebony	57,495.